D0900927

PHOTOGRAPHY,
VISION,
and
THE PRODUCTION OF
MODERN BODIES

SUNY Series, INTERRUPTIONS: Border Testimony(ies)
and Critical Discourse/s
Henry A. Giroux, editor

PHOTOGRAPHY, VISION, and THE PRODUCTION OF MODERN BODIES

Suren Lalvani

State University of New York Press

The following publishers have generously given permission to use extended quotations from copyrighted works.

From POWER/KNOWLEDGE: SELECTED INTERVIEWS AND OTHER WRITINGS by Michel Foucault, edited by Colin Gordon. Text copyright © 1972, 1975, 1976, 1977 by Michel Foucault. Compilation copyright © 1980 by The Harvester Press. Reprinted by permission of Pantheon Books, a division of Random House, Inc.

From DISCIPLINE AND PUNISH by Michel Foucault. Copyright © 1975 by Éditions Gallinard. English translation copyright © 1977 by Alan Sheridan. Reprinted by permission of Georges Borchardt, Inc.

Published by
State University of New York Press, Albany

© 1996 State University of New York

All rights reserved

Printed in the United States of America

No part of this book may be used or reproduced
in any manner whatsoever without written permission.
No part of this book may be stored in a retrieval system
or transmitted in any form or by any means including
electronic, electrostatic, magnetic tape, mechanical,
photocopying, recording, or otherwise without the prior
permission in writing of the publisher.

For information, address State University of New York Press,
State University Plaza, Albany, N.Y., 12246

Production by Marilyn P. Semerad
Marketing by Dana E. Yanulavich

Library of Congress Cataloging-in-Publication Data

Lalvani, Suren, 1954–
    Photography, vision, and the production of modern bodies / Suren Lalvani.
        p.   cm — (SUNY series, Interruptions — Border testimony(ies) and Critical Discourse/s)
    Includes bibliographical references (p.   ) and index.
    ISBN 0–7914–2717–X (hardcover). — ISBN 0–7914–2718–8 (pbk.)
    1. Photography—Social aspects.   2. Photography—Social aspects–
–History—19th century.   3. Body (Human) in art.   I. Title.
II. Series.
TR183.L28 1996   95–36567
770′.1—dc20   CIP

10 9 8 7 6 5 4 3 2 1

For Caroline and Arthi

CONTENTS

ILLUSTRATIONS

1. Camera Obscura. Observing a solar eclipse in January 1544 at Louvain. Courtesy of the Gernsheim Collection, The University of Texas at Austin.

2. Engraving of a large camera obscura. Courtesy of the George Eastman House.

3. Table camera obscura, 1769. Courtesy of the Gernsheim Collection, The University of Texas at Austin.

4. Charles Sumner, 1856 [Dagerreotype]. Photographers: Albert Sands Southworth and Josiah Johnson Hawes. Courtesy of The Bostonian Society/Old State House.

5. Gioacchino Rossini, c. 1850. Courtesy of the Gernsheim Collection, The University of Texas, Austin.

6. Alfred Tennyson, 1869. Photographer: Julia Margaret Cameron. By Courtesy of the Board of Trustees of the Victoria Albert Museum.

7. Portrait of a Couple, c. 1850. ½ plate Daguerreotype. Photographer: Marcus Root. Courtesy of the Amon Carter Museum. Mesuem No. P1989.22.14.

8. Working-class family. Birmingham, England, 1860s. Courtesy of the Cadbury Collection, England.

9. M. B. Brady's New Photographic Gallery, Corner of Broadway and Tenth Street, New York. From Frank Leslie's Illustrated Newspaper. Engraving: A. Berghaus. Courtesy of the Library of Congress, Washington, D.C.

10. Courting Couple, 1860s. Albumen Print. Courtesy of The Israel Museum.

11. Semi-nude lying on a Divan, c. 1852. Stereoscopic daguerreotype. Anonymous. Courtesy of the Gernsheim Collection, The University of Texas at Austin.

12. Life in the Harem, 1889. Photographer: Tancrède R. Dumas. Courtesy of the Library of Congress, Washington, D.C.

13. Self-Portrait in Turkish Summer Costume c. 1860. Photographer: Francis Frith. Courtesy of the Israel Museum.

ACKNOWLEDGMENTS

This work is only a fragment in an already ongoing conversation. It is a necessary fiction of a writing culture that books must pretend to be more comprehensive and conclusive than they really are. My hope is that others will write into and away from this text, appropriating what they wish, to generate rich and fruitful conversations of their own. Writing is only a temporary provisioning of space, a fragile body that announces itself only to disappear into the flesh and materiality of subsequent texts. The questions that coalesce around spaces, bodies, and visibilities will continue to disturb and stimulate me, and this remains at best a first draft. I know I will return to issues of the geography and materiality of power, albeit hopefully with more clarity.

I would like to begin by thanking my teachers, all of whom have had a profound influence on my work. Jim Carey wove a spell a long time ago, and the love I have for the field has much to do with the journeys I undertook during his lectures.

My friends Glen Mazis, Peter Parisi, Bob Coleman, Louise Hoffman, and my karmic daughter Maya have been a wonderful source of energy and kindness. There are others whose lives have deeply touched me and enabled me: Srila, the Sens, my family and of course Minal and Sunil. I reserve my greatest appreciation for my friend and companion of many years Caroline, whose presence has always been a gift.

Finally my gratitude to those who have played an important role in the production of this book and whose support, patience and encouragement made it possible: Bill Mahar, Howard Sachs, Priscilla Ross, Cindy Leach, and especially Andrea Wilkinson whose diligence and eye for detail made this a much better manuscript.

I would like to thank the following publishers for the rights to publish selections from these works:

1. Georges Borchardt, Inc., for excerpts from Michel Foucault *Discipline and Punish*, trans. Alan Sheridan, Vintage Books, New York: 1979.

2. Random House for excerpts from Michel Foucault *Power/Knowledge: Selected Interviews and Other Writings*, ed. Colin Gordon, Pantheon Books, New York: 1980.
3. Bay Press for excerpts from Jonathan Crary "Modernizing Vision" in *Vision and Visuality: Discussions in Contemporary Culture*, ed. Hal Foster, Bay Press, Seattle: 1988.

Sections of this work have been published in the following journals:

1. "Photography, Epistemology and the Body", *Cultural Studies* 7(3) October 1993.
2. "Photography and the Industrialization of the Body" *The Journal of Communication Inquiry* 14(2) Summer 1990.

ONE

A Theoretical Framework

INTRODUCTION

Beginning with the ancient Greeks, as evident in the writings of Plato and even in the case of such pre-Socratic thinkers as Heraclitus and Parmenides, vision has been provided an extraordinary status in Western philosophy, culture, and religion. Hannah Arendt has observed that "from the very outset, in formal philosophy, thinking has been thought of in terms of seeing,[1] to the extent that seeing has become the taken for granted of thought. Ocular epistemology has not only been present in the discourses of the church—hence the image of a "beatific Vision" and its claim that only the spiritually pure will "see God"—but in the emerging sciences as well, a model of vision made possible the self-transparency of the object and the production of specific truth-effects. Indeed, from Aquinas to Descartes, this most noble of senses has been deeply implicated in a narcissistic will to power and has exerted a powerful hegemony in the West.

A number of thinkers have argued that modernity consists of the powerful privileging of vision and that it represents a distinctive ocularcentric paradigm, quite different from the organization of vision in previous epochs. For instance, Heidegger has spoken of the ocularcentrism of the modern age as driven by a nihilism that reduces every presence to images and representations.[2] Derrida likewise views the hegemony of modern vision as an attempt to establish a metaphysics of presence.[3] And Nietzsche, in turn, critiqued the progressive endeavor to subjugate reality, to overcome otherness and difference, and to make everything present to the inspection of an imperial Gaze as resulting in the neces-

sary production of a seductive illusion.[4] In response, Nietzsche proposed an alternative conception of multiplying perspectives, in which it
is not the violence of light that dominates but an illuminating vision that
flickers between presence and absence, concealment and disclosure.[5]

The question of a modern vision underscores the fact that concepts of seeing must be viewed as historically specific—not only
embedded in particular ocular epistemologies organized by optical and
discursive figures, but linked to specific discourses and forms of social
power, and consequently a particular matrix for organizing the relations
between observer and observed, the visible and the invisible. Modern
perception must be viewed as a consequence of transformations in discursive and nondiscursive practices that reflect the changing structures,
conventions, and field of possibilities within which an observer will
operate.[6] The invention of photography is a crucial moment in the
development of a modern structure of vision and is both constitutive of
and constituted by a modern ocular paradigm; its operations are dependent on the larger ocular and cultural formation within which it is
deployed, its investment-effect constituted by a particular ensemble of
discourses and practices, and specific forms of subject-object relations.
In fact, in legitimizing specific forms of subject-object relations, technologies of vision like photography, embedded within particular discursive and cultural formations, organize specific relations between
knowledge, power, and the body.[7] Vision is irrevocably tied to domains
of knowledge, arrangements in social space, lines of force and visibility, and a particular organization of bodies.

In order to understand photography's relation with the body in the
nineteenth century,[8] we must not only examine the discourses and practices within which photography operated at different levels of the social
formation to produce specific bodies, but the ocular epistemology
within which these practices are constituted, shaped, and given meaning. In the nineteenth century, a powerful ocular epistemology that
organized photography's functioning at critical sites of the social formation was Cartesian perspectivalism;[9] it was a visual order comprised
of Cartesian discourses of rationality and such precursors to the camera
as the technical figures of linear perspective and the camera obscura.
An ocular paradigm with its particular delineation of the relation of perceiving subject to external world which helped establish a realist fiction

and a monadic viewpoint, it was crucial to photography's functioning within disciplinary institutions in the nineteenth century. Hence this model of vision, by determining the deployment of photographic practices, assisted in materially investing the body in power relations. Given the importance of this paradigm of vision in organizing and constituting photographic practices and producing specific effects of power, it is imperative that we explore the epistemological nature and field of its operations.[10]

AN EPISTEMOLOGICAL PROFILE OF THE CAMERA
Artificial Perspective

The modern scopic regime was ushered in with the invention of linear perspective in the Italian Quattrocento. If we are to specify the moment of its genesis, it would be the day in Florence in 1425 when Filippo Brunelleschi conducted his Baptistery-view experiments, thus introducing the Western world to the perceptual significance of the "vanishing point."[11] The experiment that is relevant to our present purposes was conducted in the following manner. On a small "half-braccio"[12] square panel, Brunelleschi painted the Baptistery, the piazza in front of it and familiar landmarks on either side, from a point within the central portal of the cathedral opposite the Baptistery. The painting itself, as Edgerton points out, would have been copied from a reflection on a mirror positioned in the very same place.[13] The mirror, serving as a base to Brunelleschi's "visual pyramid," would show all the lines of the piazza converging onto points identical with his optical plane, thus enabling him to establish the vanishing point which he then transferred in the form of a dot to the same location in the square panel. Once the painting was completed, Brunelleschi drilled a small hole through the back of the painted panel in the same position as the centric point. We may then assume that he asked a volunteer to stand in the same position, within the central portal of the cathedral opposite the Baptistery, and instructed the volunteer to hold the painted panel in one hand, and peer in a monocular manner through the back of the panel at a mirror held in the other hand directly in front of the panel which reflected the painting.[14] One may imagine that the mirror was to be lifted up or dropped down, at one moment revealing the Baptistery, and at another moment the reflection, thus rendering the illusion significant, consistent, and complete.[15] The illusion was especially significant, because the experiment not only pointed to the existence of a single, unifying vanishing point (the viewer observing the mirror would notice the lines converging to a point identical with his visual axis) but to a new geometric construction that made possible the duplication of a familiar landmark from a fixed viewpoint.

Even as Brunelleschi established the fundamental rules of linear perspective, his intent was not to explain or systematize; instead he viewed his experiments as technological feats.[16] It was Alberti, a decade later, utilizing his knowledge of medieval optics and Euclidean geometry, who grounded the experiments in a theoretical discourse known as *De Pictura*—a treatise on painting. Alberti's theory of optics, which was fundamental to his theoretical explication of linear perspective, drew on the work of three English monks: Robert Grosseteste (1168–1253), Roger Bacon (1270–92) and John Pecham (1235–92). The three monks, in turn, had drawn inspiration for their treatises on optics from the seminal contributions of such Arab scholars as the ninth-century writer Alkindi and the eleventh-century scientist Alhazen.[17] Arab scholarship had, in fact, translated and absorbed the classical Greek thinking on optics, represented by the work of such luminaries as Euclid, Galen, and Ptolemy. The circuitous nature of these influences is made clear in Alberti's opening description of the visual pyramid, which is pure Euclidean in form.[18]

> It is usually said that sight operates by means of a triangle whose base is the quantity seen, and whose sides are those same rays which extend to the eye from the extreme points of that quantity. It is perfectly true that no quantity can be seen without such a triangle. In this triangle two of the angles are at the two ends of the quantity; the third is the one which lies within the eye and opposite the base.[19]

In keeping with this geometrized model of sight, a painting then becomes "the intersection of a visual pyramid at a given distance, with a fixed center and certain position of lights, represented artistically with lines and colors on a given surface."[20] Essentially, the canvas becomes a window or flat mirror between two symmetrical visual pyramids or cones with one of the apexes representing the vanishing point of the painting and the other the eye of the beholder. The concept of "proportioné," in which the painting becomes proportional to the scene to be depicted, is clearly a product of Euclid's Theorem Twenty-one from the *Optica*: "if a straight line intersects two sides of a triangle, and this intersecting line, which forms a new triangle, is equidistant from one of the sides of the first triangle, then the greater triangle will be proportional to the lesser."[21] Thus, did this new Quattrocento mode of representation usher in a rationalization of space, insofar as it took as its basic assumption the view that visual space was *a priori*, an ordered, uniform system of linear coordinates.

In this understanding of space, the painter's canvas becomes a mirror to a reticulated, geometrized surface. Significantly, since artists relate to the objectified field from a single vantage point, their representation of the scene is such that viewers can apprehend the scene as if they were standing in the same spot. Thus perspective provides for a modernist vision in which the object is rendered inert and the subject transcendental and eternalized:

> the gaze of the painter arrests the flux of phenomena, contemplates the visual field from a vantage-point outside the mobility of duration, in an eternal moment of disclosed presence; while in the moment of viewing, the viewing subject unites his gaze with the Founding Perception, in a moment of perfect recreation of that first epiphany.[22]

This abstracted gaze of the new visual order which confronts a systematic space, infinite, homogeneous, and isotropic, signaled a radical shift from the medieval paradigm. In contrast to the Renaissance painter's devotion to perspective, the medieval artist had provided a deeply subjective vision, each element viewed separately and with little regard to a uniform and systematic representation of space: "He [the medieval painter] was absorbed within the visual world he was representing rather than, as with the perspective painter, standing without it, observing from a single, removed viewpoint."[23] Medieval vision was an incarnated vision, not the privileging of vantage points and the capture and arrest of single-point views, but rather of a vision that was tactile and kinesthetic. Furthermore, the medieval artist sought to convince the viewer of the validity of the artist's experience and the legitimacy of the representation by projecting a multileveled and multisensuous rendition of the world.[24] Renaissance perspective, on the other hand, sought to convince the viewer by means of a polarization of subject and object, and by the corresponding creation of a transcendental subject. Its particular claim, as Gombrich has argued so strenuously, is that the only real space is a space uniformly abstracted by sight.[25] In speaking of the perspectival gaze, Martin Jay observes: "The moment of erotic projection in vision—what St. Augustine had anxiously condemned as 'ocular desire'—was lost as the bodies of the painter and viewer were forgotten in the name of an allegedly disincarnated absolute eye."[26]

However, the absolute nature of this disincarnate eye became the means of legislating a new rational order, wherein the observer, delineated within a fixed set of relations, could claim the veridicality of his or her impressions. In this regard, Marshall McLuhan has disparagingly observed, that the perspectival artist's use of a reticulated screen or geometric grid to ensure the certainty of the mirroring process, is "a kind of single vision" thoroughfare to conventionalized rationality:

> The artist fixes himself in a position, allowing neither himself nor his model to move. He then proceeds to match dots on the picture plane with corresponding dots on the visual image, a rather bizarre anticipation of the head clamps of Daguerre. This is the kind of "single vision" that William Blake later deprecated as "single vision and Newton's sleep." It consists basically in a process of matching outer and inner representation. That which was faithfully represented or repeated has ever since been held to be the very criterion of rationality and reality.[27]

That linear perspective or artificial perspective is a conventional symbolic ordering of space, operating within a cultural discourse of what constitutes the real, is supported by a number of observers. For instance, several anthropologists and social psychologists have promulgated the view that perspective is not innate but a culturally learned phenomenon. In fact, Deregowski, Herskovits, and others have shown that reverse perspective, where three-dimensional objects are split and pressed apart, may be, if anything, more biologically innate than linear perspective.[28] Also, Strauss has argued in his *Psychopathology and Education of the Brain-Injured Child*, that "there is nothing innate in the human nervous system which gives us direct information concerning space. Projections of images into a space world are the result of careful focalization of certain rather subtle cues and, as such, is a learned phenomenon."[29] As McLuhan in quoting Eric Ben Hey notes: "Perception is riveted to need."[30] Similarly, Gombrich has argued "that perspective creates its most compelling illusion where it can rely on certain ingrained (cultural) expectations."[31]

The reason perspective was embraced by painters was because it underscored in their view the divine authority and moral harmony of a geometrically transcribed and ordered universe. Absorbed into the ideological discourse of the church through the metaphysical fascination with light as divine "lux" rather than perceived "lumen," perspective transformed space into a harmonic and unified expression of mathematical order and divine will. In Roger Bacon's *Opus Majus of Roger Bacon*, the transcendental is clarified as a result of geometry.

> For in Aaron's vestments were described the world and the great deeds of the father. . . . But no one would be able to plan and arrange a representation of bodies of this kind, unless he were well acquainted with the books of the *Elements* of Euclid . . . and of other geometricians. . . . Oh, how the ineffable beauty of the divine wisdom would shine and the infinite benefit would overflow, if these matters relating to geometry, which are contained in Scripture, should be placed before our eyes in their physical forms![32]

Should we be surprised that in a discourse in which the visual is privileged over the aural, the literal invested with geometric regularity should become a naturalized and rational transcription of God's truth? Seeing then takes on the magnitude of knowing: "And for the sake of all things in general, let us recall to mind that nothing can be known concerning the things of this world without the power of geometry."[33] In Dante's *Convivio*, we discover a belief common among the artists of the Quattrocento: that the "axis visualis" or the centric ray, being the shortest distance between two points, was the most Christian of rays.[34] It is no different in Alberti's *De Pictura*, for here, too, geometry is provided a theological valuation and painting functions to provide the moral order with rational coherence. "The perspectival setting itself was to act as a kind of visual metaphor to this superior existence. . . . Its major function was didactic: the improvement of society by placing before the viewer a compelling model based on classical ideas and geometric harmony."[35] In a space that functioned according to the immutable laws of God, precise frontal views rather than oblique views began to dominate painting. Figures were drawn gracefully occupying a moral tableau in harmonious proportion and gesture, all of them positioned in relation to the moral imprimatur, that "prince of rays," the centric ray, which ironically, is the vanishing point too. In this edification, the moral order is also a class order.

> Europeans came more and more to believe that things planned or seen from a central viewpoint had greater monumentality and moral authority than those which were not. . . . About 1455, the humanist Gianazzo Manetti, in his description of Pope Nicholas V's aborted plan for the Borgo Leonino, mentioned that a wide, straight avenue was to connect the Castle Sant' Angelo with St. Peter's, and that this street was to be reserved for the rich, while angular side streets were to be used by the lower classes.[36]

The invention of perspective was also in keeping with the general ocular concern for accuracy, evinced by a rising bourgeois merchant class. Banking and commerce were increasingly becoming sophisticated operations, especially with the invention of double-entry bookkeeping during this period,[37] and Florentine businessmen were in all likelihood "disposed to a visual order that would accord with the tidy principles of mathematical order that they applied to their bank ledgers."[38] Even as the spatial values of painting underwent a change, so did the temporal values attendant on its location in the social world. For, as John Berger points out, the invention of perspective coincided with the transformation of a painting into a commodity and its entry into the exchange relations of a burgeoning market system. In disclaiming the appropriateness of Alberti's metaphoric reference to a perspective painting as a window on the world, Berger responds that "its model is not so much a framed window open on to the world as a safe let into a wall, a safe in which the visible has been deposited."[39] Thus the visual representation, abstracted, and geometrically codified, simultaneously makes itself available as a commodity.

The disembodied monocular model of perspectival vision progressed in time, from an exegetical, two-dimensional, geometrical reading of the world as divine text, to a purely empirical explication of the natural world, fundamental to the advancement of the descriptive sciences. As Mitchell incisively observes:

> Aided by the political and economic ascendance of Western Europe, artificial perspective conquered the world of representation under the banner of reason, science, and objectivity. No amount of counterdemonstration from artists that there are other ways of picturing what "we really see" has been able to shake the conviction that these pictures have a kind of identity with natural human vision and objective external space.[40]

By the nineteenth century, a mechanized expression of the monocular model of vision had come into existence in the form of the daguerreotype camera. "The invention of (this) machine built to produce this sort of image, (perspectival image) . . . ironically only reinforced the conviction that (perspective) is the natural mode of representation."[41] However, a precursor to the camera, albeit a very primitive one, the camera obscura, had been in existence since Alberti's formulation and systematization of artificial perspective (Fig. 1). In fact, it is claimed that Alberti utilized the "camera obscura" in some of his experiments.[42] The "camera obscura" though initially utilized as a mechanical aid in the solution of perspective problems,[43] soon came to be used by scientists and artists as "a device for aiding graphical representation and a means for ascertaining basic truths about nature."[44] According to Arthur Goldsmith, from the viewpoint of artists, "the camera obscura filled a labor-saving need. With the aid of its projected image plus mirrors and graphs, the blocking in of complex scenes was greatly facilitated."[45]

The Camera Obscura

The "camera obscura," literally "a dark room," or inner chamber, was a function of light entering a minuscule hole in the wall of a darkened room, so that an inverted image was cast, on the opposite wall, in its natural colors (Fig. 2). Initially a room, the camera obscura soon contracted in size and even became portable (Fig. 3). Human knowing, which had become predicated on an epistemology secured by ocular vision, at the same time, as a result of perspectival principles, described and delineated the status of the observer and what constituted proper and categorical inferences about the world. But the paradigmatic model

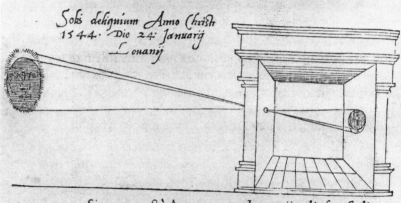

illum in tabula per radios Solis, quàm in cœlo contin-
git: hoc eft, fi in cœlo fuperior pars deliquiũ patiatur, in
radiis apparebit inferior deficere, vt ratio exigit optica.

Solis deliquium Anno Chriſti
1544. Die 24: Januarij
Louanij

Sic nos exactè Anno . 1544 . Louanii eclipfim Solis
obferuauimus , inuenimusq; deficere paulò plus q̃ dex-

Figure 1. Camera obscura. Observing a solar eclipse in January 1544 at Louvrain.

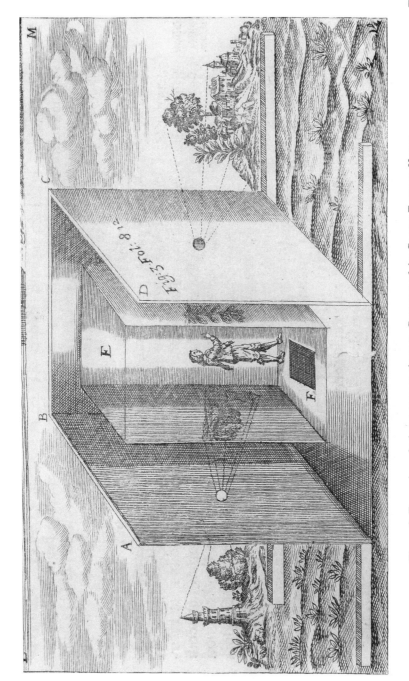

Figure 2. Engraving of a large camera obscura. Courtesy of the George Eastman House.

Figure 3. Table camera obscura, 1769

on which this visual analogue of knowing was based, was the optical and structural principles of the camera obscura.

The camera obscura was of central epistemological significance in a discursive order that included the works of Descartes, Locke, and Leibniz and the experiments of Kepler and Newton: "As a complex technique of power, it was a means of legislating for an observer what constituted perceptual 'truth,' and it delineated a fixed set of relations to which an observer was made subject."[46] According to W.J.T. Mitchell, "the camera obscura had been synonymous with empiricism, with rational observation, and with a direct reproduction of natural vision ever since Locke employed it as a metaphor"[47] for "discerning" knowledge as direct impressions of sensory experience.

> I pretend not to teach but to inquire; and therefore cannot but confess here again, that external and internal sensation are the only passages that I can find of knowledge to the understanding. These alone, as far as I can discover, are the windows by which light is let into this dark room. For methinks the understanding is not much unlike a closet wholly shut from light, with only some little opening left to let in external visible resemblances or ideas of things without: would the pictures coming into such a dark room but stay there, and lie so orderly as to be found upon occasion, it would very much resemble the understanding of a man in reference to all objects of sight, and the ideas of them.[48]

However, as Merleau-Ponty observes, Locke's conception of knowledge had been derived from Descartes. Unlike the Greeks, who had provided for an identity of the subject with the object insofar as they did not view knowledge as the possession of accurate representations, Descartes had been the first to view the mind as an inner chamber, in which "clear and distinct ideas (as representations) passed in review before a single Inner Eye."[49] It is in this inner space of the mind, which Descartes in fact compared to a camera obscura, that "in the Cartesian model, the intellect inspects entities modeled on retinal images."[50]

> For Descartes, the camera obscura was a demonstration of how an observer can know the world "uniquely by perception of the mind." The secure positioning of the self within this empty interior space was a precondition for knowing the outer world. Its enclosedness, its darkness, its categorical separation from an exterior incarnates Descartes's announcement in the Third Meditation,

"I will now shut my eyes, I shall stop my ears, I shall disregard my senses."[51]

Hence the camera obscura appeared to provide for an escape from the vagaries of human sensation and locate the observer at a privileged vantage point of objectivity. Its mode of operation based on geometrical optics and its aperture providing a fixed point of view appeared to be the embodiment of how the mind should objectively represent the world.[52] What is significant, as Jonathan Crary points out, is that binocular disparity common to the natural functions of the eye was ignored in favor of a monocular model that artificial perspective had already underwritten into the culture of seeing, and which operated conventionally to provision a space "homogenous, unified and legible," hence bereft of "any inconsistencies and irregularities."[53] Furthermore, even though monocularity seemingly provided for a transcendental viewpoint, that is, identical for an individual occupying the same point in time and place, it could also be construed as contingent on the "individual vision of distinct beholders with their own, concrete relations to the scene in front of them."[54] Nietzsche, aware of the latter possibility, concluded ironically that "If everyone had his or her own camera obscura with a distinctly different peephole . . . then no transcendental world view was possible."[55]

However, the important element to be underscored here is that the camera obscura assisted in legislating into place what Crary has referred to as "a metaphysics of interiority." For what the camera obscura represents is the obtaining of the world visually by a sovereign subject, who, enclosed and isolated in an observation space separate from the exterior world, simultaneously becomes a privatized subject. "The monadic viewpoint of the individual is legitimized by the camera obscura, but his or her sensory experience is subordinated to an external and pre-given world of objective truth."[56]

The Camera

In the summer of 1827, Joseph Nicéphore Niépce of Chalon-sur-Saône, France, succeeded in developing a primitive form of the photographic process by exposing a bitumen-coated pewter plate in the "camera obscura" to direct sunlight.[57] After eight hours the plate recorded an image of a dovecote on his estate. Louis Mandé Daguerre, a one-time painter of stage sets and owner of the Diorama[58]—a popular visual entertainment in Paris which capitalized on the general appetite of the middle class for panoramic views—formed a partnership with Niépce and together they worked to improve the process. However, with Niépce's death in 1833, Daguerre continued to work alone and in 1835 he discovered the latent process by which exposure times were reduced radically by treating the bitumen-coated plates with mercury vapor. In 1837, he finally was able to arrest the action of light on the silver halides (Daguerre had discarded bitumen-coated plates for iodized silver plates) by inserting the plates into a bath of silver chloride. Subsequently, with the discovery of hyposulfite (currently referred to as sodium thiosulfate) by the English scientist John Herschel, Daguerre used the hyposulfite rather than silver chloride to effectively fix the image on the plate.[59] By 1 September 1839, Daguerre had succeeded in reducing exposure times to six minutes.[60] That it would be Daguerre who would receive entire credit for the invention of photography and that Niépce would be overshadowed and relegated to the margins of history—as has been the case (some scholars have attempted to redress the problem and rehabilitate the latter's role)[61]—was already foreshadowed in the presentation made by the Minister of Interior to France's Chamber of Deputies in June 1839:

> It is quite by a different course, and by completely laying aside the traditions of Mr. Niépce, that Mr. Daguerre has attained the admirable results which we now behold, that is to say the extreme promptitude of the operations and the reproduction of aerial perspective, together with the full effects of shades and lights. The method of Mr. Daguerre is of his own invention and is distinct from that of his predecessor, in its course as well as in its effects.[62]

The daguerreotype, as Daguerre called his invention—a delicate, unique image, not reproducible—rapidly achieved recognition, and on 19 August 1839, the French government, having acquired the invention, presented the details of the technique to the Academy of Sciences.[63] The rapid acceptance of the daguerreotype is not surprising, given both the nature of a public imbued with a fascination for the pleasures of the visual and a period in history fundamentally characterized by a liberal faith in the idea of progress. The French physicist Gay-Lussac's own presentation in support of Daguerre's invention made to

the Chamber of Peers during that period is typical of the liberal sentiment of the times. "Everything that leads to the progress of civilization,
to the physical and moral well-being of man, ought to be the continuing
goal of enlightened government."[64]

However, it was François Arago, one of the more popular French
politicians of the period, who became one of the leading patrons of
Daguerre's invention and it was he who made the presentation to the
Academy of Sciences. His speech is interesting, insofar as it provides a
view of how photography's function and role were construed in those
early days of its inception. The speech, which began with the details of
the technique, became a laudatory evocation of the scientific uses of
photography. For instance, Arago notes with enthusiasm,

> How archeology is going to benefit from this new process! It
> would require twenty years and legions of draftsmen to copy the
> millions and millions of hieroglyphics covering just the outside of
> the great monuments of Thebes, Memphis, Karnak, etcetera. A
> single man can accomplish this same enormous task with the
> daguerreotype.[65]

As regards its uses for astronomy, he observed: "We can hope to make
photographic maps of our satellite. In a few moments of time one can
achieve the longest and most difficult projects in astronomy."[66] But
according to Arago, it was not only science that would benefit, for art
would be democratized too. Having encompassed the basic themes of
the liberal canon—democratization through technological and scientific progress—he concluded with a prophetic remark which, in retro-
spect, in its general foreshadowing of events to come, may be
characterized as ominous.

> When experimenters use a new tool in the study of nature, their
> initial expectations always fall short of the series of discoveries
> that eventually issue from it. With this invention, one must partic-
> ularly emphasize the unforseen possibilities.[67]

A Clustering of Discourses. It is worthwhile noting that August
Comte had published his *Cours de la Philosophic Positive* in 1830. His
focus on the laws of phenomenal relatedness, the study of behavior
rather than origins, as well as his general demand for scientific exacti-
tude were beginning to have a considerable influence on how the material world was to be perceived. Positivism inculcated a new

consciousness of the real and a need to objectify the real, and for many the daguerreotype provided the means for doing just that. In newspaper accounts of the time, the camera's empirical gaze is touted:

> [T]hese are the triumphs of the apparatus which Mr. Daguerre wants to call after his own name, the Daguerreotype. A dead spider has such fine detail . . . that you could study its anatomy with or without a magnifying glass, as in nature; not a filament, not a duct, as tenuous as might be, that you cannot follow and examine.[68]

The material world suddenly made available in potentially new ways, is brought within focus, delineated, described, displayed, and, as yet in a limited way, disseminated. Thus it appears a new model of perceptual truth is in the process of being instituted. Even the *British Literary Gazette* in its 13 July 1839 edition, reporting on Daguerre's first exhibition before the Chamber of Deputies, provides a celebratory evocation of the new sensibility.

> The extraordinary miniatures of such multiplied details as was shown in the street views, particularly in that of the Pont Marie, was much admired. The slightest accidental effects of the sun, or boats, the merchandise on the banks of the river, the most delicate objects, the small pebbles under the water, and the different degrees of transparency which they imparted to it—everything was reproduced with incredible exactness.[69]

What Heidegger has called a technological transforming of nature into a "standing reserve," appears to resonate in this early description of the practices of photography, and its predatory gaze is no less an "enframing."[70] Enframing requires total visibility and surveillance, and the introduction of photography as a central epistemological model for knowing operating within particular discursive orders in the nineteenth century, made possible and legitimated such a requirement. Ptolemy's intention, to have "the whole three-dimensional earth to be posited frontally before the eyes in the conventional manner of looking at a picture,"[71] seemed now more than ever a possibility to be realized.

Another newspaper *La Gazette de France* published a report on the daguerreotype on 16 January 1839, a day prior to Arago's presentation to the Academy of Sciences, noting that:

> M. Daguerre has found the way to fix the images which paint
> themselves within a camera obscura, so that these images are no
> longer transient reflections of objects, but their fixed and everlast-
> ing impress which, like a painting or engraving, *can be taken away
> from the presence of the objects.*[72]

The account itself, which defines photography as an act that counters
transitoriness by extracting from the presence of an object a particular
permanence, points significantly to a perceptual mode which Walter
Benjamin, writing almost a hundred years later, described in the following manner: "To pry an object from its shell, to destroy its aura, is the
mark of a perception whose sense of the universal equality of things has
increased to such a degree that it extracts it even from a unique object
by means of reproduction."[73] The extensive reproducibility and wide
dissemination of the image had to await further technological developments, but the seed for such a "democratization of vision" had already
been planted. In 1833, at about the same time as Daguerre's announce-
ment, Henry Fox Talbot had conceived of a process of making permanent images, which he called a calotype and which enabled multiple
prints to be produced. By the 1850s, the infrastructure enabling a
democratization of vision, or what is inversely the spectacular consumption of images, would be in place.

In John Fowles' *The Collector*, Miranda Gray, one of the central
characters of the book, notes that "when you draw something it lives
and when you photograph it, it dies."[74] *The Edinburgh Review* of
January, 1843, observed this in its panegyric on the new invention:

> But it is not only the rigid forms of art and of external nature—the
> mere outlines and subdivisions of space—that are thus fixed and
> recorded. The self-delineated landscape is seized at one epoch of
> time and is *embalmed* amid all the co-existing events of the social
> and physical world.[75]

Here, to use Benjamin's concept, the mimetic faculty is transformed
into a nonsensuous similarity[76] of the self-evident facticity of the material world. And to use the regressive expression of Benjamin's double
articulation of the collector's experience, we may surmise that the
imaginative space alluded to by *The Edinburgh Review* is a modern
space, characterized as it is by the notion of embalming, which is intrinsic to collecting and a fetishizing of the real—"the sex-appeal of the

inorganic"[77] (as Benjamin called it)—and typifies the "domesticating passions" of a monadic subject who, operating within the "cult of the individual," inhabits the "phantasmagorias of the interior."[78] For, as Benjamin noted, with the increasing division of life into private and public spheres—"the living-space becomes distinguished from the place of work"[79]—there is a corresponding psychic division, wherein "the private citizen who in the office took reality into account, required of the interior that it should support him in his illusions."[80] Thus photography underwrites the "interior," providing sustenance through a consumption of the real.[81] And what in its individuating expression is the collector's experience in the private sphere, becomes the collective experience of the archive.

However this cataloguing of the real is also premised on an interior-exterior of another kind: the mind-body dualism that is inherent within a privileging of the real solely by sight. Thus if the camera obscura functioned as a model on which the visual analogue for knowing was based and legitimized a disembodied gaze and a transcendental subjectivity which ignores the constituted embeddedness of our experience, the camera expanded and legislated that fact into everyday seeing. This is not to invoke an essence that eludes the body and which in the absence of such technologies as photography we may recover, but instead reflects the need to provide for such spaces, as may not only affirm the body as a worthwhile project but assist us in the possibility of reconstructing a different economy of bodies.

A GENEALOGICAL DISCOURSE ON THE BODY

The history of the body's constructions is a history riven with the pathological determinations of binary structurations: dualisms of hierarchical disposition which, in their demand for certainty and a metaphysics of presence, have weakened the possibility of constructing different, local, and multiple bodies in the context of a rich polysemic exploration of experiences and desires. In recognizing the hegemonic and binary rule of Cartesian ocularcentrism and its discourses, which have constituted and organized technologies of sight such as the camera, it is crucial to understand the extent to which our bodies have been subverted, made submissive, and forced to bear signs that erase the possibilities of other forms of matter, identity, and social cohesion.[82] This requires that we rethink the body by comprehending its constitution, its operations as signifying material, and its limit within the intersections of cultural and historical production, so that we may discover alternative ways of constructing our relation to it. In phenomenology, for instance, the rejection of Cartesian ocularcentrism and the centrality of the body, are in themselves critical components for understanding the nature of social existence. As Martin Jay has pointed out, in the case of both "Merleau-Ponty and Ludwig Binswanger the problematic distinction between consciousness and body was closely linked to the elevation of perspectival union with its single point of view." In *The Question Concerning Technology*, Heidegger as well had attributed the "Age of the World View" to scientific perspectivalism.[83]

Husserl for instance, despite the problems that plagued his intersubjective model, which both Merleau-Ponty and Sartre have made quite explicit,[84] developed a critique of Descartes' ocularcentric, egological gaze in which he sought to provide a place to think the "other's body" as lived experience.[85] Sartre, in turn, emphasized the incarnate nature of human existence and the body as constitutive of contingent presence in the world, especially in his description of the intersubjective dynamic between "being-in-itself" and "being-for-itself."[86] Merleau-Ponty, who had critiqued the spectatorial fissure between subject and object, referring to it as a "panoramic consciousness," drew on Paul Valéry's use of the term "chiasme" to describe the relations of the viewer and viewed[87] and provide a view of the subject as incarnated consciousness. In arguing against Descartes' view (in the *Dioptric*) of the mind as an inner chamber where sense impressions received from the outer world are subjected to the cogitations of a Cyclopean eye seeking certainty from differences, Merleau-Ponty called for the seer to abandon the inner chamber and enter into the "flesh" of the world. Accordingly, Merleau-Ponty has argued, that unlike the reflective subject who attempts to close in on itself by incorporating every other and assimilating all difference, the living body must resist closure and necessarily remains open to what is other than, and different from, itself.[88] Thus, in what Marc Richir has referred to as Merleau-Ponty's "defenestration of the cogito,"[89] the living body itself becomes the *milieu* or *chiasme* of intersecting opposites, such as interiority and exteriority, and is neither subject nor object, neither *res extensa* nor *res cogitans*. Correspondingly, embodied vision becomes the "reversible, chiasmic intertwining of the visible and invisible, the viewer and the viewed [and consequently] in the 'flesh' of the world, [is borne] the locus of positive meaning."[90]

Having reminded us of the centrality of the body, phenomenology, however, with its predisposition toward essences, is in itself inadequate for an understanding of the historical and social construction of the body and of the nineteenth-century body as a site where the most local and minute practices linked up with the large-scale organization of power. For it is at the very center of these discourses and practices that nineteenth- and early-twentieth-century photography played its particular role and must be understood. It is thus necessary to turn to Michel Foucault, whose genealogical or diagnostic account of the relations of power, knowledge, and the body provides us with the necessary framework to understand the impact of photographic practices on the body.

VISION AND VISIBILITIES

Foucault's writings are both critical and subversive of that special place accorded to vision by Western epistemology: critical because they illuminate and map the process by which a detached contemplative view, identified with the Enlightenment's passion for a universalizing reason, transforms itself into the dominating gaze of modern rationality; subversive because, as has been remarked, Foucault resorts to vision or what Certeau has referred to as a panoptical discourse to "colonize," "vampirize," and dethrone "the panoptical space of our contemporary scientific language."[91] As a consequence, Foucault's writings are characterized by a powerful ocular style that effectively deploys various optical figures: representational tableaux consisting of exemplary narratives, analytical tableaux consisting of lists of ideological rules or principles relating to a single phenomenon, and figurative tableaux consisting of seventeenth-nineteenth century engravings and photographs.[92] The immensely visual character of his oeuvre is illustrated by the fact that *The Order of Things* begins with an analysis of Velasquez's *Las Meninas*, *Madness and Civilization* with the image of the ship of fools, and *Discipline and Punish* with the horrible death of the regicide Damiens.[93]

In general, Foucault's anti-visual discourse must be viewed in the context of that shift in the twentieth century, in which vision which was at one time celebrated in French thought and culture, was increasingly being subjected to critique. A celebration reflected in Descartes' emphasis on "clear and distinct ideas" gave way, in the twentieth century, to a problematization of vision in the writings of Jean-Paul Sartre, Georges Bataille, and others. While Foucault was clearly influenced by the phenomenological repudiation of Cartesian ocularcentrism, he was not convinced that an ontology of vision constituted a sufficient critique of Cartesianism. He therefore turned instead to the writings of Bataille, Sartre, and Nietzsche to combine the elements necessary "to probe far more thoroughly than the phenomenologists the dark side of the primacy of sight."[94]

Thus, we witness, even as early as *Madness and Civilization*, the presence of an anti-visual discourse in Foucault's writings. The book opens with the Renaissance image of the ship of fools, whose symbolic cargo points to the peripatetic existence of madness, its easy cohabitance with the forms of reason: "madness was present everywhere and mingled with every experience by its images or its dangers."[95] During this period, madness was charged with a powerful eschatological significance, signifying a great embarkation that "proceeds from a point within the world to a point beyond."[96] However, following the decree of 1656, the founding of the Hôpital Général in Paris and the general confinement of the mad with the indigent, the disorderly, and the idle during the Classical age, "madness . . . ceased to be at the limits" of experience: "Oblivion falls upon the world navigated by the free slaves of the Ship of Fools. . . . Behold it moored now, made fast among things and men. . . . No longer a ship but a hospital."[97] In confinement, madness came to be displayed, "but on the other side of bars"; if it did exist, "it was at a distance, under the eyes of reason that no longer felt any relation to it and that would not compromise itself by too close a resemblance. Madness had become a thing to be looked at."[98] According to Foucault, madness, which became the object of reason's gaze, also became the subject of a blindness; the blindness of unreason, as reason "dazzled": "Dazzlement is night in broad daylight, the darkness that rules at the very heart of what is excessive in light's radiance."[99] In this context, the Cartesian distrust of the senses and its ocular concern, is an attempt to exorcise madness and exile it from the same space of light inhabited by reason:

Descartes closes his eyes and plugs up his ears the better to see the sure brightness of essential daylight; thus he is secured against the dazzlement of the madman who, opening his eyes, sees only the night, and not seeing at all, believes he sees when he imagines. . . . Unreason is in the same relation to reason as dazzlement to the brightness of daylight itself. And this is not a metaphor. We are at the center of the great cosmology which animates all classical culture.[100]

In *The Birth of the Clinic*, Foucault describes the nineteenth-century transition to modern medicine and its intensified faith in visual evidences, by invoking Sartre's "le regard" (the gaze)—the objectifying look of the other. Classical medicine was nosological and focused on the disease rather than the patient; it was a medicine of species, in which symptoms were classified, individual modulations forced to disclose the essence of the disease, and then accorded generalized treatment. However, by the end of the eighteenth century, the classificatory, abstractive vision of the physician was replaced by the clinical practitioner's gaze, "silent and gestureless,"[101] neither seeking the "essences beneath phenomena" nor being constrained by theory or imagination; here was a gaze that traversed the tangible space of the body and whose trajectory was organized by the concretely manifestable:[102] "The breadth of the experiment seems to be identified with the domain of the careful gaze, and of an empirical vigilance receptive only to the evidence of visible contents. The eye becomes the depository and source of clarity."[103] According to Foucault, this "great myth of the free gaze" had its antecedents in the political ideology of the Revolution:

The ideological theme that guides all structural reforms from 1789 to Thermidor Year is that of the sovereign liberty of truth; the majestic violence of light . . . brings to an end the bounded, dark kingdom of privileged knowledge and establishes the unimpeded empire of the gaze.[104]

The subsequent introduction of pathological anatomy introduces a new and differentiated gaze, a whole new matrix of relating the visible to the invisible. New "geographical lines" are constituted by the focus on tissual surfaces and death began to be read as "multiple and dispersed in time," instead of being provided the status of an "absolute, privileged point at which time stops."[105] By being "fixed in its own mechanisms," death "acts as a point of view on the pathological, and makes it possible to fix its forms and stages."[106] In the face of this need of the empirical gaze to make visible all invisibilities, ironically, life conceals itself, and medicine must resort to understanding the vitality of patients via their mortality.

> That which hides and envelops, the curtain of night over truth, is paradoxically, life; and death, on the contrary, opens up to the light of day the black coffer of the body: obscure life, limpid death, the oldest imaginary values of the Western world are crossed here in a strange misconstruction that is the very meaning of pathological anatomy. . . . Nineteenth-century medicine was haunted by that absolute eye that cadaverizes life and rediscovers in the corpse the frail, broken nervare of life.[107]

The anatomo-clinical method with its differential reading of cases also incorporates into the structure of illness the morbidity of individual variations. Death no longer has the same reductive function as it did during the Renaissance, that of effacing individual differences of fate in a universal gesture, but instead it is now invested with a didactic singularity: "in the slow half-subterranean, but already visible approach of death, the dull, common life becomes an individuality at last; a black border isolates it and gives it the style of its own truth."[108] And, according to Foucault, this cadaverization of life by perception, that is constitutive of individuality, becomes the model according to which the human sciences will operate in the future.

> It will no doubt remain a decisive fact about our culture that its first scientific discourse concerning the individual had to pass through this stage of death. Western man could constitute himself in his own eyes as an object of science, he grasped himself within his language, and gave himself, in himself and by himself, a discursive existence, only in the opening created by his own elimination.[109]

Similarly, in *Discipline and Punish*, Foucault points to the normalizing gaze of the examination, which by transforming the economy of visibility into the exercise of power provides disciplinary power with an invisibility, even as it imposes on subjects a compulsory visibility. This economy of visibility makes of each individual a case, just like the clinical sciences, but with the effect that describable individuality now becomes the means of domination.

In organizing an anti-visual, anti-ocularcentric discourse, Foucault speaks of the practices of power and their materialization in terms of the spaces they frame, their visibilities, their evidences, and so forth. As John Rajchman observes, Foucault's use of paintings and highly visual accounts of events are "pictures not simply of what things looked like, but how things were made visible, how things were given to be seen, how things were 'shown' to knowledge or to power—two ways in which things became seeable."[110] For instance, in order to make the argument that the Classical age assumed a transcendental observer who views the classificatory tables from a point outside of them, Foucault resorts to Velasquez's painting *Las Meninas*. In this regard, Foucault points to the absent sovereigns who are "in the painting" but unshown—except for their reflected images in a mirror positioned cleverly in the background of the painting—and notes that it is they who transcend the painting to occupy the viewpoint of the observer. The "before and after" pictures that inhabit Foucault's work also serve the same function.[111] For example, in *Discipline and Punish* Foucault discusses how crime is made visible on the body initially through punishment as spectacle, but later, in panopticon surveillance, the criminal body is permeated with a new invisible visibility. "In both instances Foucault links the two techniques of making things visible to a larger conception of seeing in the period."[112] In this manner, Foucault's methodological scheme of visualization provides "visibilities"—ways in which things are made visible during a particular period by the dynamic of knowledge and power.[113]

> Foucault's hypothesis was that there exists a sort of "positive unconscious" of vision which determines not what is seen, but what can be seen. His idea is that not all ways of visualizing or rendering visible are possible at once. A period only lets some things be seen and not others. . . . There is much more constraint in what we can see than we suppose. To see is always to think, since what is seeable is part of what "structures thought in advance." And conversely to think is always to see.[114]

And this is why Foucault is of special relevance, because as Rajchman points out, he writes about "the history of the concepts through which things were given to be seen."[115] Furthermore, he explains how those concepts of visualization were embedded in certain institutional practices. Thus, prison architecture is not just a figure of stone, an assemblage, but first and foremost a luminous form, a place of visibility that distributes the visible and invisible (the prisoners who are seen and the opaque central tower), according to the conditions established by the "light-being" of a historical formation or positive unconscious of vision of a period: "a first light opens up things and brings forth visibilities as flashes and shimmerings, which are the 'second light.'"[116] It is for this reason that Foucault focuses on the "spatial schema" of the prison, which he feels provides for a new way of seeing the criminal and the discourse of criminology. Similarly, as we will see, the "spatial and temporal" schema of photography, functioning in what Foucault (in *Discipline and Punish*) calls the new disciplinary apparatuses, not only showed what was deviant and pathological, but what was normal and efficient, and transformed the spaces of visibility through which knowledge and power would exercise their impact on the body. And photography itself was embedded in a "positive unconscious of vision" of its own: an ocularcentric regime identified with perspective pictorialism and Cartesian rationality—Cartesian perspectivalism, which was "valorized by the scientific worldview."[117]

In Foucault's materialistic conception of power, the "constructed visibility" of space, whether it inhabits prisons, hospitals, or factories, is an integral element of a "disciplinary technology," for in making visible, it helps constitute and organize subjects. The particular matrices of power, visibility and space, are organized into a new and higher level of rational calculability in Foucault's presentation of the ultimate disciplinary apparatus or machine—Bentham's Panopticon.[118] The Rousseauist dream of "a transparent society, visible and legible in each of its parts"[119] is perverted in the panopticon architecture of an overseeing Gaze. "It reverses the principle of the dungeon"[120] and in its anonymous, omniscient exercise of power represents the "architectural embodiment of the most paranoid of Sartrean fantasies about the absolute look."[121] Where once power "had only a weak capacity for 'resolution,' as one might say in photographic terms,"[122] it now inhabits an all-powerful ocularcentric apparatus for surveilling, classifying and individuating a corporeal multiplicity. As luminous arrangement or machine which passes through every articulable function and affects visible matter, the panopticon provides to architecture a normative force.[123] Foucault's interest in spaces reflects his interest in the work of the new historians, Braudel and Aries, who have both developed a history of spaces. In fact, noting that with Hegel, Bergson, and Heidegger there had been "a correlative devaluation of space which stands on the side of . . . the dead, the fixed, the inert,"[124] he argues that, "a whole history remains to be written of spaces—which would at the same time be a history of powers (both these terms in the plural)—from the great strategies of geo-politics to the little tactics of the habitat."[125]

In keeping with Foucault's own discursive strategies, "visibilities" are linked to "evidences," for after reading *Discipline and Punish*, one cannot help but view annular construction in a new light—"prisons resemble factories, schools, barracks, hospitals, which all resemble prisons."[126] His method is clearly emancipatory, for to make evident or to see[127] is also to engage in a *rupture d'évidence*, that is, to simultaneously disengage from those evidences on which our practices and discourses are predicated, and to ask how they were made self-evident. This is Foucault's attempt to "eventalize" history as in his account of the birth of the prison. For to see how events structure things and make of our seeing of them self-evident, is to see also how those events can be made unacceptable or intolerable. Power, after all, as Foucault argues, makes of its evidences an acceptability and tolerability. So to free ourselves from practices we are captive to, we must cease being prisoners of a certain way of seeing.[128] And it is because of this particular method of engagement—that is, to provide for his reader an alternate site of seeing, not outside culture but always within it (for, as we have noted, Foucault repudiates any notion of transcendental subjectivity)—that Deleuze has rightly referred to him as a great "voyant" or seer.[129] Thus, Foucault's approach, by exposing and illuminating what "each historical formation . . . reveals . . . within the conditions laid down for visibility,"[130] ultimately represents the endeavor to make visible that which remains hidden, not immediately given.

EMBODYING BODIES

Foucault's genealogy of the modern individual is simultaneously an account of the historical and cultural production of the lived body, the body's permeation by specific power relations, and its location within an expanding political field. The body has historically been the scene for the enactment of power, a surface traced by its inscription, a site for the investment of its rituals: "Power relations have an immediate hold upon it; they invest it, mark it, train it, torture it, force it to carry out tasks, to perform ceremonies, to emit signs."[131] Foucault the genealogist has especially focused on the practices and mechanisms by which the body emerged as a special site of insidious and productive power during the nineteenth century. According to Foucault, bio-power which "brought life and its mechanisms into the realm of explicit calculations and made knowledge/power an agent of transformation of human life"[132] can be traced back to the development of a new political and technical rationality which slowly began to make its presence felt in the seventeenth century. At first, he points out, this new political rationality coexisted alongside traditional political theories which operated to mask the radical changes taking place in the cultural domain. In this way, by concealing "its own mechanisms," power grants itself an acceptability and a tolerability.[133] This new political rationality that is no longer burdened by an ethical or prudential order nor tied to the fate of Machiavelli's prince but considered the state as an end in itself, increasingly began to view its subjects' bodies as a resource for the investment of an administrative and disciplinary knowledge.

> [F]rom the idea that the state has its own nature and its own finality, to the idea that man is the true object of the state's power, as far as he produces a surplus strength, as far as he is a living, working, speaking being, as far as he constitutes a society, and as far as he belongs to a population in an environment, we can see the increasing intervention of the state in the life of the individual.[134]

As a consequence there emerged a new group of administrators intent on studying the population in all its aspects and producing a knowledge that was detailed, measurable, and concrete. The lives, deaths, and miseries of individuals became the content of a new political knowledge that was bio-political in nature. A precise ordering and disciplining of individual bodies and the general methodical realization of the population resulted in the proliferation of technical manuals, the institutionalizing of a police force, and the collection of population statistics.

> Within this set of problems, the "body"—the body of individuals and the body of populations—appears as the bearer of new variables, not merely as between the scarce and the numerous, the submissive and the restive, rich and poor, healthy and sick, strong and weak, but also as between the more or less utilizable, more or less amenable to profitable investment . . . and with more or less capacity for being usefully trained. The biological traits of a population became relevant factors for economic management.[135]

The exercise of power over life coalesced around two poles. In the case of what Foucault terms as an "anatomo-politics of the human body," the focus "centered on the body as machine: its disciplining, the optimization of its capabilities, the extortion of its forces, the parallel increase of its usefulness and its docility, its integration into systems of efficient and economic controls."[136] On the other hand, the second pole of bio-power, which Foucault labels as a "bio-politics" of the population, "focused on the species-body, the body imbued with the mechanics of life and serving as the basis of the biological processes: propagation, births and mortality, the level of health, life expectancy and longevity, with all the conditions that can cause these to vary."[137] According to Foucault, the disciplining of individual bodies and the regulation of populations that had always existed to some degree earlier, came together in a new and powerful manner in the nineteenth century.

In anatomo-politics discipline takes as its object the constitution of bodies that are at the same time both docile and productive: "a body becomes a useful force only if it is both a productive body and a subjected body."[138] Following Foucault's critique of the repressive hypothesis this constitutes a functional reversal of discipline: disciplinary technologies no longer operate on the basis of suppression but the principle of production, no longer constraining but rather intensifying the value of the object of power. Where previously "they were expected to neutralize dangers," these technologies were now required "to play a positive role . . . to increase the potential utility of individuals."[139] Furthermore, the ensemble of discursive and nondiscursive practices that constituted a disciplinary technology were applied mainly to the working classes and the subproletariat. Thus, the disciplinary technologies which coalesced at the very same time that witnessed the emergence of capitalism, were not, according to Foucault, a supplementary phenomenon, but rather the precondition to the success of nineteenth-century capitalism. After all, as he points out, a prerequisite to the continued growth of capitalism was the insertion of disciplined bodies into its production apparatus, as well as the rational distribution and regulation of populations that separated the deviant, the pathological, and the unfit, from the normal, willing, and productive.

According to Foucault, the technologies of discipline are not the prerogative of any single institution nor are they isolated to the state apparatus. He focuses on the prison in order to highlight disciplinary procedures that are ubiquitous and prevalent in other sites of administrative control and reform as well. Factories, schools, hospitals, and other institutions all have recourse to them. In this sense it can be said of these disciplinary mechanisms that they emigrate: "While, on the one hand, the disciplinary establishments increase, their mechanisms have a certain tendency to become de-institutionalized, to emerge from the closed fortresses . . . and to circulate in a 'free' state; the massive, compact disciplines are broken down into flexible methods of control, which may be transferred and adapted."[140] At the same time, disciplines are not a substitute for other forms of power—the juridico-political discourses of laws, rights, and responsibilities—but rather they operate to invest these powers, concatenate them, extending their reach and expanding their efficacy so that the effects of power can be brought "to the most minute and distant elements."[141] Hence, "the real corporeal disciplines" constituted "the foundation of the formal, juridical liberties. The contract may have been regarded as the ideal foundation of the law; disciplinary technology constituted the technique, universally widespread of coercion and subjection."[142] Thus, these disciplines represent a micro-physics of power "whose field of validity is situated in a sense between these great functionings [institutional apparatuses] and the bodies themselves with their materiality and their forces."[143]

As François Ewald observes, a disciplinary society is not a society of generalized confinement in the sense of being segregational and partitioning in its effects. Indeed, the diffusion of disciplinary technologies, "far from dividing or compartmentalizing, homogenizes social space."[144] And even though disciplines are adapted to particular institutional apparatuses, they nevertheless constitute a common language in the operations of institutions. Hence "disciplinary society is a society of absolute communication."[145] As regards the *dispositifs* or social apparatuses that deploy these disciplinary technologies, Foucault observes that they are constituted by a "heterogeneous ensemble consisting of discourses, institutions, architectural forms, regulatory decisions, laws, administrative measures, scientific statements, philosophical, moral, and philanthropic propositions."[146] According to Deleuze, they may be viewed as comprising "curves of visibility and curves of enunciation" for "they are machines which make one see and speak."[147] Their historical nature is illustrated by the differential regimes of visibility and enunciation that determine the transformations of their historical existence.[148] The other two dimensions intrinsic to disciplinary apparatuses are the lines of force or power that is formed out of knowledge and the process of subjectification that is intrinsic to it.[149]

Furthermore, there are three major instruments by which discipline subjects the body to a meticulous power. They are hierarchical observation, normalizing judgments or normative sanctions, and their synthesis, the examination. In hierarchical observation, surveillance made possible by disciplinary architecture binds its subjects in an optics of power, enhancing internal visibility and refining power so that it becomes "multiple, automatic and anonymous."[150] This is power that is exercised without the alibi of a subject, a power that does not repress and whose efficacy is a function of its quasi-autonomous nature. The normalizing sanction makes possible the precise assessment of actions, the judging of individuals, the introduction of micro-penalties, and the overall distribution and ranking of individuals. The norm is that matrix which transforms discipline from repression into investment and production; along with the examination it underscores Foucault's claim that discipline "makes" individuals: "it is the specific technique of a power that regards individuals both as objects and as instruments of its exercise."[151] The compilation of dossiers in an examination, which transforms an individual into a case, not only fixes the subject in a field of writing, but in doing so, reverses "the political axis of individualization."[152]

And it is within this structural reorganization of the social, the web of data and discourse, and the disciplinary objectification of the individual, that the nascent human sciences played a significant role. The social sciences (criminology, psychology, demography, social hygiene, statistics)—located within the administrative apparatuses of prisons and hospitals, and developing their own methodologies and criteria for what constituted evidence—functioned within the general context of disciplinary technologies. According to Foucault,

> both "anatomo-politics" and "bio-politics" called for a technique of overlapping subjection and objectification. . . . The carceral network constituted one of the armatures of this power/knowledge that has made the human sciences historically possible. Knowable man (soul, individuality, consciousness, conduct, whatever it is called), is the object-effect of this analytic investment of this domination-observation.[153]

In this regard, Foucault observes that the human sciences "which [have] so delighted our humanity for over a century, have their technical matrix in the petty, malicious minutiae of the disciplines and their investigations."[154]

Foucault's account of the body's investment by disciplinary power provides an important framework for theorizing the relations between photographic practices and the body. However, Foucault's own treatment of the body does reflect certain problems and, in order to establish a firm foundation for my own examination, I have incorporated the thinking of Judith Butler. Butler has indicated that those who theorize the body treat it as a "passive medium that is signified by an inscription from a cultural source figured as 'external' to that body."[155] This is the case with Foucault's genealogical framework, in which the body makes its appearance as "the inscribed surface of events."[156] According to Foucault, the task of genealogy is "to expose a body totally imprinted by history,"[157] and it is in keeping with this project that he maintains a distinction between a body that is material and prior to signification and the processes of cultural inscription that take the body as the scene and site of inscription. For example, in *The History of Sexuality* Foucault makes reference to prediscursive sexual energies and a materiality in his evocation of "bucolic" and "innocent" bodily pleasures that prefigure the introduction of regulative regimes.[158] This is in spite of the fact that Foucault claims that "sex" is a result of the interactions of knowledge and power.[159] Hence what Foucault seems to be arguing for is a prediscursive, prelibidinal multiplicity that can somehow be freed from the regulative constraints of "sex."

As Butler has remarked, "by what enigmatic means has the 'body' been accepted as a prima facie given that admits of no genealogy?"

What is required, she argues, is "a genealogical account of the demarcation of the body as such as a signifying practice," without resorting to
the language of a prediscursive body and its disruptions.[160] Instead of
presupposing the body as a preconstituted category in the terms of a
nature/culture distinction, the aim is to examine the ways in which that
distinction or demarcation between the two is discursively produced,
maintained, and writ large into the body so as to produce culturally
coherent bodies. This requires seeing the body not as a "being" but as a
culturally constructed variable boundary of differential permeability.
And it is in Mary Douglas' work that Butler discovers the notion of the
body as permeable boundary rather than a fixed, mute facticity or uni-
tary substance that culture is then presumed to grasp and signify.[161] The
notion of the body as permeable boundary that is politically regulated
by knowledge/power configurations also speaks to the constructed
binary division between the "inner" and "outer" worlds of the subject
that help consolidate a coherent subject. However, in *Discipline and
Punish*, Foucault displaces the idea of an "interiority" by pointing to the
new disciplinary technologies which do not function on the basis of
repression but instead compel prisoners to signify the prohibitive law
on the surface of their bodies.[162] The law as the essence of their selves is
not internalized but manifests itself on the body; the invisible soul or
conscience that occupies the interior of the body is now visibly
inscribed and signified on the body. In this regard, when Foucault
announces that "the soul is the prison of the body,"[163] he means to con-
test the inner/outer distinction itself. The soul as an internal psychic
space is signified by disciplinary discourses through inscriptions on the
surface of the body that "perpetually renounces itself as such."[164] It is
hence through the signification of disciplinary discourses operating on
the body, that is through their inscriptions of exclusions and presences,
that new interiors are announced and displayed. In this manner, bodies
in the nineteenth century were invested with a powerful new permeability, their contours demarcated by the regulatory codes of cultural discourses that provide the subject with new forms of meaning and
coherence. The boundaries of the body are malleable and they are
shaped and fabricated according to the levels of permeability organized
by the different disciplinary regimes which make of the body a site of
knowledge and power. And in this structuring of the body's permeability each disciplinary discourse organizes and addresses a new "interior"

that becomes the object of power, the seat of identity, and the focus of a process of subjectivation. Photography operates in disciplinary discourses to arrest, isolate, and instantiate the body in relation to the axes of time and space; it enables the decipherment, delineation, and analysis of the body's surface. In all these ways it conspires with these discourses to accord the body a pronounced visibility and consequently render the body permeable to the operations of a disciplinary regime. Thus, the body as a boundary is continuously rewritten and intextuated by discursive regimes of power/knowledge. By regulating new levels of corporeal permeability through significations on the surface of the body, disciplinary regimes subjectify individual bodies as disciplined subjects.

POWER

Foucault's "analytics of power" influenced by Nietzsche's method of genealogy is a transposition of the "will-to-power" in terms of "knowledge is power." For both Nietzsche and Foucault, knowledge is not an *apriori* construct which is then appropriated by power but is already structured by the functioning of human interests and the relations of power.[165] Foucault's emphasis that knowledge is neither neutral nor emancipatory but linked to regimes of power, is reflective of the postmodern suspicion of reason. He views power as dispersed and indeterminate and rejects totalizing or reductionistic perspectives on power.[166] Hence the genealogies of power/knowledge developed by Foucault represent a powerful attack on both liberal and Freudo-Marxist theorists and their penchant for developing global discourses of the social totality and emancipatory and progressivist histories.[167] Foucault's concept of power/knowledge can be viewed as a grid of analysis or a heuristic device which reconstructs the history of the human sciences and society by studying the regimes of truth that condition the formation of beliefs.[168] It functions as an alternative to Marx's category of the laboring subject in illuminating the historical field and providing a critical theory of history.[169]

In Foucault's conception, power relations are viewed as intentional without being attributed to the conscious interests and intentions of a subject. In contrast to the liberal and Marxist view of power as possessed by the subject (individual or class), as centralized (state or economy), and as fundamentally repressive, Foucault proposes a model of power that is exercised rather than possessed, decentralized rather than centralized, and positive and productive rather than repressive. For Foucault the subject is a conduit for power, and even though subjects exercise power they do not possess it. Power is not possessed by the ruling classes whose ideas become the ruling ideas of an age; rather, power is a strategy in which the dominated as much as the dominating are part of the network and matrices of power. Foucault refuses to place the subject at the center of his analysis or posit a pre-given, unified subject because the constituent subject deflects examination of the process by which subjects are produced within power relations at various institutional sites. "One has to dispense with the constituent subject, to get rid of the subject itself, that's to say to arrive at an analysis which can account for the constitution of the subject within a historical account. And this is what I call genealogy."[170] Thus, in speaking of the Marxist emphasis on ideology, he responds by noting:

> As regards Marxism, I'm not one of those who try to elicit the effects of power at the level of ideology. Indeed I wonder whether, before one poses the question of ideology, it wouldn't be more materialist to study first the question of the body and the effects of power on it. Because what troubles me with these analyses which prioritize ideology is that there is always presupposed a human subject on the lines of the model provided by classical philosophy, endowed with a consciousness which power is then thought to seize.[171]

In this context Mark Poster has observed that "perhaps more than Marx, Foucault lays the basis for a materialist history of knowledge," not only because, as Poster suggests, Foucault proposes an immanent relation between knowledge and power so that discourses "are already powers and do not need to find their material force somewhere else, as in the mode of production,"[172] but also because discourses act directly upon bodies, transforming them and investing them with power relations.

Foucault's conception of the decentralized nature of power which operates independently of the conscious intentions of subjects, must also be viewed in the context of his emphasis on the highly differentiated nature of modern society. According to Foucault, modern society has "more centres of power . . . more circular contacts and linkages . . .

more sites where the intensity of pleasures and the persistency of power catch hold, only to spread elsewhere."[173] Power which is neither acquired nor seized but highly indeterminate and "relational" operates in "a multiple and mobile field of force relations."[174] It is the effect of one action on another action, so that understanding the exercise of power would include analyzing "the field of possible actions," wherein one action not only inhibits the play of some actions but increases the probability of other actions. Hence, instead of beginning with theoretical unities at the macro-level, Foucault applies a micro-level analysis to show how power circulating within a field of institutional apparatuses contributes to effects of domination at the "terminal forms" of class and patriarchy.[175] In keeping with his intentions of providing an "analytics of power," rather than a theory of power, Foucault views power as comparable to "government" in a broad sense, where "to govern in this sense is to structure the possible field of actions of others."[176]

Foucault is critical of the assumptions of the repressive hypothesis which views power as external to knowledge and anchored in constraint, submission, and censorship:

> I would . . . distinguish myself from para-Marxists like Marcuse who give the notion of repression an exaggerated role—because power would be a fragile thing if its only function were to repress, if it worked only through the mode of censorship, exclusion, blockage and repression, in the manner of a great Superego, exercising itself only in a negative way. . . . Far from preventing knowledge, power produces it.[177]

In both his studies of crime and sexuality, Foucault has demonstrated that power does not function according to the logic of repression or physical force but is productive of discourses and political technologies that constitute normative bodies and individuals.[178]

Foucault's power/knowledge configuration, according to which "power and knowledge directly imply one another," provides a corrective to ideology critique and the Marxist notion of a false consciousness. For example, in the view of the Frankfurt School, ideology is viewed as a distortion or mystification imposed via the exercise of power by the dominant class and it is presumed that once such repression is dispelled, "true consciousness" or nonideological thinking will be possible. From Foucault's Nietzschean perspective, the assumption that knowledge must be disinterested, that emancipation and truth can only be achieved in the absence of power relations, is illusory: "There is no power relation without the correlative constitution of a field of knowledge, nor any knowledge that does not presuppose and constitute at the same time power relations."[179] In response to the presumed opposition between ideology and truth, Foucault argues that the "problem is not to make the division between that which, in a discourse, falls under scientificity and truth and that which falls under something else, but to see historically how truth-effects are produced inside discourses which are not in themselves either true or false."[180] This is in keeping with Foucault's argument that the repressive hypothesis overlooks the fact that power makes possible the production of "truth." For Foucault what makes one discourse have more value than another is not its particular "truth" but its role in constituting practices. There is another reason why Foucault considers it especially dangerous for power to be viewed as external to truth. It enables an individual to falsely engage in the "speaker's benefit" and portray himself/herself as occupying a privileged position from which to view power, to promise relief, and prophesy freedom in the future.[181] Obviously the same argument can be made against Foucault's own position, but he counters the possibility by saying that he is always within and speaks from inside the discourse of power. As Jana Sawicki notes: "Foucault denies that his own discourse is free of power relations without despairing about the possibility that it can have a liberatory effect."[182] Moreover, according to Foucault, "the speaker's benefit" is merely another ploy by means of which reason dominates, transforming masks into faces, and faces into masks, producing discourses seemingly opposed to it but which are only a necessary and consequent result of its larger deployment.[183]

Mark Poster has observed that Foucault's critique of Marxism "is most threatening at the general level." It provides a strong argument for refuting "a totalizing framework that encompasses all history in an evolutionary scheme and relates all levels of society under the dominance of the mode of production." Furthermore, Foucault's "critique of the subject is sustained both at the level of the object of historical investigation (the laboring subject in Marx) and the authorial subject who writes history." After all, since knowledge is tied to power, the Marxist historian's claim to truth is a partial one. At the same time, Poster acknowledges that at the level of class analysis, "Foucault's position does not at all exclude Marxist historical analysis."[184] Deleuze is of a similar opinion, for he underscores the view that "[Foucault's] new functionalism or functional analysis certainly does not deny the existence of class or class-struggle but illustrates it in a totally different way, with landscapes, characters and behavior that are different from those to which traditional history, even of the Marxist variety, has made us accustomed."[185] Foucault has himself underscored the importance of Marxist analysis:

> It is impossible at the present time to write history without using a whole range of concepts directly or indirectly linked to Marx's thought which has been defined and described by Marx. One might even wonder what difference there could ultimately be between being a historian and being a Marxist.[186]

Indeed, as Barry Smart has shown, Foucault's work provides a revised conceptual framework with which to retheorize Gramsci's notion of hegemony. To begin with, Foucault has decentered and displaced the very ideas that have plagued Gramsci's theorizing of the exercise of hegemony—a reductionist notion of power, the role of the state, the concept of ideology. At the same time, he has placed at the center an analysis of the relations of "truth" and "power" through which "men govern themselves and others," which provides a sound basis for developing an "understanding of the exercise of power and the associated effects of hegemony in modern societies."[187] While in his functional micro-level analysis, Foucault refrained from beginning with a totalizing framework and the idea of power as the expression of a bourgeois subject, he nevertheless emphasized the presence of bourgeois hegemony in the nineteenth century. In his examination of the deployment of "sexuality," Foucault points out that the bourgeois body and class were the first to be constituted with a distinctive identity and that this process "should undoubtedly be linked to the process of growth and establishment of bourgeois hegemony: not, however, because of the market value assumed by labor capacity but because of what the 'cultivation' of its own body could represent politically, economically, and historically for the present and the future of the bourgeoisie."[188] Similarly, in discussing the development of industrial capitalism in the nineteenth century, Foucault views the political technologies of the body which permeate the social and are utilized by different institutions as "factors of segregation and social hierarchization . . . guaranteeing relations of domination and effects of hegemony."[189]

According to Smart, a Foucauldian reformulation of the concept of hegemony that moves beyond Marxist categories, requires that the social cohesion that characterizes hegemony be understood not as the product of coercion or consent but rather as the consequence of techniques and methods that constitute minds and bodies, and as the result of cultural practices which cultivate needs and desires as naturally motivated and embodied. In this regard, Foucault's analysis of the forms of knowledge and relations of power through which individuals have been objectivized and the techniques of the self in terms of which they "have learned to recognize themselves as subjects," reveals "the complex multiple process from which the strategic constitution of forms of hegemony may emerge."[190] In this revised model, the "governmentalization" of power relations substitutes for Gramsci's emphasis on the "state/civil society" dichotomy, and focus is placed on the objectifying and subjectifying techniques by which political struggle is transformed and new forms of social cohesion introduced. Foucault's analysis of the "regimes of truth" by which people govern themselves also includes attention to the role of those "specific intellectuals" who, operating in specific sectors, produce forms of knowledge and techniques invested with "truth" and reason. It is especially in the context of his examination of the production of disciplinary discourses that Foucault "offers an analytical and political purchase on the problem of hegemony."[191] This reformulated notion of hegemony, a conceptual and analytical framework that draws on both Marxism and Foucauldian poststructuralism, will provide the basis for examining the functioning of photographic practices within the matrix of knowledge/power relations and the objectifying and subjectifying practices constitutive of bourgeois power in the nineteenth century. Moreover, I will argue that photography was complicit with an ongoing hegemony of vision that would assist in the programmatic concerns and desires of this class.

Foucault has been criticized for foreclosing the possibility of progressive intervention, for not providing a direction for future action or articulating policy alternatives to combat the practices he has criticized, and for describing a power that appears inevitable, thus devaluing and eroding the forms of resistance. One of Foucault's objectives has been to challenge the scientific hierarchization of knowledge by developing critiques of both objectifying and subjectifying practices in order that those "subjugated knowledges"—"autonomous, non-centralized kind of theoretical production—whose validity is not dependent on the approval of the established regimes of thought" may be reactivated.[192] Even though Foucault has not provided any prescriptions beyond the call for a "different economy of bodies and pleasures,"[193] he has nevertheless provided us with a powerful critique of the discourses and technologies by which people have been classified, normativized, and produced as subjects with an identity. But liberal and Marxist positions are of the view that "criticism would have no point unless progress were possible, and progress means liberation."[194] Since, however, Foucault's genealogies operate on the thesis of radical discontinuity, which is crucial to his project of delegitimating the present, he is not inclined to provide historical chronologies from a progressivist perspective.[195] In contrast to Marxists who hypothesize a progress toward knowledge emancipated from power relations, Foucault's Nietzschean perspective, in which power "produces reality before it represses,"[196] causes him to view the possibility of freedom unfettered by power relations as an intellectual abstraction. But this is not the same as saying that Foucault's conception of power is empty and lacking in contrast: a society without power relations can only be an

> abstraction. . . . [However,] to say that there cannot be a society without power relations is not to say either that those which are established are necessary, or, in any case, that power constitutes a fatality at the heart of societies, such that it cannot be undermined. Instead I would say that the analysis, elaboration, and bringing into question of power relations and the "agonism" between power relations and the intransitivity of freedom is a permanent political task inherent in all social existence.[197]

Thus, the relationship of freedom to power as it is instantiated in social relations is not antagonistic but "agonistic," where each force provokes and incites the other in permanent contestation.

I have endeavored to provide an epistemological profile of the representational nature of photography's functioning within discourses of Cartesian perspectivalism, and, drawing on Foucault's genealogical focus on power, knowledge, and the body, established the basic epistemological framework relevant to my examination of nineteenth- and early-twentieth-century practices of photography on the body. Photographic practices in the nineteenth century operated at a number of sites within the social formation, taking on the functions with which it had been invested by particular discourses and practices. This in no way implies that photography is bereft of "internal" characteristics. On the contrary, its particular "intrinsic" characteristics, the product of the very discourses and practices we have just examined, made it eminently suitable for the functions it undertook within certain disciplinary apparatuses.

In the following pages, photography's relations with the body is described in terms of the discourses and practices within which it operated at three different levels in the social formation of nineteenth-century bourgeois society. In this context, I shall examine: (i) how photographic portraiture operated within a certain set of discourses and practices to socially constitute the bourgeois body, providing it meaning within an established hierarchy of values; (ii) how photography operated within a set of discourses and practices at the "anatomo-political" level, in order to surveil, regulate, and discipline the movement of deviant bodies across the social; and how it also simultaneously operated within a set of discourses and practices seeking to identify and represent deviancy itself; and finally, (iii) the nature of photography's functioning at an "anatomo-political" level in certain discourses and practices operating within the capitalist mode of production, so that "what is most material and most vital in bodies is invested in them."[198] My intent is then to determine the manner in which photography—by both representing the "exterior" body and thereby effecting the disciplining of the "interior" body—assisted in producing both knowledge and power. Finally, I shall conclude my examination of photography and its relations with the body in the nineteenth century, by locating its practices within the larger conception of seeing or the "positive unconscious of vision" that prevailed during the period.

TWO

Photography and the Bourgeois Body

INTRODUCTION

Traditional accounts of the development of photography, attest implicitly to the view that photography functioned in a beneficent manner to democratize portraiture. Seemingly there is little to quibble with in the idea that photography expanded the traditional function of portraiture that was once the privilege of the aristocracy. In time, we are told that, with the reduction of exposure times and lower printing costs, even the working classes could afford to buy representations of themselves. But this is where a certain complexity in the argument must be acknowledged, if we are to avoid a naive adherence to a narrative of linear progress or an unwavering belief in the democratic outcome of technological developments. For even while the liberalization of the economy of self-representations made possible by photography enabled those previously excluded to participate, it simultaneously ushered them into a representational system whose structure, composition, codes of operation, and internal means of making meaning bound them securely into a dominant discourse. Thus, if the particular power of nineteenth-century bourgeois portraiture is to be understood, it must be comprehended in terms of its ability to constitute the subject within a discursive field; that is, its ability to reify multiple bodies into particular types of bodies. It is then necessary to understand the political and cultural discourses within which photographic portraiture addressed the body. If, as Foucault notes, power enters deeply into the gestures, actions, and discourses of everyday lives, then photography itself, existing within a set of ideological discourses and constraints, invests the body in power relations within which it is forced to emit signs.

THE INDUSTRIALIZATION OF PORTRAITURE

The development of photographic portraiture coincided with the increasing middle-class demand for goods of all kinds and was guaranteed by their desire to represent, and inscribe historically, their arrival into the domains of finance and culture. "By having one's portrait done an individual of the ascending classes could visually affirm his new social status both to himself and to the world at large."[1] It was only a matter of time, with the middle-class push into domains previously inhabited by the aristocracy, that the methods and procedures of aristocratic glorification would subsequently yield to the new-found status of the bourgeoisie. It reflected the continuing middle-class challenge to the aristocratic monopoly of signs which Baudrillard has identified as central to the process of modernity.[2]

The painted portrait had been largely the privilege of aristocrats and the very wealthy, "but simplifications in terms of what was included in the painting, and transformations in size and materials, enabled merchants and farming gentry in the 18th and early 19th centuries to contemplate having portraits made of themselves and their families."[3] In fact, the miniature—most like the traditional large-scale portrait—became one of the first portrait forms "to be coveted by the bourgeoisie for the expression of its new cult of individualism."[4] Miniaturists who catered to the bourgeois demand had to provide a style of portraiture that while inexpensive would incorporate the signifiers of aristocratic portraiture: "Portrait painting in France at the time of Louis XV and Louis XVI [was] characterized by a tendency to falsify, to idealize each face, even that of the shopkeeper, in order to have him resemble the exemplary human type: the prince."[5] However, with the advent of photography in 1850 and the bourgeoisie firmly in place, the miniaturists had all but disappeared: "The photographers turned out an average of twelve hundred pieces annually. . . . For one-tenth the price of a painted portrait, the photographer could furnish a likeness which satisfied the taste of the bourgeoisie as well as the needs of his pocketbook."[6] Between the miniature and photography there were intermediate stages in the industrialization of portraiture and they included both the silhouette[7] and the physiontrace.

The invention of the daguerreotype, however, did not automatically guarantee the accessibility of the portrait to the new classes. Considerable refinement had to be undertaken before portraiture could be commercialized. The primitive nature of the lenses used in the daguerreotype and the insufficient sensitivity to light of the chemically-treated plates and paper, necessitated long-drawn-out and uncomfortable sittings. The commercializing of the image was also frustrated by the uniqueness and one-of-a-kind nature of the daguerreotype image, which could not be easily duplicated except by the unsatisfactory means of hand graving or etching.

Despite the difficulties attendant on the making of photographic portraits, a complex of interests, discourses, and practices would ensure its continued development. Besides the unprecedented demand for images among the middle classes, the liberal spirit of the times, motivated by an abiding faith in technical mastery and moral progress, would ensure that the incentive to develop and expand the scientific and technological knowledge of photography was not lacking.[8] Everywhere, the benefits of the new regime of secularism—quantifying, objectifying and disciplining its attachment to the "natural" and the social—were given clear and powerful expression. The development of photographic portraiture was not to be stymied.

The earliest improvements were made to cameras and lenses. Daguerre's cumbersome camera, built by Daguerre himself and sold by the optician Alphonse Giroux, weighed 100 pounds and sold for between 300 and 400 francs, a sum considered extremely high at the time. But smaller and lighter models began to be manufactured and by 1841 cameras were priced at 250 to 300 francs.[9] Although the price of plates by 1841 had been reduced considerably—from four francs in 1840 to one and a half francs in 1841—and the annual sales in Paris had reached 2,000 cameras in 1846, the price of the camera was still beyond the reach of many individuals.[10] But commercial portraiture began to take off once the Petzval lens, designed to admit twenty times as much light, was invented in 1840. John Frederick Goddard's chemical processes to sensitize the plate further were introduced that same year. Along with these developments, Hippolyte Fizeau made the image more visible and less fragile by dipping the exposed plate in a solution of gold chloride.[11] The benefits of these technical improvements were obvious in the reduced exposure times. Whereas in 1839—when photography was first introduced—the required sitting time was fifteen minutes in bright sunlight, by 1842 it was down to between twenty and forty seconds, and portrait studios began to open everywhere.

The older professions had been rendered obsolete by the technology of the camera, which meant that there were a large number of unsuccessful, unemployed, or poorly paid miniaturists, engravers, and draftsmen. They began to drift into the new occupation of photography, giving some credence to Baudelaire's caustic comment that photography had become "the refuge of every would-be painter, every painter too ill endowed or too lazy to complete his studies."[12] However, at the same time, it was the very experience of these artists which "was partly responsible for the high quality of the photographic industry during its early days."[13]

The popularity of daguerreotype portraiture in France was immediate and expanded outward from Paris into the provincial cities. Richard Beard in London, who had bought a patent from Daguerre's agent in 1841, soon owned three studios in London and netted $30,000 in his second year.[14] In the German cities of Berlin, Hamburg, Dresden, Vienna, and Bern, daguerreotype portraiture became popular, though initially not to the same extent as it did in France or England. Elsewhere in Europe the commercialization of portraiture spread, but it was in America that it gained the most rapid acceptance. "Europeans had to wait until 1841 to sit before the studio daguerreotype camera, but in America the first enterprises were opened in New York City by Alexander S. Wolcott and John Johnson, and in Philadelphia by Robert Cornelius in the spring of 1840."[15] Rudisill notes that by 1849, there were two thousand daguerreotypists in America, and Americans were spending eight to twelve million dollars annually on portraits, which represented over ninety percent of all photographic production in America.[16] In 1853 in New York alone, there were eighty-six portrait galleries sumptuously furnished, making a visit to such a gallery a social event. One of the early entrepreneurs who was extremely successful was John Plumbe who initially started out by opening a studio in Boston in 1841 and by the mid-forties owned a chain of portrait establishments in fourteen cities.[17] Mathew Brady, seeking to "vindicate true art," began catering to an upscale clientele in both Washington and New York. While the portraits undertaken by Brady, Southworth, and other notable daguerreotypists of the time were of a high quality and expensive, mechanical improvements in buffing and coating made it possible for the average daguerreotypist working in cities and small towns to charge between twenty-five cents and a dollar for a portrait, enabling a broader sector of the population to afford likenesses of themselves.[18] With the introduction of the collodion wet-plate process which allowed for the duplication of prints, and its further refinement subsequently in the collodion/albumen process,[19] commercial portraiture began to be firmly established. However, the reproducibility of the image in varying contexts, its movement as a cultural signifier across the threshold of various texts, and the corresponding production of surplus value at each of these sites had to await further technical refinements. Until that happened, what Walter Benjamin had referred to as the "cult value"[20] of the picture would remain; nevertheless the image had begun to slowly make its way into the domain of consumption.

BOURGEOIS BODIES

Photographic portraiture, especially as it was practiced in the photographic studios of the major cities of the nineteenth century, was devoted to the production of portraits of middle-class men and their families. In addition, photographs of men who exemplified middle-class values of success were gathered in albums and nationally distributed. In effect, photographic representations took as its focus three significant sites within the ideological and social formation of nineteenth-century bourgeois society: the nation-state, the family, and the individual. In its emphasis on these three sites, photographic portraiture may be said to have been comprehensive in its treatment, for each one of these sites was crucial to the construction of bourgeois hegemony.

Nineteenth-century photographic portraiture constituted its bourgeois subjects within a network of cultural, political, and aesthetic discourses; and the camera operating within a set of technical and political constraints framed and situated the body in terms of these discourses, so as to position it within a set of ideological and social relations. Given the mediated nature of the relation between camera and subject, we need to ask what were the discourses within which it sought to instantiate the body to be portrayed? How does the body in turn return that gaze? What were the particular cultural rituals intrinsic to portraiture and how did they speak to the broader culture within which they played a role? These, then, are the discourses of the body and the camera which we must confront.

Broadly speaking, the practices of nineteenth-century portraiture were united by a common paradigm in the nineteenth century: that is, the powerful and closely woven discourses of the two pseudo-sciences of the nineteenth century—physiognomy and phrenology. That this materialist hermeneutic paradigm of the self unified the nineteenth-century archive of images is borne out by Naomi Rosenblum:

> Approaches to camera likenesses, whether made for amateur or commercial purposes, ranged from documentary to artistic, from "materialistic" to "atmospheric," but whatever their underlying aesthetic mode, photographic portraits reflected from their origin the conviction that an individual's personality, intellect, and character can be revealed through the depiction of facial configuration and expression.[21]

In the discourses of physiognomy and phrenology, the surface of the body is raised to the visibility of a text, its signs deciphered to disclose moral qualities residing therein. In his *Essays on Physiognomy* published in 1789, Johann Kaspar Lavater claimed that there was a "correspondence between the external and internal man, the visible superficies and invisible contents."[22] While physiognomy's quest for empirical indices of character confined itself to the face, the science of phrenology inaugurated by Franz Josef Gall emphasized a correlation between behavioral traits and cranial shape. Phrenology proposed a map of the brain which identified specific psychic functions, whose development or lack thereof could be discerned by examination of the skull. For example, H. Lauvergne devoted his study *Les forcats considérés sous le rapport physiologique, moral et intellectuel* (1841) to examining the cranial protuberances of convicted criminals in order to verify whether they displayed a predisposition to crime.[23] Both sciences betrayed a taxonomic intention and sought to hierarchically order the social realm according to class and moral groupings. This was accomplished by rendering the body permeable to these discourses, which signified and classified the surface of the body and its particularities in order to communicate interior psychic states. The boundaries of the body are redrawn, its surfaces reinscribed by these cultural discourses so that the body may be made to articulate upon its exterior what it refuses to divulge, but which now arrives displayed in the visible light of discourse.

Popularized in the press and in the lectures of prominent physicians, these disciplinary systems were quickly "transformed into popular beliefs."[24] As Louis Chevalier points out: "Equipped with the hypotheses of Gall and Lavater, doctors in hospitals and convict prisons found no difficulty in discovering wolf-men and lion-men among their clientele. The journalists followed suit."[25] Likewise, among the arts and culture of the nineteenth century, physiognomy exerted a powerful influence.[26] In France, Gall and Lavater's characterological interpretations "were used by Balzac and other novelists and illustrators" in the "panoramic, anecdotal and prudential literature of nineteenth-century Paris."[27] The popularity of these works may be ascribed to the fact that, in America and elsewhere in Europe, where societies were undergoing rapid transformation and were characterized by fleeting interactions in an anonymous market environment, the paradigm offered a convenient hermeneutic for assessing character.[28] It was this belief—that surfaces by themselves could reveal moral depths—which was ideally the same concern that motivated the daguerreotypists to reveal the character of their subjects by a searching likeness.

In America, the introduction of the camera coincided as well with "Emerson's ocular concern for spiritual insight through perceiving nature."[29] Essentially, Emerson's philosophy presumed that by keenly observing its external manifestations one could see beyond the physical aspects of nature. Thus, the individual by transforming him/herself into a "transparent eyeball," could, through the application of "transcendental materialism," achieve unity in creation with God. This view of the camera's relation to the spiritual truth of nature is given voice by the daguerreotypist Holgrave, the protagonist of Hawthorne's *The House of Seven Gables.*

> There is a wonderful insight in heaven's broad and simple sunshine. While we give it credit only for depicting the merest surface, it actually brings out the secret character with a truth that no painter would ever venture upon, even could he detect it.[30]

The camera is thus perceived as an apparatus of "insight," by which a person's limited ocular capacity, now intensified and heightened by the camera, can discern Nature's truth. Richard Rudisill has appropriately observed that "a machine gifted with discernment of character and truth must have seemed the ultimately desirable fusion of technology and natural spirit to an age eagerly concerned with both."[31] The ease with which photography took its place within this discourse is no doubt because of the medium's particular technological process. Both the mechanical apparatus and the chemical processes replaced substantially the subjective interpretive judgment of the individual picture maker, and because the camera seemed to operate "naturally" in response to God's light in recording the image, it provided the camera its particular divine status among the transcendentalists. Whether it is the operations of a discourse that render surfaces porous and essences "readable" or the operations of the camera that are discursively constituted to grant to it the ability to produce truth-effects of a transcendental and moral sort, in both instances the ocular nature of knowing and the desire to apprehend the world through images and representations exercises a predominant influence. In the reminiscences of James F. Ryder, a nineteenth-century daguerreotypist, we see the interplay of spiritual and moral values: "The box was the body, the lens was the soul, with an all-seeing eye, and the gift of carrying the image to the plate."[32] The camera is personified as

> truth itself. What he told me was as gospel. No misrepresentations, no deceits, no equivocations. He saw the world without prejudices; he looked upon humanity with an eye single to justice. What he saw was faithfully reported, exact, and without blemish. He could read and prove character in a man's face at sight. To his eye a rogue was a rogue; the honest man, when found, was recognized and properly estimated.[33]

However, it was less a matter of surfaces disclosing rectitude and character to an omniscient apparatus, than it was a case of the same surfaces being discursively constructed to provide characterological significances and moral depths. This becomes clear when we examine the attempts that were undertaken to define national character in America.

Initially the attempt to define national character involved the construction of an archive of images, which it was presumed would disclose an American archetype.

> The portraitmakers in particular grappled with the problem of national character. Their work reflected the underlying feeling that the true nature of the American would stand revealed if only adequate representations of each citizen could be produced. Most daguerreotypists were concerned with reflecting the maximum of character in making a portrait.[34]

This desire to infer from an archive of images a representative type of national character is clearly akin, as we shall see subsequently in chapter 3, to Galton's phrenological attempt to identify through photography a "criminal type." A "mosaic of images,"[35] an American archive premised on a physiognomic logic, would presumably be held up to its people as an exemplification of American character. But the project was characterized by imprecision and ambiguity. Instead of trying to distill out of innumerable individual readings some loosely constructed optical sense of national character, the desirable option was simply to present in a reiterative manner the normative ideal. Hence the attempt to discover what constituted the archetypal American soon revealed itself as a politics bent on constructing a normative portrayal of the same.

Thus, in nineteenth-century America, an archive of images began its trajectory across the social scape with the publication of Plumbe's engravings, entitled *The National Plumbeotype Gallery,* consisting of daguerreotype portraits of national figures. Not to be outdone, Brady issued his own *Gallery of Illustrious Americans.* In the case of both publications, we encounter the desire to represent and define the national character solely in terms of a bourgeois ideal. Speaking of Brady's collection at the Crystal Palace and Anthony's National Daguerreotype Miniature Gallery, Rudisill has observed that they "were conscious efforts to display the nation in her ideal character as defined by images of the men who determined it."[36] Furthermore, in both Plumbe and Brady's expanded summaries, "the implicit assumption that the character of an individual's contribution to public life can be seen in physical features and stance"[37] testified to the continuing power of physiognomy. Naomi Rosenblum, in observing that "an even stronger belief in the conjunction of appearance and moral character is evident in the fine daguerreotype portraiture that issued from the Boston studio of Albert Sands Southworth and Josiah Hawes"[38] (premier daguerreotypists of the time), provides further evidence of the prevailing epistemology of the image (Fig. 4).

In effect, a moral icon was being cultivated,[39] due less to the special characteristics of the camera as insight machine, than to photographers operating within discourses of physiognomy, which gave them a set of typologies by which to orchestrate and adjust posture, expression, and lighting.[40] In examining the photographs of these nineteenth-century Victorians, we become acutely aware of the conventions of display regarding both dress and arrangement of the body in portraiture; we are confronted with an elaborate set of signs that symbolically evoke the bourgeois cultural ideal. There are obviously conventions that are intrinsic to the act of being photographed, for example, the self-conscious seriousness that posterity demands in this abstraction of oneself. But in bourgeois portraiture, it is especially the arrangements of heads, shoulders, and hands—"as if those parts of our body were our truth,"[41]—that give evidence of the discursive power of physiognomy (Fig. 5). And the particular "truth" they illuminate is one that is central to bourgeois ideology: that the world may be civilized by the domestication of the hand by the head. Evidence for this was to be found in the factories and industries which manifested a clear division between those who conceive and those who execute.

The political leaders of the time were not unaware of the power of these images to project "direct experience into the realm of the affective symbol in American society."[42] As one of them observed of Brady's archive of Victorian exemplars:

> The votive genius of American art has perpetuated, with the unerring fidelity with which the lens of the camera does its inimitable work, not only the likeness of form and feature, but the very expression of those in whose achievement in all walks of life the American heart takes pride, and whose memory we endeavor to glorify by whatsoever means it is in our power to exert.[43]

The political effects of a moral play of deterministic physiognomic typologies are not to be underestimated. In fact, at the heart of these images lurks an epistemology of experience, to inspire and disci-

Figure 4. Charles Sumner, 1856

Figure 5. Gioacchino Rossini, c. 1850.

pline. As Rudisill has observed, the daguerreotypist functioned not only as recorder but guide,[44] and the consequence is that such an archive, in exerting "the most salutary influence, kindling the patriotism"[45] of subjects, renews a people's commitment to the prevailing regime of sense and order. As Marcus Aurelius Root, writing in 1864, argues, in addition to the cultural enlightenment of the masses, portraiture, by displaying a pantheon of bourgeois moral exemplars, provides both an inspirational source and a moral standard to which the working classes can aspire: "The pure, the high, the noble traits beaming from these faces—who shall measure the greatness of their effect on the impressionable minds of those who catch sight of them at every turn?"[46] Root was obviously confident of the power of these images, for he unequivocally declares: "And he who beholding, on every side within his dwelling, spectacles of the class above named, derives from them no elevating moral influence, must be made of almost hopelessly impenetrable stuff."[47]

That such a public imagery, in "making ideals and qualities accessible to direct experience,"[48] would create a bourgeois icon that in turn would serve the continuing reproduction of the relations of production on which capitalist expansion is dependent, is undoubtedly due to the particular power which discourses of visual empiricism were able to exert, in order to legitimate both the epistemological validity of the camera in representing the real and the paradigmatic moral power of physiognomy. The process constitutes a multiplication of the effects of power as a result of the formation and legitimation of new forms of knowledge production.

THE DOMESTIC ECONOMY

In the nineteenth century the middle classes provided the institution of the family with a particular set of definitions, practices, and representations which played a necessary and pivotal role in the emergence of a capitalist social order and secured for the middle classes their hegemony within the social order. Central to the ideological construction of the family was the practice of bourgeois portraiture, and its representations played a significant part in affirming a set of social relations and a mode of subjectivity integral to the operations of that ideology. On one hand, the many photographs that we encounter of the middle-class family appear unremarkable because of their unrelieved consistency of pose, expression, and general format. On the other hand, their very lack of aesthetic values speaks to the presence of ideological conventions at work which reductively abstract from multiple families a singular and powerfully informing representational type. Moreover, the apparent innocence with which they offer themselves to the eye disappears once these photographs are located in the context of the discourses of the family, within whose ideological field the density of their meaning is disclosed.

By the mid-nineteenth century, struggles over the representation of gender and the proper relations between the sexes that had proceeded since the Enlightenment, had culminated in a new symbolic economy that demarcated public from private sphere and that laid the foundation for an emerging capitalist social order.[49] Even though the universal claims of greater equality and liberty made during the Enlightenment ushered in a period of genuine feminism, it was immediately contested by the majority of male thinkers who opposed increased public participation by women on the basis of sexual difference.[50] If, on the one hand, social-contract theory proposed a body undifferentiated in its ability to reason, it became incumbent upon liberal thinkers wishing to legitimize the domination of women by men, to resort to the book of nature. For example, in Rousseau's description of the state of nature, women's inherent physical and moral differences play a pivotal role in making her an unequal but complementary partner of man. In this perfect union, biological differences determine that "one ought to be active and strong, the other passive and weak.[51] As Thomas Laqueur has remarked "the creation of a bourgeois public sphere . . . raised with a vengeance the question of which sex(es) ought legitimately to occupy it. And everywhere biology entered the discourse."[52]

As early as 1765 the *Encyclopédia*, in its comparison of the female and male skeleton, concluded with the observation that "the destiny of women is to have children and nourish them."[53] In 1829, the Edinburgh physician John Barclay argued that a woman's skeletal structure was more similar in size and shape to that of a child's than that of a man's, with the exception of her pelvis which was her distinguishing characteristic. Similarly, craniological measurements of the skull supported the view that women lacked the "natural reason" that was a prerequisite for participation in the public sphere. Intelligence, like sexual identity, was innate, and women's brain size and lower intelligence were evident from their smaller skulls which were likened to those of children.[54] Consequently, into the very bones of women is written their exclusion from civil society. The smuggling of ideology into nature and reciprocally the biologization of the public sphere is evident in Comte's *Cours de philosophie positive*. According to Comte, the appropriate social roles for women was not a political question but a matter of biological evidence. In light of the view that anatomy and physiology had demonstrated the "radical differences, at once physical and moral" between the sexes, he argued that the continued stability of the family and the social order itself depended on the systematic subordination of women to men.[55] As Joan Landes has observed, "an ideologically sanctioned order of gender differences and public/private spheres . . . grounds the institutional and cultural geography of the new public sphere."[56]

The emerging order of middle-class reformers and professionals, operating in a discursive field constituted by the sciences, advice manuals, popular literature, and sermons, had begun by constructing and defining a model of the family in which the articulation of "natural" differences between the sexes pivoted on biological reproduction, which was then taken to determine both human nature and social roles. In this sense, sexual difference and the organization of sexual relations were constituted not as social but natural phenomena. A central moment in the expansion of this discourse formation was the 1843 observation by Theodor Bischoff of spontaneous ovulation in a dog, which provided scientific legitimation to the view, then current among medical men, that the woman's reproductive system was marked by an involuntary periodicity. This finding not only provided further confirmation of the "natural" differences between the sexes for professional medicine but also underwrote a view of women in which pleasure was incommensurable with reproduction.[57] Previously, Rousseau and Diderot had argued that women were innately modest, women's desire being anathematic to the functioning of civil society.[58] Later William Acton would remark that "the majority of women (happily for them) are not very much troubled by sexual feelings of any kind."[59] The same logic that deemed female pleasure irrelevant also privileged maternal love, which it was presumed had been demonstrated by spontaneous ovulation.[60] Thus, Peter Gaskell, writing in 1883, observed: "Love of helpless infancy—

attention to its wants, its sufferings, and its unintelligible happiness, seem to form the very wellspring of a woman's heart—fertilizing, softening, enriching all her grosser passions and appetites. It is truly an instinct in the strictest acceptance of the word."[61] Women, now identified with the maternal instinct, were viewed as noncompetitive, nonaggressive, tender, and self-sacrificing, qualities which provided them with a redemptive and moral power. Coventry Patmore's poem "The Angel in the House" epitomizes this idealized image of the woman.[62]

This was in sharp contrast to men who were seen as deeply divided and alienated by their participation in the market economy. The individual male was viewed not only as being able to recognize and act in his own interests but was also understood as a proprietary self, a concept which had received formulation in Locke's statement that "every man has a property in his own person." As one who exchanged his labor in the free market, this subject was inherently divided. Furthermore, since his labor was expropriated for the creation of surplus value and subject as well to the vicissitudes of the market, such a subject was also alienated.[63] However, this alienation, which expressed itself in the form of competition and aggression, was also viewed as advantageous both within the context of a narrative of self-development as well as in terms of the larger world of commerce driven by the principle that only the fittest should survive.

According to the circular reasoning of this model, males being by "nature" competitive and aggressive were ideally suited to the alienation of capitalism, while women who were given to emotion rather than reason, were in need of protection. This dictated that the public sphere be reserved as the exclusive domain of the male, whereas the private sphere would be relegated to women for the express purpose of providing succor and moral renewal to the male. The moral power of women's influence is supported in this observation by Gaskell: "The moral influence of woman upon man's character and domestic happiness . . . exercise[s] a most ennobling impression upon his nature, and do[es] more toward making him a good husband, a good father, and a useful citizen, than all the dogmas of political economy."[64] Thus while the reproductive system of women had been invoked to delineate and stabilize that sphere of the capitalist economy responsible for the reproduction of labor power, women's labor, instead of being accounted for in economic terms, was cast in emotional and moral language.[65]

In general, the binary opposition ratified not just the sexual division of labor but a whole host of cultural and economic practices including the sexual division of political rights. In its far-reaching effects, "[t]his representation of woman constituted the basis . . . for the fundamental model of male identity in capitalist society." Moreover, the gender difference not only became the basis for determining the roles and rights of men and women but also operated, as we have seen, to create an opposition between the public sphere characterized by alienation and the domestic sphere where it was assumed to be absent.[66] Thus, a discursive construction of the woman's body, which denied that body the possibility of formulating its own pleasures and interests, and which placed its desiring in the service of patriarchy, provided the terms on which to establish a nonalienated sphere of feminized morality that would balance and compensate for the struggles males would have to undergo in the public sphere. Correspondingly, the domestic ideal functioned as a desirable alternative that men labored to achieve and this, in turn, served to consolidate bourgeois power. At the same time, "the cult of domesticity helped to relieve the tensions that existed between the moral values of Christianity, with its emphasis on love and charity, and the values of capitalism . . . pervaded by the spirit of competition."[67] But this is not to say that during the nineteenth century the binary opposition between the sexes was not culturally contested. The domestic ideal was constantly in need of "extensive ideological work," especially given the incongruence between the ideal and what was attainable, as evidenced by the "problem" of large numbers of unmarried working women or "redundant women" as W.R. Gregg termed them in 1862.[68]

Nineteenth-century portraiture, in functioning to bring the body of ordinary experience to visibility and to think it into a normative order, became a disciplinary practice essential to the cultural reproduction of the individual and the family. What needs to be understood is that portraiture is always about public display, even if the photograph is limited to private consumption. There is an attending to the discursive, the cultural, and the social that is implicit in the portrait. The portrait registers both social disposition and cultural intention which, communicated by way of the displayed body, legitimizes a particular discursive and ideological formation. That is to say, social attentiveness and cultural intentionality communicated via the represented body are ideological elements and constitutive of ideological practice. Drawing on Clifford Geertz's description of the function of art, it can be said that portraiture "materializes a way of experiencing"; it "brings a particular cast of mind into the world of objects where man can look at it."[69]

Photographic portraiture, in confining its production largely to the display of individual males on the one hand and depictions of the cult of domesticity on the other, explicitly modelled and endorsed the symbolic separation between the public and private spheres of bourgeois life. The portrait photographs of individual middle-class males bear witness to, testify to, and evoke the autonomous category of the bourgeois self; they display the gendered body engaged in a performance of that destiny which is linked to the assumption of a proprietary self. The alienation that is productively expressed in aggression and competitiveness finds its reflection in the portrait, which reiterates the form of that alienation in its display of self-as-other. Simultaneously, the photo-text of bourgeois portraiture evokes the idea of the male as recipient of socially sanctioned rights, and all of this, silently written into the expression and topos of the textualized body, manifests itself in the self-governance of rationalized display (Fig. 6).

In portraiture we discover that the representation of individualism "derives its power through the citations that it compels" from the photographed body.[70] If, as Freud argued, "the ego is first and foremost a bodily ego" or if it is an "imaginary morphology," which Butler asserts is secured through regulatory schemas, we can expect the normative production of identity to be constantly projected onto and textualized in relation to the surface of the body.[71] Hence, in these photographs we encounter males whose enactment of identity, whose desire for coherence and normative representation, is idealized and circumscribed according to corporeal significations. Photography then becomes a performative practice of such "interiors" as respectability, character, sex, and so on, conveyed via bodily significations whose meanings are guaranteed by the discourses of physiognomy, phrenology, and gender.

At the same time, the family portrait, by providing a normative representation of the family through pose, lighting, and a set of typologies, typifies and idealizes the family and helps renew a whole train of commitments to the domestic ideal (Fig. 7). Here is a representational space in which industriousness and cunning come to roost in their domesticated other—morality. And where the familial body is sat

Figure 6. Alfred Tennyson, 1869.

Figure 7. Portrait of a couple, c. 1850.

foursquare and solid in the center of the frame, the sexual division of labor anchored in the gendered subjectivities of husband and wife; the male's body conducts itself with public authority; his wife on the other hand, a more private figure, appears as the dutiful support, with signs of their conjugality arranged in regular and decorative intervals about them (Fig. 8). In the family portrait, experience is idealized and compressed in a representational tableau; the family is instantiated in frozen ritualized display; as cliché and quotation it is oddly superficial in content; and as an image it is seemingly reticent but that is because it is so firmly anchored in the ideological terrain of a middle-class paradigm and requires very little explication for its subjects. While the portrait "appears" to be denotational—pointing, stating, announcing—beneath the coded expressions of its subjects lurks the discursive regime of the dominant culture they inhabit; power emanates from a unified, determinate space—the privileged site in front of the camera—and the system of differences that constitutes the photograph, is at one and the same time the textured fabric of dominant social relations.

What is more, for the nineteenth-century sitter, being photographed in a studio represented a ceremonious occasion. And ceremonies, we are given to understand, symbolically affirm and celebrate specific discursive and ideological formations. The sitting thus carries with it the elements of theater as the subjects establish, by means of conventions that include both the practices of the camera and body, a metonymic performance of a discursive field. And it is the metonymic nature of the photograph that provides to the family portrait its compressed content, its patent obviousness, its self-evident nature.

However, ideology is not limited to its performative expression in the studio but is elaborated upon in the seclusion of the middle-class home;[72] for in returning the "gaze" of a family member, its seamless surface uninterruptable, the portrait reproduces a fantasy of the normative statement. In the mode of intersubjectivity established between family member and portrait, we are confronted not with a simple record, but with the expression of a sentiment that disciplines.[73] Hence, within the enclosed family, which had become the agent and scene of discipline, the family portrait takes its rightful place. For even though the family unit, bound by cords of reciprocal love and obligation, does not manifest itself in its entirety on the surface of the photograph, the portrait, being a veritable showcase and establishing the normative

Figure 8. Working-class family, Birmingham, England, 1860s.

"scene" of the family with its appropriately gendered subjects, its self-evident hierarchy, and passive children on display, nevertheless evokes a discipline of love. Here is a pedagogy that not only seeks to bind the child in the present but also to construct an ideal basis for familial memory.

The portrait, in turn, generates other cultural spaces of normative and ritualistic value. The photograph album as family chronicle, is a collection of nineteenth-century private lives engaged in social moments—the coming of age, the picnic, the engagement, the marriage—with bodies striking poses or in repose inhabiting esplanades, drawing rooms, pavillions, and promenades anchored in social time, space, and class, representing simultaneously familial memory, living social document, and genetic record. As one observer has noted, these settings "leave the Victorians exactly where they want to be, framed in distant, conventional poses which deflect the examining eye."[74] The family album is both a document of social assertion and a sentimental register; it represents a domesticated space of cultivated, nonproductive appearance, which has been carefully scripted, arranged, and suspended before the camera to record; as such these photographic documents, counterposing continuity to the ruptures of daily life, confirm the power of domestic fictions to conceal the contradictions of lived experience.

Moreover, in portrait after portrait, the family appears "as an autonomous emotional unit [that] cuts across class and power relations to imply that everyone shares the same experience."[75] The regulation of images, in providing for "a common sexual and economic goal" and in enabling ideological oversight to permeate the private realm, plays "a central role in the development of the . . . ideology of the family."[76] For example, Marcus Aurelius Root, writing in America in 1864, makes such a utilitarian claim for the salutary effects of photographic portraiture on the working-class family when he notes: "To what extent domestic and social affections and sentiments are conserved and perpetuated by these 'shadows' of the loved and valued originals, everyone may judge. The cheapness of these pictures brings them within reach, substantially, of all."[77]

Besides the discourses that we have already considered which inform the practices of nineteenth-century photographic portraiture, certain cultural and technical practices were pursued, and their consequences were no less ideological. As already argued, photographs are not simply representations but are representational in that they are permeated by a system of values and an intelligibility which endow their subjects with meaning. Lest we forget, the camera image is a sliced, framed, and cropped piece of reality. Are we surprised then that in nineteenth-century portraiture, the camera does not address its bourgeois subjects with the blunt frontality with which the criminal, the insane, the poor (as in Jacob Riis photographs), and the colonial subject are forced to confront the camera's gaze; rigid frontality signified the bluntness and "naturalness" of a culturally unsophisticated class ("pose de l'homme de la nature") and had a history, in the satire of Hogarth and Daumier, that predated photographic portraiture.[78]

The head-on stare in such cases should be read in contrast to the cultivated asymmetries of aristocratic pose, for pose is a function of leisure while frontality confirms the complete lack of it. Leisure, or that which signifies freedom from the necessity of reproducing the body, makes possible not only conspicuous consumption but representation of the body as symbolic text. Freed from its brute facticity, the body is reconstituted and mediated by the photograph as text and posed as cultural value at some distance from itself. In general, the preparedness and display of the body signalled a heightened awareness among middle-class citizens that the body, appropriately attired and arrayed, was definitely a cultural and class signifier in a society increasingly mediated by visual interaction.[79] With the democratization of fashion, the awareness of the body as a zone of signification proliferated downward through the social hierarchy.

Finally, what can we say or what should we say about the photographer's studio, that apparatus for producing visibility? An exploration of the spaces of the upper-class photographic studio or gallery as it came to be called, may provide us with an effective manner of making evident what was involved here. The upper-class gallery consisted of three major functioning spaces: (i) the reception room, (ii) the studio where the subjects were transformed into images, and (iii) the factory space of production.[80] In the reception room, the walls were hung with iconic representations (Fig. 9). Marcus Aurelius Root describes the function of this space, as one decorated and embellished with portraits of "the leading types of characters which might be expected among the sitters, and to be calculated to call into vivid action the feelings pertaining to these characters."[81]

Figure 9. M.B. Brady's New Photographic Gallery, corner of Broadway and Tenth Street, New York.

The second space, that is, the studio space, is in effect a fabricated space, a theatrical space outfitted with props designed to promote the public self of portraiture. It is a space for constructing metonymic signs that evoke the necessary impressions and experiences. A synecdochically organized space, it often conveys itself as a drawing room—that center of bourgeois domesticity; at other times, the space is a balcony off the main drawing room—a captain's bridge for a captain of industry, the statesman's platform of rhetoric; or the space becomes simply a place to promenade. As such it was designed to evoke the necessary symbols of the family and the social order that comprise the bourgeois milieu and within which its subjects are positioned. Is it coincidental, then, that some of the large-format "cartes-de-visite" were entitled Promenade, Boudoir, and Imperial Panel, conjuring up the very spaces that the photographs framed? These are the spaces that savour the hegemony and presence of a particular class: spaces not of labor, but of cultivated leisure, characteristic of a capitalist class; and through their use of Grecian columns and voluminous drapes exude a civilizing and civilized air. In photograph after photograph, we witness rooms and figures—a panoramic view of the bourgeois on parade under the idolatrous gaze of the camera.

The "ground of intelligibility" of portraiture, as Alan Trachtenberg refers to it, or the "regime of sense," is to be found operating in this space.[82] For here we discover photographers, deeply involved in discourses of physiognomy and phrenology, as they wield their insight machines supposedly disclosing character with a discerning intent. However, as already demonstrated, what the photographer possesses is really a set of physiognomic typologies to render the subject in the manner of the very iconic images displayed reverently in the reception room. The cycle is complete and thus a new image enters the symbolic order of the portrait as public self, signified and encoded by a system of conventionalized signs. And, finally, we encounter the concealed factory space of production, with its division of polishers, coaters, and mercuralizers busily at work processing photographs for their distribution, to those eagerly waiting to be ushered into a transaction with the public community of images, transcribed and circumscribed by a moral icon of representative character.

Thus, on the one hand, the camera, by democratizing the image, provides those previously invisible with the opportunity to be visible as subjects of their own representations. On the other hand, however, the representational system discursively produces them as objects of that visibility, for that visibility is at one and the same time ideologically binding. But there are pleasures to be had in conforming to dominant ideology and the subjectivity proposed by representational adherence ("plaisir"). And there are other pleasures too; for the photographer's studio, with its props and the resulting photo-text with its typologies, soon available to all classes, enables individuals to momentarily conceal their working-class backgrounds and be made visible in the light of their aspirations. Hence, lived differences are subsumed in the homogenous syntax of an idealized typology functioning as bourgeois icon.

THE OTHER WITHIN

I wish, however, to counterpose against this economy of representations, against the self-assured fixity of these images and their seamless portrayal of the libidinal organization of bourgeois patriarchy, a different set of images from the nineteenth-century archive. Photographic history has generally had little to say about the intersections between imperialism and industrialism within which nineteenth-century photography is implicated. For this reason, as David Bate suggests, it has been "complicitious with . . . a colonialist gaze."[83] I hope both to rectify this neglect and to illustrate that patriarchal ideology not only underwrites the conventional portraiture of the family but extends into those operations which function to fetishize the representations of the Other. These latter images, which are implicated in the webs of an imperialist discourse and are a direct result of the colonial encounter, function as a zone for the projection and the displacement of male fantasy. The field of domestic representations must be expanded to incorporate these images because they are part of the order of its hidden realm, its barely concealed repressions, and are therefore revealing. It is a field of representations wherein the Other becomes a terrain for the forces and energies of suppressed desire; here difference and disavowal disturb and unhinge the dominant field of bourgeois portraiture while underscoring the ambivalence of a bourgeois discourse. What is prohibited by the libidinal economy of domestic relations, whose continuance is essential to the maintenance of the industrial order, is (re)presented, (re)oriented, and (re)located in the Other.

During the nineteenth century the Orient became a favored destination of the bourgeois imaginary. Writers like Flaubert and Gérard de Nerval and adventurers like Richard Burton took up residence in the Orient and began to produce a large body of Oriental-style writings. These writings which ranged from the purely archaeological—Lane's *An Account of the Manners and Customs of the Modern Egyptians*—to works that were spectacular in form and dreamlike in content, were bound by a remarkable discursive unity.[84] As a consequence there emerged an oriental world "governed . . . not simply by empirical reality but by a battery of desires, repressions, investments and projections."[85] What was true of literary works and travel accounts was also the case with Orientalist painting.[86] As Nissan Perez notes, by the 1840s the demand for photographs of the Orient was such that a number of European photographers resorted to producing in their studios in the West, genre scenes with Oriental subjects (Figs. 10 & Fig. 11). These staged Oriental scenes were to exert considerable influence on "later styles of representation, including even those of photographs executed in the Orient in authentic surroundings."[87] By the 1850s, however, a number of commercial photographers, especially from France and England, had established studios in the Near East to cater to the tourist trade, or travelled to and from the Orient to supply the demand in the home market.[88] This intensive photographic activity represented what the nineteenth-century critic Francis Wey called "les conquêtes pacifiques" (the peaceful conquest) of the Orient.[89]

Western photographers who travelled to the East encountered the Orient in much the same way as had their literary predecessors, and their work reflected the prevailing discourse: "Even if the images were taken *dal vero* [from real life] and their arrangement and composition reflected a certain truth and objective reality, in the end they were still false. . . . The Orient remained embedded in the private fantasies and imagination of the Westerner. Most photographers could not free themselves from the mental image they brought with them to the Orient; they forced the hard reality into visual fantasy."[90] In the nineteenth century, for instance, the colonial fetish of the harem was such that the news photo agency Underwood & Underwood introduced a popular series of stereo images entitled "Favorites of the Harem," featuring erotic images of scantily dressed women in a pseudo-Oriental interior. The photographer Tancrède Dumas, who resided in Beirut, contributed

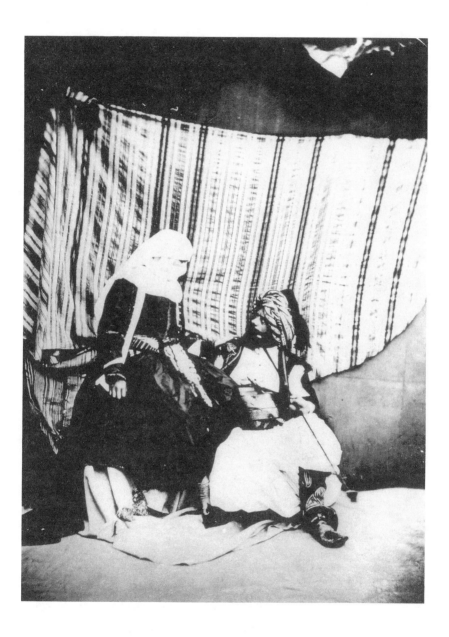

Figure 10. Courting couple, 1860s.

Figure 11. Semi-nude lying on a divan, c. 1852.

to the traffic in Orientalist photography by fabricating a harem scene through a crudely executed photomontage (Fig. 12).[91]

What we discover in these images is that desire and threat coalesce in the formations of erotic and political projections. In the images which feature European men dressed in native costume and lounging in casual, slothful poses, mimicry is engaged in the fantasy of identification with the despot (Fig. 13). These photographs reflect the Western male subject's desire to partake in the mythic fantasies of sexual domination figured by the Orientalist discourse on the harem.[92] The scenography of despotism provides for an erotic fantasy of the powerful patriarch with monopoly control of all women and is reminiscent of Freud's description in *Totem and Taboo* of the family prior to Oedipal Law.[93] Projected in general onto the Orient, this fantasy has the effect of transforming the Orient into a supplement, an exotic locale to be penetrated as sexual phantasm (Fig. 14). We see this in a number of photographs of the period, where the intent was to blatantly unveil and transform the Oriental woman into an object of scopophilic desire, to make of her body a ready availability (Figs. 15 & 16).

As Perez informs us, many of these women who were "photographed in evocative poses were no doubt prostitutes." In some cases, as the portrait of the Nubian model testifies, they were blind and may have been unaware of what was happening (Fig. 17).[94] And hence, ensnared in her darkness, the other woman is bared to the perverse illumination of the colonial subject's gaze. Since, in nineteenth-century Europe, sex was normatively tied to the bourgeois concept of the family, what is repressed is then displaced and transferred onto the Other, who is forced to function as the scene of prohibited desire and licentious pleasures. "Just as the various colonial possessions—quite apart from their economic benefit to metropolitan Europe—were useful as places to send wayward sons, superfluous populations of delinquents, poor people, and other undesirables, so the Orient was a place where one could look for sexual experience unobtainable in Europe."[95]

At the same time, however, the Other woman also portends danger, because even though her sensuality is a promise of the prohibited libidinal power of women, that in itself poses a threat to Western male identity and the polarized categories of its constitution. "Like the mirror-phase 'the fullness' of the stereotype—its image as identity—is

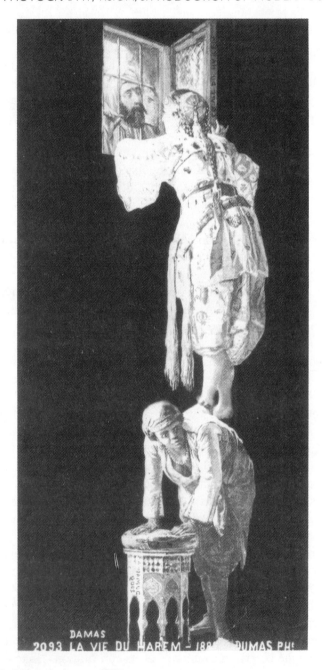

Figure 12. Life in the harem, 1889.

Figure 13. The photographer Francis Frith in Turkish summer costume, c. 1860.

Figure 14. Almée, late 1840s.

Figure 15. Nubian woman, 1860s.

Figure 16. Oriental dancer, 1860s.

Figure 17. Blind Nubian woman, 1890s.

always threatened by lack."[96] It is also for this very reason that the colonial subject tends, in keeping with a phallocentric discourse, to view the colony as woman, seductive, dangerous, portending even death in terms of the effacement of selfhood. Thus the Other woman is simultaneously instantiated in the double bind of a colonial discourse, which either objectifies her for a narcissistic gaze (erotism) or views her as potentially threatening to the male psyche. It is in terms of this dynamic that repressed male desire transgresses the domestic economy to fetishize the Other.

The structural ambivalence of colonial mimicry should also be understood in the context of the bourgeois male who journeyed to the Orient and was primarily motivated by a disenchantment with a rational social order and a desire for self-discovery. "Many of the early Oriental amateurs began by welcoming the Orient as a salutary 'derangement' of their European habits of mind and spirit."[97] Hence Richard Burton escaped a stifling Victorian moral regime and Kinglake affirmed in *Eothen* the value of the Orient as a place for remaking oneself. This impulse to reinvent the self, expressed in terms of a displacement posited on the Other, also constitutes a threat, insofar as it poses the possibility of identification with the Other (the despot) and hence the potential effacement of the colonial subject's identity.[98]

As Alan Grosrichard, in his study *Structure du Serail*, points out, the myth of Oriental despotism is not only about untrammelled domestic patriarchal authority but about state political power too: *le grand serail*, in effect combining a sexual with a political monopoly of power.[99] "In a despotism the citizens have no more rights than the women and slaves in a patriarchal household. Thus, the image of the seraglio is crucial to the scenography of the Orient precisely because it conflates state and household. The patriarch and the Shah [the phallus] merge into one."[100] The threat of political absolutism which dispenses with the rule of law is a source of anxiety for the West and is projected onto the screen of the Other, even as domestic patriarchal authority which signifies a singular male (despot) and a plurality of women (harem) is a source of desire. Hence the photographs of the Orient which function as the site of displacement of erotic and political fantasy, disturb and render ambivalent the libidinal economy of bourgeois patriarchal relations expressed in the dominant economy of bourgeois portraiture. And, at the same time, photography's twin functioning within the discursive regimes of capitalism and imperialism makes it possible for what is repressed in the domestic order to be displaced onto the body of the Other, so that the Other operates as the site of specular desire.

A SPECTACULAR ORDER OF IMAGES

Even with the sudden explosion of representations brought about by the arrival of the "carte-de-visite" and the consequent onset of scopophilia in the nineteenth century, the irony is that the visible geography of the self in all its expressible variety and difference arrived in the structured sameness of the traditional bourgeois portrait. The "carte-de-visite," patented by André Adolphe Disdéri in 1854, would, however, go a long way toward establishing that economy of images Oliver Wendell Holmes called for: "there must be arranged a comprehensive system of exchanges, so that there might grow up something like a universal currency of these banknotes, or promises to pay in solid substance, which the sun has engraved for the Great Bank of Nature." [101] Disderi had realized that, given the potential demand for photographic portraiture, it was as yet available to a relatively few. His ingenious idea was to produce a "carte-de-visite" portrait photograph of 3½ × 2½ inches. This consisted of a paper print mounted on a slightly larger card, a print produced by use of a special camera equipped with four lenses and a moving plate-holder capable of taking eight exposures at one sitting. [102] Furthermore, since unskilled labor could be utilized for many of the operations, the "carte-de-visite" could be sold inexpensively. A single negative and a dozen exposures sold at one-fifth the usual cost. Whereas earlier a single print had cost anywhere from fifty to a hundred francs, Disdéri charged twenty francs for twelve photographs. [103] The radical changes in format and cost dramatically increased the accessibility of photographic portraiture even among the lower classes.

The introduction of photography to a wider public at the Industrial Exposition of 1855, part of the spectacle of the Paris World's Fair, further served to boost Disdéri's business; soon his studios—which were in effect well-run factories, staffed with a large number of assistants—were able to offer a forty-eight-hour service on hundreds of copies. [104] The industrialization of the image had been taken up with renewed vigor and as a result the image was provided with a new level of mobility. Disdéri constructed his conventional portrayals[105] through a liberal use of props. He utilized the method to excess when he concocted his scheme to package portrait collections of contemporary celebrities, a practice which was taken up on an international scale by photographers elsewhere in Europe and America. As the popularity of "carte" portraits increased, works of art, famous monuments, and fashionably attired women, in addition to celebrities, appeared on them, and soon people were avidly exchanging and collecting these images in ornate albums produced to satisfy the new craze (Fig. 18).

But as Rosenblum has indicated, the significance of these celebrity images went far beyond their immediate impact as a popular pastime. They pointed to the impact that the image as public discourse and exchange in urban communication could exert on the cultural and political domains.

> Both the moderately gifted Jenny Lind and the unexceptional Lola Montez became cult figures in the United States largely owing to their promotion through carte portraits. Lincoln is said to have ascribed his election to the Presidency at least in part to Brady's carte of him when he still was an unknown.[106]

Royalty, realizing that here was a powerful symbolic environment that they could harness to their own benefit, provided permission for their royal likenesses to be made into "carte" portraits for distribution to their subjects. Mayall managed to sell 100,000 copies of his photographs of the Royal Family.[107] On the death of Prince Albert, Queen Victoria's consort, 70,000 portraits of the prince were sold.[108]

The expanding middle-class ideological formation, the cultural demand for representations, and entrepreneurial zeal had combined to introduce a new direction to photography;[109] in turn, it helped establish the basis for a spectacular economy of images. It was not that the older regime of disciplinary sentimentality and moral influence had been suddenly overturned, but rather that in parallel manner the regime of the spectacle had begun to operate.[110] The introduction of serial production, especially in the case of the "carte-de-visite," had meant the introduction of a radically new sign—"in a series, objects become undefined simulacra of each other."[111] The image was entering a whole new configuration, an assemblage of technical and cultural practices, that

Figure 18. Artists' portraits, c. 1866.

increasingly privileged serial production and concommitantly the circulation and proliferation of signs severed from a referent.

At about the same time, the first retouched prints made by Franz Hafstaingl, a renowned German lithographer of art works and portraits, were exhibited at the Paris Industrial Exposition. Soon afterward, "the bourgeois insistence on a 'pleasant' prettified self-image led to the practice of retouching"[112] portraits. The introduction of the first anastigmatic lenses, which enhanced the optical capability of the camera so as to provide images of unusual clarity, exacerbated the tendency toward retouching. The process of retouching further emphasized the radical contingency of the image, now increasingly divorced from its referent. Courbet, in turn, retaliated by mounting a banner over the entrance of the gallery at which he was exhibiting his work, a banner which bluntly announced in opposition: "Realism."[113]

This expanding economy of images which announces the world as image, inaugurated the prehistory of the spectacle. Thus we discover in 1860 Felix Nadar, the well-known French portraitist, descending into the catacombs of Paris to retrieve sights never before seen. Nadar's career epitomized the confluence between the emerging regime of the spectacle and surveillance. For in 1856 he took the first aerial photographs of Paris while flying in a balloon, and became indispensable to the French military because he was able to photograph the movements of the German troops during the German siege of Paris.[114]

In 1878 Charles Harper Bennett developed a gelatin dry plate which made it possible for exposure times to be reduced to one twenty-fifth of a second. With the reduction in exposure time, the tripod became dispensable and the camera's new mobility was announced in a wide variety of hand-held cameras. With the use of the "detective cameras," average citizens could now partake of the visual culture of the city by engaging in surveillance or voyeurism without the risk of being detected or embarrassed (Fig. 19). With the introduction of George Eastman's Kodak in 1888, photography was introduced to millions through a fully industrialized process of mass production.

During this same period, manufacturers began to produce dry plates and, as a result, photographers no longer had to prepare the plates themselves. In this manner, the basis for a photofinishing industry was established, even as function by function, component by component, the production process was dismantled from its unity and basis in one

Figure 19. Snapshot. Courtesy of the George Eastman House.

individual and reassembled in manufacturing spaces elsewhere. If the amateur photographer was displaced from his or her traditional position, so was the portraitist, who had not long ago displaced the miniaturist and engraver. The portraitists' only alternative was to enter the very nexus of relations they had indirectly brought into existence, by opening photographic stores to cater to the new clientele of amateur photographers.[115]

The latter part of the nineteenth century not only witnessed the establishment of the photofinishing industry and the mass production of hand-held cameras, but also the introduction of the half-tone plate, which at last made possible the economical and endless reproduction of photographs in magazines, books, newspapers, advertisements, and so forth. Along with the capability of sending photographs by wire transmitter, these developments signalled a fundamental transformation in the status of the image. Where previously the camera had been made mobile, now the image received an increased level of circulation and exchange. Where earlier technical efforts had concentrated on increasing exposure rates of a single image, these new developments multiplied the extent to which individuals would be exposed to images. In newspapers, magazines, and advertising, the photograph became the perfectly consumable image, because it could be thrown away as soon as it was consumed.[116] The image, always vulnerable to a number of interpretations, now received a mutational form in being able to express a multiplicity of meanings depending on the context in which it occurred. It had now become a hyper-commodity, a continuously renewable commodity in new contexts, producing a surplus of sign-value with each new exchange.

THREE

Photography and the Deviant Body

INTRODUCTION

Michel Foucault has identified the emergence of a new regime of power which gradually evolved throughout the eighteenth and nineteenth centuries in Western Europe. During a period of great demographic changes and general urbanization, this power established itself in the scientific and legal institutions; and the discourses produced functioned to implicate the body within the demands of social engineering and the humanistic rhetoric of reform, to comprise a disciplinary bio-politics. In this political technology of the body, the instrumentalities of discursive power intercede at the level between the functioning of the institution and the bodies themselves, establishing a "micro-physics" of power which organizes the body deeply in a circular logic so that the formation of knowledge and the increase of power reinforce one another. Power is no longer simply the perpetuation of ideology in its ideational and expressive form, neither is it crude and unadulterated physical repression; but, rather, it is now positivized as discipline that permeates its objects with a new and luminous visibility. Power thus imbricates the discourses, the actions, the very gestures of everyday living and by this means inserts itself into the capillaries of the social body.[1]

THE EMERGENCE OF THE CRIMINAL

In his revolutionary document *Dei delitti e delle pene*, first published anonymously in 1764, Cesare di Beccaria made the following statement to his readers: "Observe that by justice I understand nothing more, than that bond, which is necessary to keep the interest of individuals united; without which, men would return to their original state of barbarity. All punishments, which exceed the necessity of preserving this bond, are in their nature unjust."[2] The influence of Montesquieu is evident as is the reference to Rousseau's social contract. Beccaria not only proclaimed the equality of all before the law, but he censured authorities for their arbitrary and excessive use of power and denounced torture and the death penalty. What the *Dei delitti* announced was a "whole new conception of . . . justice" based on enlightenment principles[3] and it represented a fundamental attack on the foundations of the criminal justice system. It became the rallying cry for an educated urban class who resented the tyranny of the church and the state. Desirous of finding new and efficient ways of protecting and advancing their economic needs, they became the most ardent reformers and supporters of the classical system of justice.

According to the theory of the social contract that Beccaria and other humanist reformers drew on, crime no longer constituted an assault on the body of the sovereign but rather a violation of the contract which the collective body had agreed to uphold. Since it was the collective body that had been victimized by the crime, it was within the rights of society to punish. Citizens had freely obligated themselves to observe the social contract and accept punishment if they transgressed it; and such punishment derived from the need to protect the rights and freedoms of individuals against possible usurpation by others. The standard according to which justice would be meted out was based on the common humanity of the parties to the contract, since any crime implicated both the criminal and the general society. No longer would punishment be viewed as a retribution exacted in a spectacular display of public excess that marks, maims, and breaks the body of the condemned in order to reconstitute the body of the sovereign.[4] The excess and immoderation that attended sovereign punishment would be supplanted by a more rational and lenient distribution of justice.

Did the new reforms represent the voice of compassion and humanity confronting the tyranny of an oppressive system? Or did they harbor the desire to punish not less but to punish more effectively, through rational means, because the traditional methods of retribution no longer appeared to be as effective? In England the proliferation of penalties in the eighteenth century that sought to criminalize customary rights inhibiting the development of commercial activities,[5] meant that between 1765 and the end of the Napoleonic Wars, the number of offenses punishable by death had increased from 160 to 225, under the new Bloody Code.[6] Given the severity of the punishment, it was not surprising that "persons, lay and official, who administered the criminal law, invented and indulged in practices which almost nullified the capital penalty."[7] The law had become unpredictable and under this system it was a matter of chance and speculation whether a particular criminal would be convicted or not. In 1818, of 13,567 persons who were tried for capital offenses, 8,958 were convicted, 1,254 were sentenced to death, and 97 were executed.[8] Since the new game, vagrancy, and embezzlement statutes were being selectively enforced, the middle classes with property at stake complained that the failure to penalize petty crimes only encouraged petty criminals to proceed unhindered toward the commission of more serious crimes.[9] The reformer Samuel Romilly observed that, since the multiplication of capital offenses, only 15 percent of those guilty of capital crimes were being executed, compared to the mid-eighteenth-century figure of between 50 and 75.[10] Matters were further exacerbated by the awareness that the efficacy of public hangings as a deterrent value had become quite suspect: "[T]he physical confrontation between the sovereign and the condemned man must end; this hand-to-hand fight between the vengeance of the prince and the contained anger of the people, through the mediation of the victim and the executioner, must be concluded."[11] The disproportionate use of power to affirm the invincibility of the prince produced itself as a surplus that both threatened and unified the crowd, which more often than not transformed the solemn ritual into a popular bacchanal "in which rules were inverted, authority mocked and criminals transformed into heroes."[12]

With the demand that the death penalty be abolished and the advocacy of punishment guaranteed to redress the wrong done to society, the question of the reform of the criminal became a central issue: "The immediate principal end of punishment is to control action. This action is either that of the offender, or of others: that of the offender it controls by its influence, either on his will, in which case it is said to operate in the way of reformation; or on his physical power, in which case it is said to operate by disablement: that of others it can influence no less otherwise than by its influence over their wills; in which case it is said to operate in the way of example."[13] Bentham's statement coalesces the fundamental principles of the classical system of punishment, which substitutes for the excesses of an omniscient and brutal revenge the transparent light of reason and the triumphant humanistic coda of reformation and deterrence. Following Beccaria, Bentham observed in his *Introduction to the Principles of Morals and Legislation* (1780) that "all punishment in itself is evil. Upon the principle of utility . . . it ought only to be admitted in as far as it promises to exclude some greater evil."[14] According to Bentham's "felicity calculus," criminals were rationally capable of weighing the pleasure derived from the crime against the quantum of punishment that would result. Motivated by the force of reason, the new system of punishment proposed to shift the application of the punishment from the body to the mind of the criminal. But to devise a system of proportional justice required that a comprehensive body of knowledge be established in which each crime and its corresponding punishment could be objectively coded. Thus, a system of jurisprudence that seemed to express "the perfection of reason"[15] was called for. The new system of justice proposed not only more humanitarian punishment but greater efficiency in application.

A legal discourse that founded its right to punish on a social contract "had to be presented as deriving from enlightened reason in continual progress, to justify the relations of direct domination it imposed."[16] For in the actual administration and exercise of justice, ideological valuations and differences of class and gender continued to play a constitutive role in determinations of guilt. As a number of scholars have observed, the emerging middle classes benefited greatly from the new criminal justice system.[17] Not only were they protected from the whims of aristocratic privilege, but they soon came to occupy positions of authority within the new judicial system which enabled them to enact laws that reflected their changing needs.[18] A case in point was the Master and Servant Act of 1823. It instituted a differential system of punishment, according to which employers could only be fined for a breach of contract, while employees were subject to the rigors of criminal prosecution.[19]

THE PENITENTIARY

But before resistance could actually develop against the system of judicial representations, which was anyway quite flawed, a new and more efficient system of punishment was introduced with the prison as its centerpiece.[20] In England, prior to 1775, imprisonment was rarely used as a form of punishment.[21] Besides ritualized punishments like hanging, whipping, and pillory, transportation of convicts to the colonies, where they would provide much needed labor, was the dominant practice. Prisons were utilized primarily to confine debtors and as a transitional place to house criminals who were in the judicial process. As a general rule, those prisons that existed were run by private contractors and, lacking formal supervision from outside authority, they were altogether riddled with abuses and injustices.[22] In the face of criticism directed against the death penalty and increasing evidence that petty crimes were not being prosecuted because of the severity of the penalty, judges and magistrates realized the need for a punishment that was intermediate between hanging and transportation: "It was necessary to find an intermediate penalty, combining "correction of the body" with "correction of the mind.""[23] In England, in a debate before the House of Commons (1810), Samuel Romilly argued that the deterrent value of punishment was being weakened by the present "lottery of justice." Echoing Beccaria, he advocated that the solution lay in the certainty of punishment rather than severity of punishment: "So evident is the truth of that maxim, that if it were possible that punishment as the consequence of guilt could be reduced to an absolute certainty, a very slight penalty would be sufficient to prevent almost every species of crime, except those which arise from sudden gusts of ungovernable passion."[24] The war with America which suspended convict transportation, and increases in both population and crime, all contributed to a strain on the existing system of prisons and increased as well the pressure for reform.

In this transformation of the "epistemologico-juridical" formation, which coalesces humanist reforms with that of a disciplinary technology, "the humanization of the penal system" is correlative with "the knowledge of man."[25] Punishment must now act on the criminal's soul, his perversity; it must act in depth and silently upon his inclinations, will, and aptitude and in doing so it inserts into the legal process a whole body of knowledge whose effect is the transformation of the criminal's body according to a new set of power relations.

> It would be wrong to say that the soul is an illusion, or an ideological effect. On the contrary, it exists, it has reality, it is produced

> permanently around, on, within the body by the functioning of a
> power that is exercised on those punished. . . . This real, noncorpo-
> ral soul is not a substance; it is the element in which are articulated
> the effects of a certain type of power and the reference of a certain
> type of knowledge.[26]

The criminal had become an expanding discursive field for the conduct
of investigations, experiments, observations, and classifications by a
host of experts or disciplinary technicians who would distribute the
question of the criminal beyond the purely legal realm and into the
moral, medical, and biological realm. It is within what Foucault refers
to as this burgeoning "political anatomy"—elements, materials, and
discourses that function as relays and support for the knowledge power
relations that transform bodies into objects of knowledge[27]—that photography would play its particular role. It would simultaneously function to discipline and regulate the body of the criminal as well as
apprehend the "soul" of the criminal.

John Howard's *The State of the Prison,* which appeared in
England in 1777, became the basis for the Penitentiary Act of 1779.[28]
The book was a systematic documentation of prison abuses and a comprehensive program for a political technology of the body. It stimulated
a reform movement which included both doctors who were revolution-
izing institutional hygiene and industrialists like Josiah Wedgewood,
who were the originators of the factory system and scientific management in England.[29] The introduction of a political technology which
took as its sources a materialist psychology, Catholic monastic tradi-
tion, Dutch Protestant asceticism, and middle-class reformism, would
fashion out of its discursive web a salvation for earthly use by the state.
Howard's belief in the universality of sin was the basis for his con-
tention that the state had a moral obligation to the criminal and it underwrote his conviction that the criminal was capable of being reformed.
His vision of imprisonment conceived in terms of Quaker pietism was
that of purgatory, suffering, and solitary introspection; secluded from
the corruptions of the senses, the criminal would be forced to confront
the self.[30]

But the transformation of the soul would only be possible if the
body were subjected to the rigorous functioning of a disciplinary
machine, which included the wearing of uniforms, cellular confinement, fixed hours of rising, reading of the Bible, prayer, work, and con-

stant supervision. That the body was a visible template of the soul was provided scientific legitimation by Hartleian materialism, which effaced the mind-body distinction by claiming that pathologies of the psyche were rooted in the body, inasmuch as disturbances of the bodily system registered themselves on the psyche.[31] Thus, the boundary of the body is configured so that it becomes permeable, a conduit by means of which the interior psyche can be effected; but it is also the surface on which pathologies of the self register themselves. "Materialist psychology implied that a regimen applied to the body by the external force of authority would first become a habit and then gradually be transformed into a moral preference. Through routinization and repetition, the regimens of discipline would be internalized as moral duties."[32] However, the religious dimension in Howard's reformist discourse also enabled him to contradictorily assert that, in addition to submitting the body to a disciplinary regimen, the value of punishment lay in inducing social guilt in the criminal.[33]

But as the reformers of the 1770s, especially Bentham, were aware, if punishment must be relied on to produce guilt, its efficacy in this regard was dependent on its moral legitimacy. This in turn required that discipline in the penitentiary appear to be both rational, impartial, and benevolent.[34] Within this program of "scientific humanity" which would seek to reconcile "deterrence and rehabilitation, punishment and reform," punishment would no longer be left to the capricious authority of a private contractor but was to be brought directly within the functioning and guidance of the state; punishment was too crucial to the exercise of class rule to be left unsupervised in private hands.[35] The reform movement institutionalized itself in 1817 with the formation of the Prison Discipline Society, and as a consequence of the society's efforts the Gaols Act was passed in 1823. Bentham's design for the panopticon was utilized in the construction of new penitentiaries including the prison at Bury built in 1805, the Millbank penitentiary completed in 1816, the Pentonville penitentiary which opened in 1842, and in a number of county prisons. With the building of the new prisons, employers who had formerly punished their servants themselves, now turned increasingly to the state, which had become the new locus of impartial power. Where once magistrates were men well-known in a particular community and the keepers of jails were private entrepreneurs who made their living off the incarcerated, by the last quarter of the century "all of these operations had been centralized under the control of the state, and power became the attribute of the system rather than of a person who happened to be in a position of authority. The transfer usually marked the entrance of the public as the supposed beneficiary of the new processes of power."[36] The reforms continued into the mid-nineteenth century, with the establishment of a national prison inspectorate in 1835, and this was soon followed by the professionalization of prison staff.[37] The prisons themselves had become total institutions, their inhabitants occupying a separate, isolated, but highly formalized social system.[38] New fields of knowledge and power were developed with the proliferation of administrative bodies involved in the management and reform of criminals.[39] Knowledge of the criminal was advocated by economic, political, and judicial bodies, thus increasing the importance of the subject in social discourse.

Ignatieff notes that, in England by 1835, 85 percent of the arrests were for common crimes such as vagrancy, disorderly conduct, prostitution and so on, and that those who were incarcerated, were in prison "simply because they were poor."[40] In France during the same period, "most convicts, both men and women, were members of the laboring classes, from semiskilled and unskilled jobs."[41] This was to be the pattern especially for the first three-quarters of the century. "Thus a criminal justice system which systematically imprisoned and punished the 'lower classes' derived its legitimacy from the community presupposed by the Classical School."[42] Threatened by what they perceived as disorder, it is of little surprise that the penitentiary exerted such a strong hold on the imagination of middle-class reformers; it represented in microcosm their ideal of a perfect society—disciplined, hierarchical, and completely visible in all its aspects.

THE LABORING AND DANGEROUS CLASSES

Circulating at the center of the discourse on criminality in the nineteenth century was the idea of "dangerous classes" or, as it was later to be referred to, the "residuum." Used interchangeably with "laboring classes," for much of the nineteenth century, it liberated criminality from the its legal confines and made of it a multifarious instrument of social control. The discourse on "dangerous classes" coalesced notions of vice, depravity, disease, and poverty in an interconnected web of concepts derived from biology, sociology, and morality, and in so doing, authorized the intervention of a number of groups, all of whom sought to suppress crime or what had become synonymous with it—disciplining certain sections of the working class.[43]

During the early part of the nineteenth century, the educated classes, under the influence of Malthus' predictions of zero economic growth and the possibility of mass starvation, were much alarmed by the tremendous increases in population (the population in Europe having increased from 140 million in 1750 to a total of 266 million by 1850).[44] In the view of the educated classes, it was the laboring poor who, lacking in moral restraint, multiplied "like animals in the dark cellars and airless garrets of the cities."[45] According to H.A. Frégier, bureau chief of the prefecture of the Seine in 1838, these were the "dangerous classes" who, having joined "to vice the depravity of destitution,"[46] are inclined to a life of crime. Those who lived in the utmost extremes of poverty and destitution also posed a more immediate political threat. Writing in 1840, Eugène Buret observed: "Isolated from the nation, outlawed from the social and political community, along with their needs and miseries, they struggle to extricate themselves from this terrifying solitude and, like the barbarians to whom they have been compared, they are perhaps meditating invasion."[47] This fear was not unjustified. In Paris, for example, a rise in the price of bread almost inevitably meant the occurrence of riots. Hence the letter from the Prefect of Police to the Minister of Interior on 27 October 1827: "It is imperative to see that the price of bread does not go higher than 3 sous the pound."[48] The "dangerous classes" were thus doubly dangerous, a potential threat to both property and government.

This general insecurity must be understood in the context in which cities like London and Paris, and later New York, were perceived by the middle classes. Overpopulated and poorly managed, marked by disease and expanding slums, the cities were viewed as symptomatic of a general malaise and moral deterioration in society; and it was the poor, the underemployed, and unemployed who bore the stigma of this dystopian view. In their apprehension of a sick society in which images of vice, prostitution, poverty, disease, and crime blended, the middle classes linked the discourse of crime to such fields as "sanitary science" and "social hygiene."[49] In the course of the nineteenth century, the problem was further compounded by the social distance between the classes made wider by their sharp geographical separation in the city. As Marie-Christine Leps has demonstrated, in France as well as in England, newspaper reports on crime "reiterated hegemonic truths about the "lower orders" in general and the "residuum" in particular."[50] The result produced in the public both an abhorrence of crime and a respect for the value of established institutions.[51] With the decline in the traditional forms of control based on daily contact, paternalism, and deference, the poor districts loomed as an immense, unknown territory in the minds of the middle classes, a source of anxiety, fantasy, and fear.[52]

In France, for instance, the laboring poor came to be viewed as a race apart: "The workers [are] savages by reason of their precarious existence. . . . The life of the industrial proletariat and the savage alike is at the mercy of the hazards of life. . . . They [are] alike, too, in their perpetual roving. . . . It is from the ranks of this population, which is far larger than is supposed, that the paupers are recruited, the enemies who threaten our civilization."[53] Savages by virtue of their "inequality before life and death" also "made this people different in bodily appearance and doomed [them] for that very reason to every sort of ugliness and degradation."[54] In Chevalier's view, the "social struggles in Paris during this period cannot be understood unless it is realized that it was based upon physical, and, even more specifically, morphological foundations."[55] The writings and investigations of Lavater and Gall, of course provided credence to the popular belief that individuals and classes possessed specific physical characteristics that corresponded to particular moral qualities. Hence, the drawings of Daumier and Travies are revealing in their depiction of the lower classes as hideous, bestial, and ferocious.[56] In newspaper accounts of street incidents, "the physical appearance of the laboring classes was the same as that attributed to the dangerous classes."[57] In England, author and journalist Henry Mayhew described the lower classes as a wandering nomadic horde that preyed on the industry of a more civilized tribe. Each of these groups, the nomadic and civilized, was described by Mayhew as separate races, differentiated in terms of their physical, intellectual and moral characteristics. Thus, the "nomadic" lower classes were characterized by their aversion for "regular and continuous labor," their violent passions, their lack of morality and, perhaps worst of all, by a "looseness" of "notions as to property."[58] In this way, the laboring and criminal classes came to be recognized as belonging to a single group and their physical and economic distress ascribed to moral deficiencies.[59]

In England the presence of the casual poor, indistinguishable to many in the bourgeoisie from criminals, was primarily a consequence of social and economic dislocations created by the Industrial Revolution: "the decline or collapse of old staple industries, and the growth of new industries parasitic upon that decline: industries characterized by low wage rates, irregular employment, and the subdivision of skilled processes into unskilled ones. These conditions provided the efflorescence of a casual labor market of almost unparalleled dimension."[60] By the 1860s, the middle classes, no longer under the sway of Malthusian theory, but their fear nevertheless sharpened by the bread riots of the period, began to view the "dangerous classes" not in terms of poverty but pauperism and the demoralization of the working class. In the view of the middle-class reformers who were to establish the Charity Organization Society (C.O.S.) in 1869, it was sentimental and indiscriminate charitable giving by private and public organizations that had encouraged the "clever pauper" and steadily demoralized the poor.[61] The solution was to systematize charitable-giving, instill in the recipient the obligation which attends gift-giving so that charity may be utilized as a form of social control, and provide close supervision and guidance of the poor through the establishment of settlement projects.[62] In this manner, charity was to become a science, managed by those of the professional middle class who had the requisite expertise and knowledge. In fact, under the banner of "scientific humanism," the C.O.S. became a "pioneer of 'casework' and thus laid the foundations of modern social administration."[63] As part of their disciplinary program, the C.O.S. also attacked the institution of outdoor relief arguing that the poor should be directed instead to the workhouse.[64] As Steadman Jones notes: "no . . . concession was made to the problems of the casual laborer; if he begged, that was because he was 'demoralized'; if he was unemployed, that was because he was not really interested in work."[65] If in the 1860s the "dangerous classes" were viewed through the lens of "demoralization," by the 1880s they would be viewed as "degenerate." Whether economic and social problems were transferred onto a moral plane or, as in the case of the 1880s, onto a biological plane, the fact remained that in both cases they functioned to

leave intact the existing structures of authority. Throughout the nineteenth century the laboring and dangerous classes were to become the
object of a number of investigations by disciplinary technicians, each
using different techniques of knowledge production, each producing
new domains of visibility.

STATISTICS AS A MORAL SCIENCE

A political rationality, no longer obsessed with the fate of the
monarchy but which considered the state as an end in itself and correspondingly embraced "the idea that man is the true object of the
state,"[66] resulted in the emergence of a burgeoning administrative apparatus and the statistical appropriation of the body by the new professional order of specific intellectuals—disciplinary technicians and
social scientists.[67] Moral science, as it came to be called—this fetishistic control of data, seemingly motivated by philanthropic desires but
aimed at the preservation of the state—"brought life and its mechanisms into the realm of explicit calculation and made knowledge-power
an agent of transformation of human life."[68] Traditionally, there had
been an interest in the population insofar as it impacted on considera-
tions such as military recruitment and taxation. In this increasing rationalization of the state, however, the population for the first time was
carefully delineated, categorized, and displayed in a numerary of fine
partitionings. "It represented an overt political response by the state.
Find out more about your citizens cried the conservative enthusiasts
and you will ameliorate their conditions, diminish their restlessness,
and strengthen their character."[69] Thus, "Life became not only an object
of thought but an object of power; it was not merely individual living
persons who might be subjected . . . but Life itself, the life of the
species, the size of the population, the modes of procreation."[70] The
organic, assimilated to the fine mesh of a statistical grid, effected the
commonplace and the traumatic in equal and sundry measure. Death,
sickness, and life expectancy were defined in uniform, if arbitrary, categories. "Enumeration," after all, as Hacking points out, "is hungry for
categories."[71]

The criminality of the "laboring and dangerous classes" and its
relation to poverty, climate, sex, and so forth, was a central source of
concern in statistical studies produced by philanthropic societies, penal,

and government institutions. In England, *The Journal of the Statistical Society of London* published several studies on the "lower orders." In France, the first criminal statistics, *Compte général de l'administration de la justice criminelle en France*, were published in 1827. These statistics detailed the number and kinds of crimes with a breakdown of the age, sex, occupation, and education of the defendants.[72] Even the relationship between the crime rate and the price of bread received attention. In Bavaria, Georg von Mayr, in his study of crime and the price of rye for the period 1835 to 1861, concluded that an increase in the price of grain by half-groschen called forth one more theft per one hundred thousand inhabitants.[73] This obsession with the potential criminality of the laboring poor generated an explosive desire for a numerical arrest of their proclivities and pathologies and, in turn, functioned to reinforce the anxiety that attended the subject. Thus, in France we discover that by 1834 there were so many numbers that every salon spoke in fear, and with full knowledge, of the "croissance effrayante" [the buzzword of the day] of crime, sanity, prostitution, vagabondage, vagrancy, and suicide.[74]

According to Chevalier: "the proliferation of the criminal classes . . . was, over the years, one of the main problems of city management, one of the principal matters of general concern."[75] At the center of this expanding statistical immurement of deviance, and the individuals most responsible for its technical refinement in the first part of the nineteenth century, were the French lawyer André-Michel Guerry and the Belgian astronomer and statistician Adolphe Quetelet. Quetelet's work is especially significant and worth examining because, as we shall see, photographic identification of the criminal body relied on Quetelet's conceptual construct of the average man ("l'homme moyen").

As Haskins notes, Quetelet's work was a culmination, a veritable bringing together of two previously mutually exclusive traditions in the nascent discipline of statistics. One school, represented by statisticians such as Muenster, Achenwall, and Conring, had utilized verbal description and took as its object of analysis "the whole life and organization of the state."[76] Muenster, for example, in his *Cosmographia* (1536), had examined "the geography, history, manners and customs, industries, commerce, political and ecclesiastical organization, and military power of all known countries."[77] And it was, in fact, Achenwall who had formulated the definition of statistics in his *Vor bereitung zur Statswissenschaft der europaischen Reiche* published in 1784: "Before we begin to observe the constitution of the most important European states of today, it will be fitting to make some general remarks on 'Statistik,' as that discipline which is concerned with this object."[78] The function of these works was to ascertain the strengths and weaknesses of a state and thereby serve as a guide for political control. On the other hand, the school of Political Arithmetic, represented by statisticians such as Derham and Sussmilch, had a narrower focus, and were dependent largely on techniques of enumeration and calculation.[79]

Quetelet, however, combined the two approaches, drawing on the emphasis developed by Achenwall and the verbal statisticians, while nonetheless establishing completely the Political Arithmetic "conception of statistics as a method of observation based on enumeration and applicable to any field of social inquiry."[80] Furthermore, he perfected the method of census taking, brought attention to both the importance of criticizing sources and the significance of managing of data so as to maximize correlations, and generally established progress toward the uniformity and comparability of data.[81] He was, as Haskins notes, undoubtedly influenced by Malthus, Laplace (Quetelet was Laplace's pupil), and Fourier, whose four-volume series *Recherches statistiques sur la ville de Paris et le department de la Seine*, consisting of tables of population and mortality, mathematically expressed the average duration of life.[82]

Both Guerry and Quetelet utilized the data published by the *Compte général de l' administration de la justice criminelle en France* in their studies. While Guerry developed a cartographic method to represent crime rates of different areas, Quetelet utilized the data to develop the notion of "propensity of crime," which depended on factors such as sex, race, and so on. What struck Quetelet most was the statistical regularity or "fatality in the production of crime."[83]

> Thus we pass from one year to another with the sad perspective of seeing the same crimes reproduced in the same order and calling down the same punishments in the same proportions. Sad condition of humanity! . . . We might enumerate in advance how many individuals will stain their hands in the blood of their fellows . . . almost as we can enumerate in advance the births and deaths that should occur.[84]

The statistical regularities to which Derham and Sussmilch had provided a theological valuation, arguing that the mathematical ratios testified to a divine order, Quetelet believed were revealing of an existing social order.[85]

> Society includes within itself the germs of all the crimes committed, and at the same time the necessary facilities for their development. It is the social state, in some measure, which prepares these crimes and the criminal is merely the instrument to execute them.[86]

Such an observation appeared to contradict the theory of classical jurisprudence predicated on free will and its preclusion of social factors. Quetelet hesitated to rule out individual responsibility,[87] but by providing a scientific interpretation he elevated the regularities to the status of social laws, the causality of which depended on social conditions, thus grounding "moral statistics" (a term A.M. Querry had coined), in social science.[88] Furthermore, Quetelet developed a table of mortality differentiated by sex in order to establish the first actuarial tables in Belgium.[89] The studies undertaken by Quetelet were a precursor to sociological investigations into crime that would be undertaken by the government, the police and various philanthropic societies.

But, more significantly, Quetelet gave his own unique interpretation to the normal law of error by introducing his concept of the average man ("l'homme moyen") which according to him represented perfection in terms of both physical characteristics and moral goodness. Initially, in *Sur L'homme* written in 1835, Quetelet viewed the average as the mean between an upper and a lower limit. But after 1835, the concept of the average man was extended by Quetelet to include moral and intellectual qualities as well:[90] "I show that the law of accidental causes is a general law which is applied to individuals as well as to peoples and which dominates our moral and intellectual qualities as well as our physical qualities."[91] Hence, the average man is both a biological and moral type, a mean around which actual men are distributed according to the law of normal error. Quetelet referred to the normal law of error as the law of accidental causes because he was of the opinion that the average type was a product of constant causes and variations from the type, a consequence of accidental causes. Accordingly, utilizing the normal law of error, Quetelet did a number of studies on the physical properties of the average man, which established a precedent for subsequent studies in the physical measurement of criminals for reasons of identification.[92]

POLICING

The increasing bio-political rationalization of the social, and the political technologies of the body it engendered, was given further impetus in the nineteenth century by the establishment of a disciplinary apparatus of overt coercion—a uniformed police force. But even the police force could not operate only on the basis of coercion; it depended on a general environment of consent and belief in disciplinary techniques and moral supervision.[93] The power acquired through the surveillance of this disciplinary apparatus produced new knowledge about its subjects, which, in turn, required systematic procedures of documentation within which photographic evidence would play a prominent role.[94] Thus, "the conditions were in play for a striking rendezvous—the consequences of which we are still living out—between a novel form of the state and a new and developing technology of knowledge. A key to this technology from the 1870s on was photography."[95]

In England, during the Anglo-Saxon period, it had been the collective responsibility of each township or hamlet to apprehend and punish an offender and, in general, maintain the King's Peace or be fined for not undertaking its common-law obligations. But with the rise of capitalism, the gradual break-up of traditional agrarian relations, and the rapid growth of vagrancy, pauperism, and crime, there emerged in the nineteenth century a realization that common-law conceptions of social order and responsibility no longer prevailed.[96] In the absence of the customary fabric of social order, it became imperative, with property at stake, for the emerging structures of capital to be provided with an institution of surveillance that would enforce a new era of social discipline.[97] In keeping with Lenin's observation that the state is the instrument of capitalist domination, the institution of police must be viewed in "its modern form (as having) emerged from class struggle under industrial capitalism."[98] As Sidney Harring observes, in establishing a police force, the capitalist state reserves for itself the monopoly over the legitimate use of violence and coercion. After all, the potential to deploy force in the event that other social mechanisms fail, is understood to be a significant aspect of the state's power.[99] The rise of

Luddism in 1811 and the initial attempts of the working class to organize itself only served to underscore to the propertied classes the need for a centralized system of policing and surveillance. The repressive welfare schemes introduced to combat pauperism (considered as the root cause of crime), the increase in the number of capital offenses, and the constant resort to the military to protect the property and lives of the bourgeoisie were definitely not in themselves long-term solutions; they alone could not create a disciplined and stable society.[100] The function of a uniformed police force took on new urgency and meaning.

> Once the class begins to organize, to agitate, to demonstrate, you need a force which has all the appearance of independence, which cannot be seen to be visibly taking sides in the class struggle, but which is merely there to enforce the law. The genius of the British ruling class is that they realized the need to have such a force and set about creating it. [101]

As a result of the Police Act of 1829, proposed by the Home Secretary Robert Peel, the first steps were taken toward transforming the role of the watchman under common law into a member of an organized, disciplined force governed by a hierarchy of supervisors and operating under a system of regulations and codes. This is not to say that the measure did not meet with resistance. The upper classes feared government spying and the lower classes simply loathed the new police force, calling them "Peelers" or "Peel's bloody gang."[102] Though initially limited by size and jurisdiction to a small section within the Greater London area, the control of the newly established police force was systematically extended to other urban areas by the Municipal Corporations Act of 1835 and finally to the counties and rural provinces by the Parliament Act of 1856.[103]

In general, this increasing regulation of behavior by depersonalized and rational legal forms[104] was concomitant with the general trend toward bureaucratization in the nineteenth century. In the case of a uniformed police system, this rationalization not only represented a cleverly erected buffer in the class struggle, but also pointed to the increasing socialization of the costs associated with the reproduction of labor, which was already evident in such areas as street construction and public health.[105]

Municipal governments' entry into the realm of heretofore private services represents nothing less than the socialization of the task of reproducing the labor force. In effect, the capitalists turned over a portion of that function to municipal government, because government could accomplish the same result, at public expense, far more efficiently and more legitimately than could the capitalists themselves.[106]

The development of a centralized apparatus of surveillance and discipline, in the semblance of a uniformed police system, must be understood within this context. The police, by functioning as a disciplinary institution, provided the control and fundamental stability necessary for the comprehensive and efficient exploitation of the working class. Marx has similarly indicated that the capitalist state "employed the police to accelerate the accumulation of capital by increasing the degree of exploitation of labor."[107] In fact, even presently, the police assist in reproducing the social relations of production daily through the functions of law enforcement, surveillance, and a network of informers.

As Bunyan argues, the success of the police lay in reassuring the middle classes and vested interests that the capabilities and resources of the disciplinary apparatus would not be used to spy upon them but rather would be deployed against criminal activity and political opposition.[108] The fears of the bourgeoisie, as such, were surely unfounded, for it was largely the working class that came under the considerable scrutiny of the police. Until a systematic form of documentation of criminal bodies and their acts (within which photographs would subsequently play a central role) was in place, patrolling was imperative, because the only way criminals could be caught was if they were apprehended in the act. Thus, in search of the criminal element, the police resorted to rigorous patrolling of the working-class districts.[109] However, to members of the working-class communities, the constant surveillance was intrusive and it was not uncommon that a policeman about to make an arrest was attacked by neighborhood groups.[110] Furthermore, Harring has observed of American cities during the nineteenth century, and it was true of other major European cities at the time, that the patrolling by police served to reinforce the spatial division and classification of the city.

The boundaries of such neighborhoods were clearly understood by all, and their meaning was not simply geographic. . . . Whole sections of the city were off limits to members of some classes, either informally through fear, or semiofficially, as police picked up and questioned strangers. Notions about class society that may seem abstract now were concrete and obvious in the late nineteenth century.[111]

The police were no less active in countering political opposition. For instance, in 1833 the National Political Union of the Working Classes protested against the government's use of police spies to infiltrate their organization, which they rightfully argued they had indirectly paid for, under the belief that the police were there to protect their lives and property.[112]

The police clearly served to operate as a shield between the bourgeoisie and militant sections of the working classes. Direct confrontation between master and wage laborer would be avoided if a third force intervened. Nonetheless, on the face of it, a contradiction appeared to exist. As T.A. Critchley notes, "To the police fell the unenviable task of appearing to oppress the working people from whom most had come."[113] But, as Harring observes, even though the police drew a large number of its recruits from the working classes, internally it stabilized itself by reinforcing the loyalty of its rank and file through the creation of career tracks, by professionalizing its functions, and generally clothing its oppressive mechanisms in the value-neutral language of the law.[114] Confirmation is offered in this regard by Bunyan, who notes, "The first of the new policemen were invested with the full authority of the law and instilled with a value system antithetical to their class origins. And through frequent parades, inspections, and drilling they were slowly turned into a disciplined and obedient force."[115]

Thus, a policed society was gradually legitimated and, in turn, the policing system as a politically neutral force was validated both by the conditions which gave rise to it, and by an ideological strategy which positioned the police as providing a valuable service to all (Fig. 20).[116] Even the working class received some measure of protection by the police from robbery and attack in the streets, even if such "protection" only served to justify the intensive surveillance of working-class neighborhoods. "Moreover," as Bunyan points out, "the need to give some

Figure 20. New York police, an early photograph.

security for the working man and his family was essential if they were to accept that policing was in their interests."[117]

With the establishment of the Criminal Investigation Department (C.I.D.) in 1876, which by 1886 had a staff of eight hundred, the police apparatus possessed, in addition to a sizable force in uniform, a powerful and shadowy body of plainclothes officers.[118] Not to be overlooked is the connection that lay between an expansionist colonial army operating abroad and an internal force deployed at home to maintain the domestic reproduction of the relations of production. After all, the "Commissioners of the Metropolitan Police [in Britain] during its first hundred years were drawn almost exclusively from those with a background of military or colonial experience."[119]

Across the channel in France, there emerged, even prior to the nineteenth century, a far more powerful police system than that which existed in either America or Britain at the time. According to Philip Stead, the "pattern of constitutional reversals dominating French political history since 1789, such reversals so often being the consequence of the government's loss of control of the streets,"[120] goes a long way in explaining why the French government established such a powerful and comprehensive apparatus for maintaining public order and for gathering of intelligence about its own people. Earlier, during the *ancien régime*, the monarchy, keen on countering the power of the landed gentry, established a centralized police system. From 1667 to 1789, the Lieutenants General of Police (a position first instituted by Louis XIV), secured public order in the streets of the capital by crushing mobs and staving off the possibility of riots by controlling the food supply and the prices of food. They also eradicated what was perceived at the time as the root causes of crime—darkness and dirt—by illuminating the streets (in 1697 Paris was lit by 6,500 lanterns placed 20 yards apart) and by a program of social hygiene (the paving of streets, the destruction of criminal lairs and the control of prostitution, etc.), and generally organized and regulated the arterial flow of crowds by building streets and bridges.[121] The general structure of policing established during this period and whose powers Napoleon had expanded tremendously, survived into the nineteenth century. During the revolution, the police had been the focus of bitter criticism and antagonism, since they were the most visible presence of monarchial authority and oppression, and that situation did not change much during the nineteenth century. Rigorous documentation of the citizenry was revived, and a detective organization staffed by criminals and run by the infamous Vidocq, who was himself a criminal, generated considerable knowledge of the population at large.[122] In the second half of the nineteenth century, Napoleon III, realizing the precariousness of his rule, further expanded the centralized system of policing, broadened its powers, and literally converted France into a police state.[123]

Thus, by the end of the nineteenth century there had been established in the major capitalist states a powerful policing system of considerable proportions. Linked institutionally with the penal system, the reform school and the factory, and bound to the reformatory-disciplinary nexus of capitalist social relations, the police began to operate in the midst of the working class. As Foucault notes, in quoting from a police manual during the reign of Louis XIV, "the true object of the police is man";[124] and the mode of surveillance was made all the more effective by the production of a new textual practice, at the center of which operated the incontrovertible testimony of the photography.

PHOTOGRAPHY: APPREHENDING THE CRIMINAL

In 1883, Alphonse Bertillon, a minor French bureaucrat, utilized Quetelet's concept of the average man in a discursive apparatus which combined and organized, by means of a filing system he had invented, photographs, anthropometric descriptions, and physiognomic details to successfully identify and classify criminal bodies. Bertillon was motivated by the need to eliminate recidivism and, in fact, through the utilization of the technology of surveillance that he instituted, he did manage between 1883 and 1893 to identify 4,564 recidivists.[125] Until the use of Bertillon's "anthropometrical signalment," the French police, more apt to be concerned with political suspects rather than a systematic method of detection and recording of criminal activities, had given little thought to a method of identification. What methods there existed, were, to say the least, both crude and cruel. "Up to 1832 in France a barbarous method of identification of criminals was still permitted by the statute; they could be branded with a red-hot iron."[126] In 1840, when photographs were first utilized to identify criminals, facial expressions, "which as often as not disproved the fallacy that the camera never lies,"[127] and problems of classification clearly posed problems sufficient enough to discourage the effective deployment of photography: "The collection of criminals portraits had already attained a size so considerable that it has become physically impossible to discover among them the likeness of an individual who has assumed a false name."[128] Consequently, the French police resorted to such clumsy methods as paying officers five francs for each offender recognized as having been arrested previously, and the result itself was inevitable: "Corrupt officers induced prisoners to admit to a previous conviction on the promise of a share of the five franc piece."[129]

Bertillon, however, revived the use of photography by effectively inserting the technology within a discursive framework which, drawing upon statistics, exact anthropometrical measurements, and a physiognomic transcription of the body, produced the individual criminal's body as a clearly defined and identifiable text. He developed his "anthropometrical signalment" by first subjecting each criminal body to eleven measurements. "He had chosen those parts of the body which could most easily be measured accurately. They were the length and breadth of the head and of the right ear, the length from the elbow to the end of the middle finger, that of the middle and ring fingers themselves; the length of the left foot, the height, the length of the trunk (*buste*), and that of the outstretched arms from middle to middle finger-end."[130] Furthermore, these parts of the body were not only susceptible to accurate measurement but could also be conveniently and quickly measured with the simplest of instruments (Fig. 21).[131] Utilizing "the statistical techniques which Quetelet (and) his father"[132] had taught him, Bertillon deduced that the probability of two individuals sharing the same eleven measurements was of the order of one in four.

The series of measurements in the "anthropometrical signalment" were also accompanied by a brief description of identifying marks, such as scars or warts, and by a pair of photographs, one of which provided a frontal view and the other a profile of the criminal's head (Fig 22).[133] "It was one of the gravest of faults of the classical police photograph that neither the pose nor the lighting conditions was standardized (Fig. 23)."[134] Bertillon, however, realizing that the semantic value of the photography lay in its function as a conclusive proof of identification, sought to effect a representation of the criminal's body that was "neutral." With this in mind, the focal length was standardized and the body of the criminal exposed to an "even and consistent lighting."[135]

Figure 21. Bertillon measurements. Measuring the left foot.

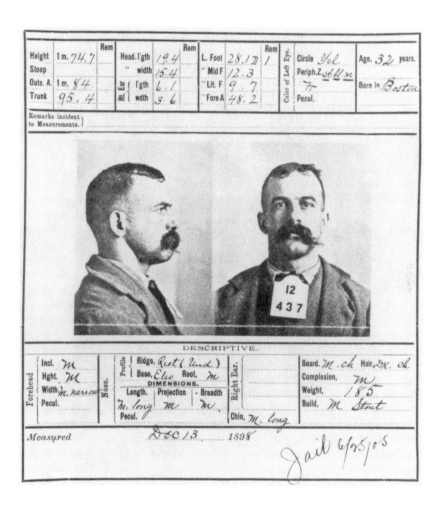

Figure 22. Anthropometrical signalment.

Figure 23. An early British photograph of prisoners, Glasgow, 1865.

Furthermore, the problems posed by facial expression, which had thwarted previous attempts at photographing criminals, was neutralized by the use of the profile view. It was not unusual, after all, for criminals being photographed to struggle and screw up their faces in a tight grimace so as to render ineffective for identification purposes the representations elicited from them (Fig. 24). "Of what good can these twisted and unnatural faces be? Were their owners met in the streets their countenances would be composed. They would be altogether free of these distortions, by which they have tried to cheat the purpose of the police in photographing them."[136] The result was that while the profile view served its purpose in thwarting an individual criminal's expressivity, the frontal view enabled both ease of identification and detection on the streets by patrolling policemen.[137]

Finally, the classification of the immense number of criminal photographs was effected by the use of Quetelet's average man. The anthropometrical signalment placed on individual cards was organized by below average, average, and above average measurements into the grid of the filing system that Bertillon had invented.[138]

> [Bertillon] divided his cards into three groups corresponding first to the length of the head—the first for the large, the second for the medium (or average), and the third for the small heads. These three groups were again subdivided in terms of a large, medium (or average), and small width of the head, making nine groups (3^2) in all. These nine groups were again subdivided in terms of the small, medium (or average), and large left middle-finger, making twenty-seven groups (3^3) in all.[139]

With another similar subdivision in terms of the large left little finger producing a total of eighty-one groups, the cards were arranged in a filing cabinet with eighty-one drawers (nine horizontal and nine vertical rows). Thus, the filing cabinet could carry the anthropometric descriptions of many thousands of criminals, "with a properly balanced distribution of the cards throughout the drawers,"[140] enabling easy and convenient access to each card. The value of Bertillon's filing system is confirmed by Rhodes' observation that, "the science of identification could never have been applied in practice had it not been possible to devise a system of classification and arrangement which was practi-

Figure 24. Attempting to photograph a prisoner, New York.

cally foolproof and which made it possible to find the description required with the minimum loss of time."[141]

The filing system, as a technology for surveillance, provisions a powerful new space for the monitoring and classification of individual criminal bodies; their independent pathological traces, their innumerable acts of violence against the social body, are now made indelible and brought forth to a new and heightened level of visibility by this "identity" and "difference" machine, which, operating within the classicist desire for tabular representations, reproduces and reifies the body as a new locus for rationalist and disciplinary practices.

Essentially, the filing system is a practical solution and represents a primitive form of a model operating on the basis of an anticipatory logic and constituted by both temporal and spatial variables. Even though the filing system at first strikes one as a spatial configuration, it is at the same time a model that operates on a temporal systematization of the universe it is constructed to model. For one thing, it is premised on an anticipatory logic providing for future identification of the criminal and proof of recidivism. Secondly, it is a model of duration, updated and constantly seeking to model the trajectory of the criminal body through social space. To be effective, surveillance seeks to anticipate throughout its gaze every possible movement; every permutation and combination of motion, bodies, and forces within the field of visibility of the disciplinary apparatus must be calculated in advance into its grid of knowledge. Furthermore, the power of surveillance increases as the particular universe surveilled is broken into its componential parts and then recomposed into a model that is run at rates faster than the real world it models. At the same time, the subjects it surveils receive only a componential view of that same reality. Thus, effective surveillance takes place when the space to be surveilled and dominated is open to the full gaze of power, but remains fragmented to the surveilled.

For our present discussion, it suffices that we acknowledge the temporal valuation inherent in any technology that models the universe it seeks to surveil, combining the repository force of an archival method with the mobility of an anticipatory logic, as exemplified by the lowly technology of the filing cabinet. While within the context of the filing system, the photograph is a particular image isolated for examination; in the case of the emerging science of criminology which sought knowledge of the criminal "type," the photograph becomes a representative image.[142] Additionally, Bertillon sought to make the process of identification more efficient by a transcription of the criminal's face in terms of descriptions of particular features creating what he called a *portrait parlé* or "speaking likeness."[143] Sectional photographs of the features of different individuals, for example, the forehead isolated, half the profile, the ears alone, and so on, were produced, measured as to whether they were below average or above average in size, and generally compared, contrasted, classified, and described.[144] In this manner, a physiognomic grid of substantial semantic value, comprised of both numerical expressions and brief verbal descriptions, was established, thus making for more consistent and accurate identification of the pathological or deviant body (Fig. 22).

As a consequence of Bertillon's introduction of penal photography, the surface of the body enters the realm of new visibilities, its aspect and features put to a single use: the incarceration of anti-social bodies. Each distinguishing mark, each scar, the measurement of limbs, the deployment of frontal and profile views are enmeshed in a discourse that forces these bodies to betray themselves, to disclose their biography of crime, and thus enable their organization within a matrix of knowledge/power relations. In this way, the body becomes permeable to the principle of surveillance and the gaze of power flickers over these bodies, isolating, neutralizing, standardizing and reducing them, one and all, to the topography of power. Power makes of the signs of the criminal body a textual practice.[145] The body is objectified, divided, analyzed and organized into a cellular structure of space (the file index)—the representative architecture of surveillance; it is individuated, transformed into a subject and subjected, a discursive object within a disciplinary apparatus.

Furthermore, the photograph's value as evidence is incorporated within the "examination" or interrogation.[146] The "examination" with its attendant "rituals, its methods, its characters, and their roles, its play of questions and answers, its system of marking and classification,"[147] engenders "a whole domain of knowledge, a whole type of power."[148] Through both the operations of photography and the documentary practices of the examination, criminals are made visible to a panopticon technology that locates their deviancy within a "network of writing" that "captures and fixes them."[149] In this manner, the biography of the criminal is afforded a new level of individuality. Not "the chronicle of a man, the account of his life, his historiography, written as he lived out his life [and which] formed part of the rituals of his power,"[150] but a lowered threshold of describability that makes of this description "a means of control and a method of domination."[151]

> The examination as the fixing, at once ritual and "scientific," of individual differences, as the pinning down of each individual in his own particularity . . . clearly indicates the appearance of a new modality of power in which each individual receives as his status his own individuality, and in which he is linked by his status to the features, the measurements, the gaps, the "marks" that character- ize him and make him a "case."[152]

Despite the competition received from the synechdochal finger- print system, wherein the tactile trace although visually apprehended substitutes for the visual inscription of the whole body, Bertillon's sig- naletic was received enthusiastically and subsequently adopted world- wide.[153] Bertillon's legacy continues into the present, for forensic science, or what the French refer to as "criminelistique," owes much to the photographic techniques that Alphonse Bertillon introduced.[154] For example, it was Bertillon who developed metric photography which made it possible to record the scale of the scene photographed and hence note the exact position of the body and its relation to other objects at the scene of a crime.[155]

THE 'TALKING SCAR'

The deployment of photographic representation against the crimi- nal's body enabled the state to increasingly identify the subpopulation of recidivists and imprison them. The irony, however, is that the recidi- vists began to function as "key agents in the diffusion of new subcul- tures" of protest in prison.[156] One of the forms this protest took was the production by prisoners of their own set of bodily representations in reaction against the state (Fig. 25). The criminal's tattooing of his own body did not represent, contrary to the claim of Cesare Lombroso and others, a mark of atavism, but instead functioned both as group identifi- cation and as distinguishing marks of status.[157] The criminal's tattoo which Alexandre Lacassagne labeled in his study as "a veritable talking scar" within the milieu of the prison,[158] represents the criminal's pro-

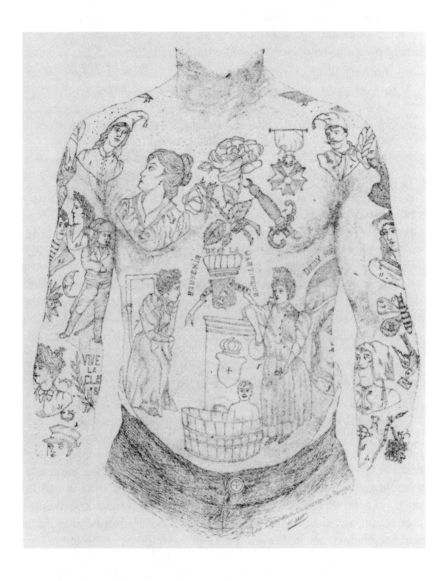

Figure 25. Tattooed torso of a prisoner, Nîmes, France.

duction of his own body as communal text, and operates in an interesting contrast to the *portrait parle* or "speaking likeness" that surveillance produces to isolate his body. In tattooing as a self-imposed form of identification, the body's boundaries are topographically signified to convey the criminal's participation in a community that stands in opposition to the depersonalization of the prison. Tattoos that adorned the bodies of prisoners of the period, displayed such statements as "Martyr for liberty," "Prison is waiting for me" and "Death to the bourgeoisie," and functioned symbolically to affirm the common values of defiance and protest against a dominant social order.[159] But tattooing was not restricted to the males, for female prisoners tattooed themselves as well. However, unlike the males, they did not resort to sexual imagery but instead chose depictions of motherhood and romance. All of this indicates "that prisoners were not an inert mass, a passive population on which the new disciplinary system acted without reaction or resistance." In fact, as O'Brien informs us, "inmate interactions in the context of subcultural behavior were as important to the daily operation of the prison as work orders and instructional schedules."[160] Other forms of subcultural resistance included prison argot that helped establish among the incarcerated a sense of autonomy and an alternative structure through which rights, obligations, and status could be defined and expressed.[161] Furthermore, against the bourgeois condemnation of the boundary crossing that is homosexuality and the middle-class reformers' anxiety about such sexual pollution, the prisoners, both male and female, freely engaged in this form of sexual expression; it became the basis of love, affection, and power among inmates and the means by which they overcame the isolation and depersonalization of prison life.[162]

In France, the rates of recidivism, which had begun to increase after the mid-nineteenth century, had by the end of the century reached such an extent that "two of every five imprisoned men and one of every four imprisoned women were repeat offenders."[163] The increase in the rates were a direct result of post-institutional surveillance of the released prisoner. Post-institutional surveillance reflected both "a general disillusionment with the reformatory promise of penitentiaries"[164] and the belief that the punished criminal represented a continuing danger to society.[165] Motivated by the desire to separate the dangerous classes from the working classes, the system of surveillance prevented former criminals from residing in major industrial and manufacturing sectors where they would most likely find work. The consequence was that "under this new and rigid residence requirement . . . the former criminal resorted to crime in order to survive."[166] Hence, as the nineteenth century wore on, the penitentiary, in turn, began to be seen less as an institution of reformation than one of retribution and penal quarantine.[167] The high rates of recidivism similary served to underwrite the belief in a hardened underclass of habitual criminals with the effect that attention soon shifted to the biology of crime.[168]

PHOTOGRAPHY: APPREHENDING CRIMINALITY

Unlike Bertillon, Francis Galton was not inclined toward the techno-surveillance uses of photography and the compiling of criminal biographies, but instead used photography to construct composites that would reveal a genetically determined criminal type.[169] Bertillon was interested in controlling recidivism, while Galton was determined to maintain the "pedigree" of established social classes through a program of selective breeding.[170] However, while Galton's particular deployment of photography was motivated by different intentions, his methods were nonetheless based on the same statistical principles articulated by Quetelet. Like other studies in phrenology, his use of composite images of criminal types also revealed an unshakable belief in visual empiricism.[171]

Francis Galton's work in criminology may be located at that crucial juncture of the "cross-fertilization" of the social sciences and the biological sciences.[172] The ideology of social Darwinism, securely embedded in ideas of evolutionary change and a liberal political economy, "became a means of explaining the differences between races and between classes"[173] and was the epistemological site within which Galton began his experiments. In keeping with this general biologization of sociocultural phenomena, Galton intended to analyze the hereditary faculties of different individuals, classes, and races and, more significantly, sought to establish a program of social and political control for the improvement of the species. "Eugenics," a term first introduced by him, thus emerged as both a science and a political program.[174] The idea that eugenic theory had clear practical implications is indicated by Galton's definition of the term provided in his will endowing a

Chair of Professor of Eugenics at the University of London: "the study of . . . agencies under social control that may improve the racial qualities of future generations either physically or mentally."[175]

On the one hand, eugenics was utilized to justify the dominance of colonized nations by Europeans, on the grounds that these nations were characterized by a racial stock inferior in physical, intellectual and moral "fitness." For example, in his book *Hereditary Genius*, written in 1869, which represented Galton's first attempt to measure the statistical distribution of intelligence, he noted that "the number among the negroes of those whom we should call half-witted men is very large."[176] That his research was clearly motivated by this general desire, is evident from a questionnaire Galton administered to colonial teachers, in which one of the questions asked of the respondents was the following: "Children of savages who have been reared in missionary families have been known to throw off their clothes and quit the house in a momentary rage and to go back off to their people among whom they were afterwards found in contented barbarism. State authentic instances of this, if you know any, with full particulars."[177]

On the other hand, at home in Britain, eugenics was conveniently used to explain differences in social privelege. In this regard, Galton was intent on "constructing and drawing upon an account of British society according to which the characteristics of that society were fundamentally the result of the measurable hereditary make-up of the individuals composing it."[178] As we have noted, Quetelet had applied the techniques of error theory to human data and had showed that physical characteristics follow the law of frequency of error. In *Hereditary Genius*, Galton, following in Quetelet's footsteps, applied the law of frequency of error to human data except that, in Galton's *apriori* model, it was mental characteristics which were portrayed as following a normal mathematical distribution. "This is what I am driving at—that analogy clearly shows there must be a fairly constant average mental capacity in the inhabitants of the British Isles, and that deviations from that average—upwards towards genius, and downwards towards stupidity—must follow the law that governs deviations from all true averages."[179] As Mackenzie notes, while from an error-theorist's perspective, variability or "error" was something to be controlled, an orientation which "militated against the treatment of variability as a phenomenon in its own right,"[180] for Galton, the eugenist, "variability was the potential source of racial progress"[181] and, hence, intrinsically significant. In keeping with this strategy, Galton drew on Charles Booth's social survey of London and mapped Booth's social-class categories onto his distribution of intelligence along a bell-shaped curve, so that those in the lowest social strata were also the groups with the smallest quotient of intelligence or "civic worth." Thus starting at one end of the distribution were "criminals, semi-criminals, loafers and some others," followed by those "very poor persons who subsist on casual earnings, many of whom are inevitably poor from shiftlessness, idleness or drink"; just above this group and moving closer to the center of the distribution were those "supported by intermittent earnings," either because they were shiftless or simply poorly paid; this group was followed by the numerically largest group which occupied the center of the distribution and, as was to be expected, was comprised of the respectable working class. Moving toward the high end of the distribution, and proportionately fewer in number, were the "better paid artisans and foremen," and "the lower middle class of shopkeepers, clerks and subordinate professional men, who as a rule are hard-working, energetic and sober." Finally, occupying the upper limit of the distribution, were groups possessing the highest intelligence or "civic worth": "They found great industries, establish vast undertakings, increase the wealth of multitudes and amass large fortunes for themselves. Others whether they be rich or poor, are the guides and light of the nation, raising its tone, enlightening its difficulties and imposing its ideals."[182] Apparently in Galton's eugenic theory of society, the higher the social class, the greater the quantity of innate qualities, and the lower the social class the smaller the presence of innate qualities and capacities.

It was on the basis of this theory that Galton introduced specific policies designed to improve the hereditary make-up of future generations. The policies put forth were double-edged and comprised of both a "positive eugenics" and a "negative eugenics." Essentially, Galton's sociopolitical program intended the establishment of measures that would inhibit the rate of reproduction among eugenically inferior groups in society ("negative eugenics"), while at the same time encouraging groups endowed with superior moral, physical, and intellectual characteristics ("positive eugenics"). His own view of the program was that of a benign hastening of the process of natural selection. "What nature does blindly, slowly and ruthlessly, man may do providently, quickly and kindly."[183] Thus, Galton and other eugenists called for the permanent segregation of those groups considered a "racial danger"—"habitual criminals," "the insane," and so forth—and for the sexes to be kept apart to prevent procreation. In instances where it was difficult to isolate individual cases, the eugenists argued for a strategy of "mass selection" undertaken through intelligence tests and scholarship achievement tests.[184] In the likelihood that there would be resistance to the idea that the number of children an individual could have would depend on the level of intelligence of the particular individual, an alternative proposal was to rely on the admittedly approximate correlation between eugenic worth and social position in terms of earnings.[185] As Mackenzie notes: "The advantage to the eugenist on this focus on earnings was that social and economic policies and institutions that had been developed for quite other reasons could be manipulated for eugenic purposes."[186] Thus, those families who depended on public financial assistance or on private charity could be controlled eugenically insofar as the consequences of having two or more children would be a cessation of financial aid.[187] This strategy was complemented, on the other hand, by a policy of "positive eugenics" in which, as in the case of one proposal considered by the eugenists, the rich would be provided income-tax allowances for each child they had. In fact, in 1914 the Eugenics Education Society "did campaign for eugenic reform of the income tax."[188]

Galton's book *Inquiries into Human Faculty*, where the term "eugenics" first appeared, was published in 1883, during a period when assumptions concerning the effectiveness of strategies utilized to moralize and control the "residuum" of criminals, prostitutes, the "casual poor," and, in general, the unproductive stratum in society (which also included lunatics), were brought into question by a series of reports and revelations.[189] The economic distress of the "residuum" was no longer attributed, as in the 1860s, to pauperism, but instead was viewed through the lens of hereditary urban degeneration. "It was generally believed that the casual poor were largely composed of the growing degenerate stratum of city life. If this were so, then the ultimate causes of their poverty and distress were neither economic nor moral but biological and ecological."[190] The economic depression of the 1880s had also meant a dramatic increase in the casual "residuum," with increasing numbers of the respectable working classes facing chronic unemployment. The result was that the upper-class bourgeoisie anxiously viewed itself under the threat of being socially levelled and engulfed by an underclass, which was also slowly being swelled by the ranks of the respectable working class. The increasing incidence of strikes and riots, and the ominous fact that socialist leaders from the newly founded Social Democratic Federation were appealing to the "residuum" as well as the respectable working classes under the banner of relief from unemployment, served to underscore the threat of social upheaval.[191] According to the liberal leadership, it was imperative that a clearer distinction be made between the respectable working classes and the "residuum" if social order were to be maintained. However, "the counterpart of wooing the respectable working class, in the new type of liberalism, was the espousal of a more coercive and interventionist policy towards the residuum."[192] Thus Galton's proposal for segregation of the "dangerous classes" found support in the economist Alfred Marshall's call to expel the "residuum" to labor colonies. It is in the context of the fears about this "residuum," now viewed as "dangerous not only because of its degenerate nature but also because its existence served to contaminate the classes immediately above it,"[193] that Galton's eugenics program must be understood. As Greta Jones notes: "Eugenics was able to integrate two aspects of late nineteenth-century culture—fear of working class disorder and discontent and the rise in their numbers."[194]

> I do not see why any insolence of caste should prevent the gifted class, when they had the power, from treating their compatriots with all kindness, so long as they maintain celibacy. But if these continued to procreate children, inferior in moral, intellectual and physical qualities, it is easy to believe the time may come when such persons would be considered as enemies of the State, and to have forfeited all claims to kindness.[195]

The "residuum" or underclass whose numbers had to be regulated for their own sake, lest they may be viewed later as "enemies of the State," was comprised of populations most likely to destabilize the moral and, simultaneously, the economic order.

> The proportion of weakly and misshapen individuals is not to be estimated by those we meet in the streets; the worst cases are out of sight. We should parade before our mind's eye the inmates of the lunatic, idiot and pauper asylums, the prisoners, the patients in

hospitals, the sufferers at home, the crippled, and the congenitally blind . . . our civilized stock is far more weak through congenital imperfection than that of any other species of animals.[196]

In this regard, David Green has rightly observed that "to eugenics the paupers, the unemployed, the criminal, the insane and the invenerately ill were considered not as social categories but entirely as natural ones."[197]

Intent on identifying hereditary characteristics, Galton turned to phrenology and physiognomy, and, influenced by Cesare Lombroso's work on criminals, he set about analyzing the "biology of crime." Like Lombroso and Havelock Ellis before him, Galton made use of anthropometrical measurements, and emphasized the examination of the head and facial features to identify a distinct criminal type whose physiology would correlate with an immoral and atavistic states but unlike them, and in keeping with the eugenics movement in general, he insisted on a wider application.

> The really scientific method would be to apply the tests on whole sections of the labouring classes of society including the criminal. . . . [It] seems clear that a scientific criminal anthropology which is to cover the whole ground must deal with the idle, the vagrant, the pauper, the prostitute, the drunkard, the imbecile, the epileptic, and the insane, as well as the criminal.[198]

Thus, in his *Essays in Eugenics*, Galton classified "loafers" as being part of that same category which included criminals and those deemed unfit, the word "unfit" bearing clearly in its wake the prescription of demographic regulation.[199]

In need of finding a way to document the physical particularities that would summon forth the criminal type, Galton turned to photography. In 1878, utilizing identification photographs of convicts, Galton created a composite of the criminal type—a hybrid of superimposition fabricated by a rudimentary combination of optical and statistical procedures. The process consisted of simply taking successive images of the subjects to be photographed, each image superimposed on the previous and occurring on a single plate, with each image provided a fractional exposure depending on the number of subjects to be photographed. If thirty subjects were to be photographed (statistical constancy, according to Galton, being produced by thirty such pictures), then each subject or, rather, image was provided one-thirtieth of the required total exposure.[200]

Galton, it is clear, felt that he had invented a powerful methodological procedure; however, at the center of this was the haunting desire for *l'homme moyen*:

> The process is one of pictorial statistics, suitable to give us generic pictures of man, such as Quetelet obtained in outline by the ordinary numerical methods of statistics, as described in his work on *Anthropometrie*. From these numerical data he calculated and laid down upon paper the average positions of those points, and therefrom constructed sketches of the typical man at various periods of his growth, like Flaxman's drawings or Retsch's outlines. By the process of composites we obtain a picture and not a mere outline. It is blurred, something like a damp sketch, and the breadth of the blur measures the variability of individuals from the central typical form.[201]

This was a tautological pursuit, assuming what it set out to prove, and at its illogical center "the symmetrical bell curve now wore a human face."[202] About his criminal composite, Galton observed: "The individual faces are villainous enough, but they are villainous in different ways, and when they are combined, the individual peculiarities disappear, and the common humanity of a low type is all that is left."[203] Galton's procedure of composite images, introduced in 1877, gained wide use and composites of criminal skulls appeared in both the 1895 French and Italian editions of Lombroso's *Criminal Man*. In fact, one of Galton's own composites was featured on the frontispiece of Havelock Ellis's 1890 edition of *The Criminal*.[204]

Both G.R. Searle and D. Mackenzie have argued that the development of eugenics was initiated, supported, and promoted by the new professional middle class who were of the view that a program of eugenics undertaken by the state would continue to legitimate their function, insofar as such a program would envisage a prominent role for them.[205] For example, Mackenzie, in his examination of the membership of the Council of the Eugenics Education Society in 1914, concluded "that the society's activists were drawn almost exclusively from the professional middle-class."[206] Furthermore, Searle points out, that in eugenic propaganda the professional middle class always appeared as the "heroes of the play," while the working class was denigrated and the aristocracy and business class bitterly criticized for injudiciously marrying for wealth rather than genetic worth.[207] Also, insofar as eugenics argued for the demographic regulation of the population in favor of those who possessed intelligence and intellectual expertise, it clearly legitimized the social status of the professional middle class. Thus even though eugenics attempted to present itself "as an objective description of nature and a set of policies in accord with nature, [it] reflected social interests and social relationships."[208]

The professional middle classes were to be both differentiated from the capitalist classes, since they (the professional middle classes) owned neither capital nor land, and from the proletariat, since their labor was both mental and superior to manual labor. They envisioned a society based on meritocracy—"for them trained and qualified expertise rather than property, capital or labor, should be the chief determinant and justification of status and power in society,"[209]—and sought to further their interests by a professionalization of the economy.

> [T]he eugenic solution to social problems, employing as it would the statisticians' figures, the biologists' studies, the psychologists' tests, the social workers' case reports and ultimately the psychiatrists' scalpel, was one which would give potentially full play to the skill of the developing scientific profession.[210]

Even though the professional middle classes were a distinct class with neither capital nor physical labor to offer, as long as the intellectual capital they provided could be harnessed to the needs of capital, their interests were not divergent from the capitalists. According to Mackenzie, the eugenists "were committed to change within the framework of capitalism. To seek to make the state more efficient, capital more productive and the labor force 'fitter.' "[211] Furthermore, as Mackenzie points out, the eugenists identification with capitalist thinking is evident from their view that the rate of wages was a good indicator of an individual's innate qualities, and illustrates Lucaks' notion of 'reification'—the reduction of people and social processes to a quantitative state of enumeration.[212] Correspondingly, L. Levidow has argued that the modern measurement of intelligence favored by psychologists who are eugenically biased is a product of the very same thinking that makes of human labor an abstract quantitative power for capital. The individual becomes an abstract individual, the "proprietor of abilities, technically defined, ordinally comparable and valued instrumentally."[213]

With the emergence in the nineteenth century of institutions functioning within the juridico-legal apparatus of the state and the production and circulation of discourses on crime and criminality that proliferated around these sites, photographic practices were deployed to produce a disciplinary politics of the criminal body which engendered new knowledge of the very subjects it produced and correspondingly expanded the power of a centralized state. Photographic practices functioned, on the one hand, in the organization of a surveillance technology to exhaustively catalogue and apprehend individual criminals and, on the other hand, it operated within a constellation of overlapping discourses comprised of criminology, statistics, phrenology, physiognomy, and eugenics, which sought to identify the biology of the criminal in order to intervene in the demographic reproduction of the deviant and the generally unfit. The function of these discourses and practices, which entangled criminality in a web of concepts drawn from morality, hygiene, rationality, social position, and biology, was to authorize and legitimize the social management, discipline, and control of the lower classes, at a time when these classes were perceived as posing a serious threat to an expanding capitalist order.

VISIBLY INSANE

Following from that "great reorganization of relations between madness and reason"[214] which culminated in the birth of the asylum, photography was also utilized in the mid-nineteenth century to apprehend and delineate the signs of madness. By the 1880s the mentally insane would comprise the "residuum" that threatened the race with degeneracy; hence it became imperative to isolate and realize that body, to make it disclose its dark and hidden recesses to the clarified light of discourse. Functioning as irrefutable proof within a regime of truth which assigned to it the status of objectivity, photography operated to revitalize the discourse on the physiognomy of the insane. In the words of Hugh W. Diamond, superintendent of the women's section of the Surrey County Lunatic Asylum and a member of the Royal Photographic Society, the most important advantage in utilizing photography in the "science" of physiognomy, lay in its ability to record "with unerring accuracy the external phenomena of each passion, as the really certain indication of internal derangement."[215]

Underscoring the identification properties of the photograph, Diamond noted: "the portraits of the insane . . . give to the eye so clear a representation of their case that on their re-admission after temporary absence and cure, I have found the previous report of more value in calling to mind the case and treatment, than any verbal description I may have placed on record."[216] This belief in the photograph's ability to accurately identify, (re)present and (re)collect the insane, inevitably led to the suggestion that it be deployed to surveill and regulate them. In the words of T.N. Brushfield, superintendent of the Chester County Lunatic Asylum: "In the case of criminal lunatics, it is frequently of great importance that a portrait should be obtained. . . . [I]f they do escape from the asylum they are doubly dangerous to the community at large, and they may frequently be traced by sending their photographs to the police authorities."[217] This belief also meant that the photograph was invested with a powerful autonomy that not only furnished credence to the view that it could function in clinical description "as an accurate substitute for the presence of the patient,"[218] but in many instances allowed the photograph to testify to the state of madness unencumbered by verbal interpretations that would have otherwise anchored appearance in a diagnostic or classificatory model; the photograph pictorially substituted for the proof of madness. Thus Dietrich Georg Kieser, whose *Elements of Psychiatry* was the first textbook illustrated with photographs, observed this in his introduction: "The photographic portraits are complementary to the living physiognomy, showing what the case study reveals in words."[219]

In the course of this discursive accumulation premised on the veracity of the photograph, John Conolly, the reformer of British asylums, ascribed to the photograph the capability of outlining and, in turn, regulating the permeable boundary between madness and normalcy— between "the ordinary expression of the passions and emotions" and "its exaggeration in those whose reason is beginning to remit its control." Thus to the photograph is granted the capacity for instantiating every trace, every singular vestige of madness—"there is so singular a fidelity in a well-executed photograph that the impression of very recent muscular agitation in the face seems to be caught by the process."[220] However Conolly, unlike Kieser, accompanied each photograph with written descriptions of the case, thus tacitly acknowledging the need for textual information to supplement visual empiricism. This was similar to Alphonse Bertillon's linking of shorthand written descriptions—"speaking likeness"—to the photograph, as a way of neutralizing the difficulties associated with visual empiricism.[221]

As Sander Gilman points out, for all the insistence of the objectivity of the photograph and under the guise of it, the portrayals of the insane during this period were simply a reiteration of stereotypes and conventions established in the works of Esquirol and others (Fig. 26). We see this in the work of both Hugh Diamond and Max Leidersdorf where the photographs depict the insane in the manner that Esquirol had, that is, with their hands concealed (Figs. 27 & 28).[222] The invisible presence of a straitjacket makes itself felt. Bound from within or whether bound from without, the body appears rigid and withdrawn: an interpretive confluence, representing either the self-imposed exile of madness or the restraining hand of reason. In certain photographs, as in B.A. Morel's portrayal of a cretin, the decision has been made to depict a prominent physical deformity (goiter), which then functions as the "iconographic sign of the physiognomy of insanity (Fig. 29)."[223] In this way, Morel intended that the insane would identify themselves as a separate category representing "the invariable, distinct and immutable characteristics which distinguish the natural race from its degenerate variants." Furthermore, in these portrayals, the insane are repeatedly represented in the manner we have come to associate with the photographic representation of criminals: frontality and a plain background (Fig. 30). According to the classificatory scheme by which the body is produced as an object of physiognomic discourse, mania takes on the following characteristics: "marked by the bristled hair, the wrinkled brow, the fixed unquiet eye, and the lips apart as if from painful respiration."[224] What are we to make of this, if not the fact that these visible aspects derive their meaning precisely in relation to that of a functioning classical norm, Athenian in origin: "an ample brow, a clear and steadfast eye, a firm and well-proportioned mouth."[225]

In 1887, influenced by the view that there was a direct association between diseases of the mind and pathology of expression, William Noyes decided that, instead of photographing individual expressions reflecting particular mental aberrations, it would be useful to visually depict general pathological states. Inspired by Galton's work, Noyes

Figure 26. "Melancholia" from the essay on "Folie" by Esquirol in the *Dictionnaire*.

Figure 27. Puerperal mania. A lithograph based on one of Hugh H. Diamond's photographs.

Figure 28. "Madness with epilepsy" from Max Leidersdorf.

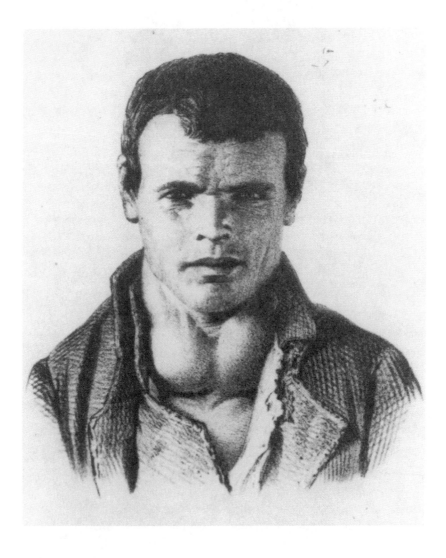

Figure 29. Cretin. Based on a Baillanger photograph from B.A. Morel's *Atlas*.

Figure 30. "Melancholia." Photograph by Browne.

developed a composite by taking multiple exposures of male and female patients suffering from general paresis with the intention of proving visually a pathologic type (Fig. 31): "The . . . composite photograph of general paresis is made from the portraits of eight patients, three females and five males. . . . The percentage of females is higher than in the natural ratio of the two sexes in the disease. The cases are all in the second stage of the disease, and their individual portraits show the marked characteristics of general paresis."[226] Inasmuch as photography was viewed as a mode of representation that provided for objective, unmediated observation, "the connection between seeing and photographing the insane [had been] closely made."[227] Hence, photographic practices operating in a series of discourses which sought to see right into the body in relation to its surface particulars, produced the body as mute testimony of its own deviance. Here we are faced with bodies that perform for the eye the discourses written onto their bodies.

Figure 31. Composite portrait of a general paresis. Photographer: William Noyes, 1899.

FOUR

Photography and the Body of the Worker

INTRODUCTION

I n the nineteenth and early part of the twentieth century, photography—operating wholly within the confines of a capitalist logic and within the analytical space of a panopticon apparatus (the factory)—became an effective instrument of the technician-engineer's attempt to wrest control of the processes of production from skilled labor, to strip such labor of those skills, and significantly to fracture the very body of the laborer along an axis of time and motion. Photography was part and parcel of a managerial discourse in "anatomo-politics" that envisioned an engineering of the body of the worker in terms of the efficient concerns of capitalist enterprise. And labor—which Marx had presupposed as exclusively human, in that it was purposive action guided by intelligence[1]—was now transformed in its capitalist mode to a process of "ballet-mechanique." This severance of conception from execution (the material embodiment of the Kantian dichotomy)—produced by the objectification of labor and the subsequent analysis and fragmentation of the body of the worker into units of elementary actions made possible by photography's active seizure of work—resulted in the training, disciplining, and reordering of the worker's body, so that his or her motions were organized only along the most efficient trajectories of capital accumulation.

The insertion of photography into the discursive field of management and the capitalist process of production, as a mechanism of objectification and as an instrument of subjection, is within the broader parameters of the desire and power of capital to know, realize, and control labor in its own image. The utilization of photography takes place within what Michel Foucault has referred to as the "circular process" of knowledge and power: "an epistemological thaw through a refinement of power relations; a multiplication of the effects of power through the formation and accumulation of new forms of knowledge."[2] It is central to the process which sought to supervise, codify, and deploy in place of the skilled worker, the body of the unskilled worker, engendering in its wake a further refinement of the capitalist relations of power.

In the disciplinary apparatus of capitalist production, the human body enters "a machinery of power that explores it, breaks it down, and rearranges it." A "political anatomy," which is also a "mechanics of power," was being born.[3] As Foucault argues, these disciplinary techniques, in abstracting and dissociating the power of the body, enhance the forces of the body in terms of its economic utility, equipping it, for instance, with a greater "aptitude" and capacity, while seeking to diminish its political forces by reversing such energies and transforming them into "a relation of strict subjection."[4] A body that is docile is at once a useful body, becoming obedient as it becomes more useful.[5] While none of the disciplinary techniques utilized were new, "by being combined and generalized, they attained a level at which the formation of knowledge and the increase of power regularly reinforce one another. . . ."[6] Power as Foucault points out, is also positive in its effects, creating as it does new realities, new domains of objects, and new "rituals of truth."[7]

To the inevitable question of the genesis and evolution of photography's role in the (de)composition of the worker's body, it would be overly simple, but nevertheless not wrong, to observe that it was a corollary of all those processes, micro and macro, that capital harnessed to itself in the pursuit of controlling the social body politically and economically. The use of photography in the rationalization and objectification of skilled labor must also be understood in the context of the general emphasis on technical rationality which the emerging metadiscourses of the sciences ushered in and legitimized during the nineteenth century. Furthermore, the consolidation of a powerful new professional class in the nineteenth century—the engineers, operating as agents of capital—served to accord to rationalization and efficiency the status of normative values and the means by which control over skilled labor could be established. Indeed, as we shall discover, the instrumental realism of photography is deeply implicated in an ideology that claims the autonomy of science and technology as productive forces.

The systematic appropriation and use of techniques of discipline by capitalism in its bid to control completely the mode of production and subjugate labor to its will, slowly evolved in degrees of intensity and in phases throughout the nineteenth and early part of the twentieth century. It is necessary both to delineate and clarify this process. It is a process which at one and the same time represents both the origin and development of what we so glibly refer to as management, which, ironically, did away with "that inductive sign of the human essence," the hand, and "the civilization of the hand."[8]

EARLY ATTEMPTS AND FAILURES TO CONTROL WORKERS

Prior to 1880, the organization of capitalist production evolved from the decentralized "domestic system"—work performed in innumerable tiny domestic workshops—to a variety of relatively centralized subcontracting systems. During this early phase, capitalists, in emphasizing their cost structure and resorting to intermediaries for the management of labor,[9] disregarded "the difference between labor power and labor that can be gotten out of it."[10] In fact, Pollard has referred to this buffer arrangement between skilled labor and manufacturers involving skilled intermediaries as "a method of evading management."[11] The reluctance of manufacturers to bring skilled workers under their direct supervision and reorganize the processes of work, meant that workers not only controlled the manner and pace of their work but also that labor embodied a unified expression of conception and execution.

Despite the fact that the contract system continued in many machine shops into the twentieth century, "the power and independence of the contractors"[12] with regard to the relations of production became increasingly unacceptable to capitalists. Indeed, by 1900 the centralized control of labor at a single site, represented by the new factory system, was becoming the norm. In America the majority of the 4,500,000 wage earners were employed "in factories with more than 500 employees."[13] In 1870 there were only a handful of large factories, concentrated in textiles. By 1900, however, there were 1,063 factories with 500–1,000 wage earners.[14] The iron and steel plants had usurped the position of the textile companies to become the largest American factories.[15] Complexity in manufacturing operations evidently contributed to the large size, but it also reflected a growing understanding among capitalists that disciplinary control over the workers (skilled and unskilled) could be more easily effected by a centralization of employment, by, in fact, gathering the workers in one place.[16] The way was thus paved for the extensive and intensive use of salaried foremen and the close supervision and surveillance of skilled labor; the exploitation of the workers would be closer at "hand"!

The utilization of the salaried foreman undoubtedly brought the skilled worker more intimately within the disciplinary architecture of the factory. In many machine shops, the foremen were the collectors of cost data, and prior to a more organized temporal ordering of the production space by means of automatic time clocks and card systems, they were management's timekeepers. Not unlike the contractor, the foremen were skilled workers themselves and their usefulness to management depended to a great extent on their technical knowledge of the production process in the machine shop. While the foremen were management's insertion into a production process as yet outside its particular epistemological control, they were also its disciplinarians. The basis of their disciplinary method was physical compulsion and verbal bullying, which in common factory parlance came to be known as the "driving method."[17]

The foreman also acted as a rate-setter in factories where the piece-work system was the common basis of correlating productivity with incentive in terms of wages. Based on their own work experience, foremen were quite capable of estimating the capabilities of individual workers and arriving at the wage rate for piece work. However, there was one major problem with the piece-work system. When it succeeded as an incentive, and skilled workers began to produce more, and correspondingly were paid more for their productivity, the manufacturers—alarmed by the fact that the workers were now receiving a significantly higher pay than they had under the day wage system—often cut back the piece rate to what the workers would be making under day work, in effect penalizing the workers for being productive.[18] In such a situation the workers in turn responded by producing just enough to make the going wage. The incentive to produce more was thus nullified.

It was apparent to the workers that the manufacturers wished to seek optimum productivity, while at the same time not wishing to reward the workers commensurately. In order to protect themselves as a group from such exploitative practices, skilled labor sought to control those ambitious or naive among them who attempted to produce above the generally agreed-upon level, and in effect sought to thwart the foreman's and general management's ability to establish norms regarding the required levels of productivity and output. And despite threats, profanity, and dismissal of individual "troublemakers," skilled workers began to redefine the actual value of their labor in terms of the exchange rate manufacturers wished to establish, by operating below their own potential. Unable to control the value of their labor power (wages), skilled workers were determined to control the extent to which they labored,[19] and consequently control the rate of surplus value, much to the chagrin of the capitalist manufacturers who wished to extract as much labor as they could without compensating the workers.

This pattern of output restriction emphasized the limitations of the foremen's supervisory control over skilled labor, and their power was further eroded by the attempts of unions to weaken, by formal means, the wage-setting authority of foremen. Unions such as the Amalgamated Association of Iron and Steel Workers negotiated contracts with iron manufacturers, placing restrictions on how much labor could be extracted from their members.[20] From the manufacturer's point of view, it was soon realized that the intermediary role of the foreman had ceased to have its particular usefulness and that a more systematically rationalized appropriation of labor had to be initiated. This awareness was further underscored by a spate of strikes between 1880 and 1920. Initially, companies in responding to strikes resorted to every possible anti-union tactic—spies, provocateurs, the blacklist, the recruitment of thousands of strike breakers—as they sought crudely to dismantle the power of labor.[21] Standard Oil, Swift, Armour, Pullman, Pressed Steel Co., and the Bethlehem Steel plants were sites of some of the most violent confrontations during the pre–World War I era.[22]

In the capitalist attempt to control the pace of labor, in its attempt to temporalize the body of the worker, the strike by labor represents a temporal dislocation of that process. It indicates a mobilization of time against the monopolization of space/property by capital. However, as a strategy to control labor, anti-union tactics and the overt display of capitalist power only served to reconstitute the body of labor in the everyday domain. Power wore a very visible face, a face contorted by its own intensity, and it risked the elevation of the victim into an object of pity and admiration. Punishment had become spectacle and could only be counter-productive. Discipline must reverse the lines of visibility: power must become less visible and the body of labor must be raised to a new and different level of positive luminosity. Power could then "leave the domain of more or less everyday perception and enter that of abstract consciousness; its effectiveness . . . seen as resulting from its inevitability, not from its visible intensity."[23] In doing so, it would culminate in the organization of a domain in which the body of labor would be subjected "to infinite examination and . . . compulsory objectification."[24] The consequence was a disciplinary apparatus of intense registration that would accumulate a whole mass of documents, visual and written, on the working body. A new ethics of control written along a politico-anatomy register would reappropriate the motions of a working body, in time making it more decipherable, legible and manipulable, spinning in its wake an incipient epistemology of the body—scientific management.

THE 'DISCIPLINE' OF SCIENTIFIC MANAGEMENT

As Pollard and others have noted, the impetus for the rise of scientific management, which ushered in the erosion of the traditional foreman's ad hoc control over the laboring process, was not only the increasing size and complexity of manufacturing operations, but the emergence of a new technical elite—the engineer, who embodied the instrumental reasoning necessary for solving the technical problems besetting the capitalist, and who simultaneously provided the methods for rationalized management of a refractory artisanal labor.

Ironic though it may seen, the engineer was a product of the union of the sciences and the mechanical arts.[25] But as a union, it favored the engineer rather than the artisan, for it would be the engineer who would seize technical and managerial control of the labor process and abolish whatever control artisans, because of their skills and knowledge, had over the mode of production. The circuits of knowledge would be reversed. Even more so, the union would indeed favor the capitalist, for the engineer was the agent of capital.

> Even in his strictly technical work the engineer brought to his task the spirit of the capitalist. His design of machinery, for example, was guided as much by the capitalist need to minimize both the cost and the autonomy of skilled labor as by the desire to harness most efficiently the potentials of matter and energy. The technical and capitalist aspects of the engineer's work were reverse sides of the same coin, modern technology. As such, they were rarely if ever distinguishable: technical demands defined capitalist possibilities only insofar as capitalist demands defined the technical possibilities. The technical work of the engineer was little more than the scientific extension of capitalist enterprise; it was through his efforts that science was transformed into capital.[26]

Knowing that improvements in machinery and the technical infrastructure were insufficient to guarantee the capitalist's success and their own success, more and more engineers took on managerial positions.[27] They began to apply their technical expertise not only to the engineering of materials but also to the engineering of people.[28] Consequently, engineering became not only "the science of controlling the forces and utilizing the materials of nature for the benefit of man" but also "the art of organizing and of directing human activities in connection therewith."[29] This thinking had become indispensable for engineers and synonymous with professional advancement.[30] More importantly, the engineer was also the exponent of efficiency, which increasingly represented the utilitarian solution to an instability that was evident both within the corporate order besieged by labor unrest and in the larger social order riddled with class tensions.[31] In fact, in 1882 the U.S. House Committee on Education and Labor, worried about labor unrest, began an investigation into the relations of labor and capital.[32] Four years later the Haymarket bombing occurred.

It was into this environment that Frederick Winslow Taylor, formerly foreman, engineer, and then plant manager, introduced "scientific management" and became the leading exponent of the systematic management movement. According to Merkle, "The formal goal of the Taylor system," represented no less than an attempted "reconciliation of capital and labor."[33] But as a reconciliation formed in the neutral language of technical expertise and celebrative of efficiency as an end in itself, it only sought to better disguise behind its instrumental, positivist, pseudo-scientific reasoning, the terms of its new-found exploitation and "reconciliation" of labor to the capitalist mode of production. As Braverman, in substantiating David Noble's argument, correctly points out, scientific management "lacks the characteristics of a true science because its assumptions reflect nothing more than the outlook of the capitalist with regard to the conditions of production."[34] Scientific management—with its complex synthesis of organizational techniques which had been present earlier as "a disconnected series of initiatives and experiments"[35] but were now unified by an ideology of science[36]—represented at its very center an ambition to realize Bentham's panopticon principle that a good design could supersede supervision.[37]

To begin with, Taylor sought to extract from labor the maximum output from a working day's labor power. Having been a foreman in the machine shop at the Midvale Steel Company (1878–90), he was not unaware of the problem faced by systematic "soldiering" or output restriction that workers engaged in when doing piece work. Furthermore, he was aware that such behavior on the part of workers was not unreasonable: "After a workman has had the price per piece of the work he is doing lowered two or three times as a result of his having worked harder and increased his output, he is likely to entirely lose sight of his employer's side of the case and to become imbued with a grim determination to have no more cuts if soldiering can prevent it."[38] However in Taylor's view, the problem lay in the fact that workers, by virtue of their knowledge and skill, retained control over the processes of labor—that, indeed, "workmen . . . possess this mass of traditional knowledge, a large part of which is not in the possession of management."[39] Hence, employers are forced to "derive their knowledge of how much of a given class of work can be done in a day from either their own experience, which has frequently grown hazy with age, [or] from casual and unsystematic observation."[40] As a consequence, management is reduced to turning the work over to the workman and then hoping merely to induce "each workman to use his best endeavors, his hardest work, all his traditional knowledge, his skill, his ingenuity, and his goodwill, in a word, his 'initiative,' so as to yield the largest possible return to his employer."[41] This was obviously an inefficient and insufficient solution. In order to put an end to "soldiering" and derive from skilled labor the maximum possible output what was required was

> the deliberate gathering in on the part of those on the management's side of all the great mass of traditional knowledge, which in the past has been in the heads of the workman, and in the physical skill and knack of the workman, which he has acquired through years of experience.[42]

In this discursive appropriation and reconstruction of work, the engineer, given his special expertise and instrumental knowledge, would play a central role.

> The duty of gathering in all of this great mass of traditional knowledge and then recording it, tabulating it, and in many cases finally reducing it to laws, rules, and even to mathematical formulas, is voluntarily assumed by the scientific managers.[43]

Thus, despite Peter Drucker's disingenuous claim that in its search of a higher output, scientific management simply represents an "organized study of work, the analysis of work into its simplest elements,"[44] the fact is that "[scientific management] is intended to be a science of the management of others' work under capitalist conditions."[45]

Whereas division of labor under capitalism had meant the analysis of a process and then its division and distribution among many workers, what Taylor proposed and implemented was the breakdown of each worker's procedure of working on a particular task, the reorganization of its elements into the most efficient configuration, and then its return to the worker as an accelerated process. In pursuit of this objective, Taylor turned his attention to one of the most important and skilled trades of the time, that of the machinist, considered "the sine qua non of modern industry."[46] He proceeded by reducing and systematizing the metal cutting process—generally involving a number of different skill-related decisions—into twelve variables, which he then represented in a practical "slide rule" that could be used to instruct a worker of little skill and no mathematical training. Rather than relying on knowledge, experience, and skill, the workers were forced to work from a quantified list of sequential movements provided by the planning department.[47] Thus, by rendering skilled workers dependent on management, Taylor instituted the "dissociation of the labor process from the skills of the workers,"[48] which, in turn, enhanced management's ability to produce "docile bodies."

Furthermore, in keeping with his effort to gain control of the work process and extract from workers the optimal amount of labor power, Taylor undertook what he called "the scientific study of unit times." Under such stopwatch studies, for example, even shoveling dirt is broken down into "fifty or sixty elements"[49] such as, "time filling shovel and straightening up ready to throw," "time throwing one shovelful,"[50] and individually timed (in hundredths of a minute or per foot walked) so that any job requiring shoveling can then be quickly calculated as requiring X amount of time depending on the timed elements it includes. In this regard, time-motion study represents the "temporal elaboration of the act"[51] characteristic of a disciplinary apparatus, which subsequently achieves its most powerful expression in Gilbreth's use of photography.

In order to determine the time of each of the elements, Taylor utilized only what he called "first-class men,"[52] men who he claimed were physically suited to the job but who most often were physically exceptional specimens. It was on the basis of the work done by these "first-class men" that he established the principle of a "fair day's work" and the subsequent rates to be paid.[53] In this manner, by subdividing work and timing its elements, the workers were "tuned up" to machine speeds[54] and their motivation enlisted by a differential piece-work rate that attempted to demonstrate the connection between increased output and an increased wage rate. The rate was punitive if one worked below the required pace but increases in output beyond a point were not reflected in the differential rate, because Taylor believed that anything over a thirty to sixty percent increase in a worker's pay would be spent on drink.[55]

Thus, the temporal imperatives of a capitalist efficiency ethic, the soul of its disciplinary apparatus, subjects the body of the worker to exhaustive use. Surveillance, as Foucault has observed, is crucial to the power of a disciplinary apparatus: "The exercise of discipline presupposes a mechanism that coerces by means of observation; an apparatus in which the techniques that make it possible to see induce effects of power, and in which, conversely, the means of coercion make those on whom they are applied clearly visible."[56] In this regard, Taylor's time-motion studies are not without their surveillance components.

> This case or "watch book" is another device. . . . It consists of a framework containing in it one, two, or three watches whose stop and start movements can be operated by pressing with the fingers of the left hand upon the proper portion of the cover of the notebook without the knowledge of the workman who is being observed. . . . There are many cases, in which telling the workman that he was being timed in a minute way would only result in a row, and in defeating the whole object of the timing.[57]

What Taylor, in effect, did was introduce Bentham's panopticon architecture into the factory space. It was an internal architecture of detailed control that would function "to transform individuals: . . . to provide a hold on their conduct, to carry the effects of power right to them, to make it possible to know them, to alter them."[58] For instance, we are told that the planning department and its functions are to be placed as closely as possible to the center of the shop or shops; the managers, and their assistants, "should, of course, have their offices adjacent to the planning room, if practicable; the drafting room should be near at hand, thus bringing all of the planning and purely brain work of the establishment close together."[59] Hence, conception extracted from the worker's body is instituted in the planning department and the planning department becomes correspondingly the central gaze of the disciplinary apparatus constituting bodies in terms of days and tasks, as it analyzes all orders, provides step-by-step instructions by which each casting is to be made, maintains time cards on a daily basis, maps the route each piece takes in production, and generally coordinates the flow of work even as it standardizes representations of its own organizational processes.[60] Labor dissociated from the labor process makes for a tractable manual force and a cost-efficient solution: "There is no question that the cost of production is lowered by separating the work of planning and the brain work as much as possible from the manual labor."[61]

As for the mass of documents generated by this systematized surveillance, they provide for "the pinning down of each individual in his own particularity,"[62] for they indicate the output of each worker, the hours he has worked, and hence "the individual differentiations make possible for a classification of all bodies."[63] Foucault observes that "in discipline it is the subjects who have to be seen"[64] and the apparatus of writing produced by Taylor's planning department organizes an economy of visibility and simultaneously an economy of power by fixing, arresting, regulating, and maintaining calculated distributions. Each instruction card in its disciplining function, in its charting of routes and distribution of tasks, in its subsequent returns, each timetable in its formation of days and enumeration of tasks locating each body in time, together are maps of the part and representative of the whole architecture.

> The disciplinary apparatus would make it possible for a single gaze to see everything constantly: A central point would be both the source of light illuminating everything, and a locus of convergence for everything that must be known: a perfect eye that nothing would escape and a center towards which all gazes would be turned.[65]

Furthermore, the individuating observations that were initially undertaken provisioned an analytical space in which further observations, differentiations, and classifications could be generated, creating, in turn, and spawning new methodologies and knowledges of management control. The panopticon, once instituted, is a privileged site for observing, analyzing, and modifying behavior. And in its attempt to make visible, to know at a glance, the planning department operates as a diagram of power to establish a finely detailed supervision of bodies, spaces, and functions.[66] In this regard, Taylor's system of "functional foremanship" provides for an exact geometry for distributing and multiplying supervision at each level. For example, in addition to four types of "executive functional bosses" who directly supervised the machine shop—the "gang-boss," the "speed boss," "inspectors," and "repair bosses"—there were four other functional foremen who operated from the planning department: the "order and route clerk," the "instruction card clerk," the "time and cost clerk," and the "shop disciplinarian." Under Taylor's plan, surveillance becomes both more specific and functional, integrating and intensifying the disciplinary space at every moment. As Foucault indicates, in order to increase its productive function "[surveillance] [has not only] to be broken down into smaller elements" but it is necessary to "specify the surveillance and make it functional."[67] This is exactly what Taylor had instituted. Furthermore, even though surveillance operating in Taylor's disciplinary apparatus is carried out by individuals, it generates a power both autonomous and anonymous:

> The power in the hierarchized surveillance of the disciplines is not possessed as a thing, or transferred as a property; it functions like a piece of machinery. And, although it is true that its pyramidal organization gives it a "head," it is the apparatus as a whole that produces "power" and distributes individuals in this permanent and continuous field.[68]

The reasons for establishing such a network of functional and supervisory relations provide an insight into the nature and functioning of this machine Taylor had erected. First, he notes the advantage of increasing the points of surveillance: "Certainly the most marked outward characteristic of functional management lies in the fact that each workman, instead of coming in direct contact with the management at one point only, namely through his gang boss, receives his daily orders . . . from eight different bosses."[69] Drawing on the analogy of the classroom, Taylor asserts: "In such a school the children are each day successively taken in hand by one teacher in his particular specialty, and they are in many cases disciplined by a man particularly trained in this function."[70] As Foucault has noted, as with the school, so with the workshop, "the minor techniques of multiple and intersecting observations"[71] provide for an overall functioning of power. But where does the greatest potential of Taylor's "functional foremanship" lie?

> The full possibilities of functional foremanship, however, will not have been realized until almost all of the machines in the shop are run by men who are of small calibre and attainments, and who are therefore cheaper than those required under the old system. The adoption of standard . . . methods throughout the shops, the planning done in the planning room and the detailed instructions sent them from this department, added to the direct help received from the four executive bosses, permit the use of comparatively cheap men even on complicated work.[72]

Thus, the disciplinary apparatus of scientific management, in its attempts to neutralize what Foucault refers to as "horizontal conjunctions"[73] ("soldiering"), in its deployment of time to train, surveil, and extract from bodies a maximum of force, in its utilization of "tactics of distribution,"[74] in its use of "reciprocal adjustment of bodies"[75] to generate an increased utility from a multiplicity, in its surveillance, assessment, and classification, in all of this it sought to intensify the effects of power and, correspondingly, the creation of both useful and docile bodies. It is into this disciplinary apparatus of the capitalist mode of production that photography is introduced. Its effects are as deconstructive of the body as they are powerful.

PHOTOGRAPHY AND THE INCEPTION OF A MOTION ECONOMY

Taylor had used photographs in his book *On the Art of Cutting Metals*. Some of the photographs were plates depicting the best method of forging a standard cutting tool, and others were close-ups of various tools in the process of wear from use, and yet others of tools in the process of forging. While Taylor had restricted the use of photography to examining individual tools of production, it was Frank Gilbreth, one of his disciples, who brought photography to bear on the body of the worker in pursuit of what he called a "motion economy."

Frank Gilbreth's work in photographing motion was essentially a product of the investigations conducted in the last quarter of the nineteenth century by both Etienne Jules Marey and Eadweard Muybridge into the physiology of animal and human locomotion. In an age of Freud and the unconscious, the desire here is for the new empirical vigilance instituted by the camera's gaze to disclose that which is initially hidden, to play upon the solid opaque surfaces of the body, and reveal that which is not privy to the first disclosure of organic sight.[76] Gilbreth, however, improved upon their methods between 1911 and 1912, and directed his efforts toward an efficient re-engineering of the worker's body. Taking the rationalization that Taylor had initiated deeper into the physiology of the worker, Gilbreth would operate at a newer and higher level to abstract, classify, and deploy in standardized motions that which was previously concealed from management.

Despite the fact that Taylor had displayed a limited interest in the industrial uses of photography, in emphasizing a "science of work" predicated on observation, "he had been most influential in paving the way for photography."[77] Gilbreth, a fervent believer in Taylor's scientific management who joined Taylor's circle in 1907, began to first utilize photography to study the motions of journeymen bricklayers, so that he could discover the most efficient methods of work and standardize them. In the book *Motion Study: A Method for Increasing the Efficiency of the Workman*, in which he examines bricklaying, Gilbreth's use of photography is most rudimentary. Its intent is simply to demonstrate, as with some plates entitled in the imperative mode: "Wrong way to pick up a brick" and on the facing page "Right way to pick up a brick." In spite of being rudimentary, these photographs demonstrate the overriding desire for a normative body that is at once an efficient body. However, these photographs are the consequence of analysis rather than being analytical. For example, in a section of the book devoted to "stringing mortar," the work of the best bricklayers is observed, broken down into its elements, photographed, and timed.[78]

> [P]hotograph the various positions in which the hands, arms, feet and other parts of the body involved in the operations were placed, and record the time taken in moving from one position to another by one method, as related to the time taken in moving from the same first to the same second position by another method.[79]

The most efficient way of "stringing mortar" is then presented in a sequence of photographs, showing the positions of various limbs, the particular grip with which a brick is to be picked up, the positioning of the implements to provide for increased efficiency, and so forth.[80] In the book *Applied Motion Study*, co-authored with his wife, Gilbreth presented a list of variables of motion which included: acceleration, automaticity, combination with other motions, path, length of motion, inertia, and so forth. However, the detailed breakdown of work began to take place when he introduced his concept of "micromotion."

"Micromotion" was first systematically implemented at the New England Butt Company in 1910. The company had already reorganized itself according to Taylor's principles of scientific management and concluded that Gilbreth's motion studies could increase efficiency even further. Taylor's stopwatch studies, though useful, did not provide for an accurate recording of each unit timed, nor had it been able to provide a record of the surrounding conditions, which the camera had been able to provide Gilbreth in his early bricklaying studies. Furthermore, the elementary units in Taylor's stopwatch studies were essentially, as Gilbreth pointed out, "groups of motions": "They were elementary only with relation to the stopwatch, with which it is impossible to record accurately the time of an element of a motion, since it takes two decisions and two motions to press the stopwatch."[81] Furthermore, even leaving aside reaction time, in the absence of photography, under Taylor's method, the accuracy of the description of a "group of motions" depended upon the powers of observation of the individual doing the recording. However, with the use of a camera and a microchronometer (a speed clock), even smaller units of motion could be recorded and timed.[82] Since, in Gilbreth's view, Taylor's method did not account accurately for the motions of the worker, he referred to Taylor's work as time studies, rather that time-motion studies.[83]

At the New England Butt Company, employees were ushered into what was referred to as "the betterment room," which resembled a typical workshop organized for the manufacturing of dress braid machines, except that the walls had a grid pattern on them similar to the backdrops Muybridge had used. The camera was then utilized to record the employees' motions while they worked. Work is here reconstructed according to the demands of the capitalist disciplinary apparatus, and the camera itself served a double purpose, as an empirical instrument yielding "scientific proof" and as a pedagogical instrument for readjusting the worker's body against a standardized grid which visually aided in the measurement of the duration and distance of the work movement. The narrative pattern utilized in this pedagogy of the worker was a chronologically-based "before" and "after" approach, the same method that was to become so popular in advertising's rhetoric on the therapeutic effects of the commodity.[84] The camera recorded the worker's initial performance which then was played back to the worker, while Gilbreth, pointer in hand, instructed the worker on how to minimize certain motions and how to do away with others altogether. After this meticulous disciplining of the body, the worker's performance on the task was once again recorded to register the improvements. "As in works of melodrama, these early films were planned to have a happy ending, proving the values of scientific observation and instruction."[85]

In his studies of "micromotion" Gilbreth had used a hand-cranked motion-picture camera which included in each frame both the motion of the worker and a microchronometer registering time. Furthermore, in addition,

> An ordinary reliable clock was placed alongside the micro-chronometer, in order to serve as a check upon its inaccuracy, if any occurred, and also to provide a record of the time of day that the study was made in the resulting picture. Temperature and humidity records were included upon the picture. Signs, describing the place where the investigation was being made, the name of the investigator and the date, were placed for an instant in the field, and thus became a part of the permanent record.[86]

Despite the comprehensiveness of these records, Gilbreth discovered that it was difficult to visualize the path of a motion, and it was not possible to measure the length with precision from the observations of the motion-picture film alone, "as there is no summary or recapitulation of all the motions of a cycle or operation in any one picture."[87] He thus turned to photography again, to solve these problems and invented the "chronocyclograph" method which was basically a modification of Marey's own invention, the geometrical chronophotograph.

However, photography itself posed a problem, insofar as complex motions resulted in blurred images. To solve this difficulty, Gilbreth substituted Marey's luminous tape with tiny electric bulbs attached to the particular limbs being studied (Fig. 32). Instead of blurred images, the motion paths registered as linear shapes on the photographic plate. "An ordinary photographic plate or film was exposed during the time that he [the worker] performed the work, and recorded the motion path described by the light as a white line, something like a white wire. . . . This line was called a 'cyclograph.'"[88] The orbit of the motion had been registered, but the time taken by the motion path needed to be visually depicted too. In order to account for relative time, relative speed, and direction of the motion path, Gilbreth introduced a properly timed, pulsating interrupter into the circuit which was adjusted to record the duration of the motion. The "chronocyclograph" method now depicted the motion, light path or cyclograph as a series of dashes (Fig. 33). Gilbreth subsequently added directional arrowheads pedagogically indicating the path of the motion to the worker (Fig. 34). To provide for a more

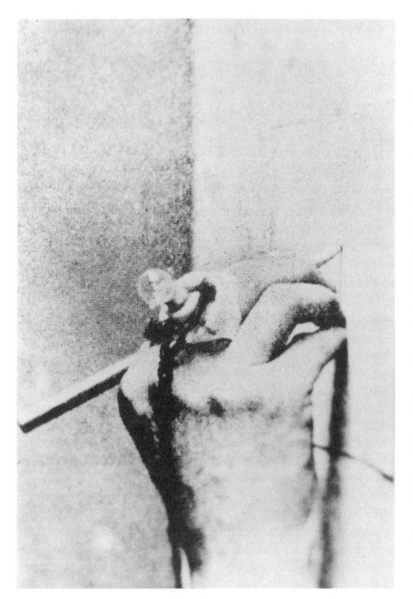

Figure 32. Electric finger bulb attachment designed by Gilbreth for chronocyclograph study.

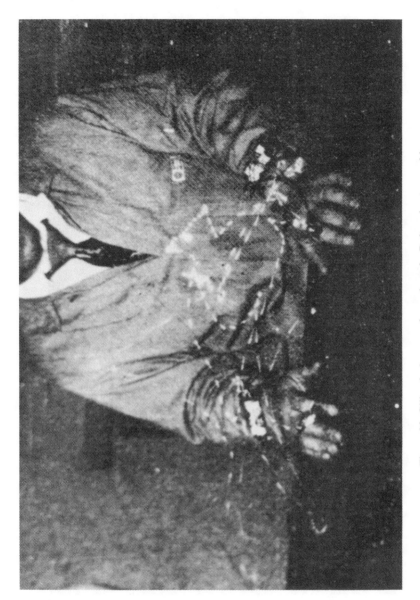

Figure 33. Gilbreth chronocyclograph study. Bolt and nut assembly.

158

Figure 34. Close-up of bolt and nut assembly.

accurate measurement of the distance traversed by a particular motion, Gilbreth introduced a cross-sectional screen ("penetrating screen") into the photograph through multi-exposure methods.

> The resulting photograph gives the path of the motion laid along the cross-sectioned plane divided into any space elements desired. The penetrating screen, therefore, now furnishes the last desired feature for measuring and recording, namely, the exact distance of motions. This, in combination with the foregoing list, now gives us records of exact speed.[89]

To Gilbreth, the chronocyclograph made possible a scientific analysis of work. The functions of the chronocyclegraph, according to him, were:

1. It illustrated the fact "that the subdivision of the motion cycle is the important element." Accurately recorded by the chronocyclograph, the motion cycle could be analyzed, standardized and then synthesized into a recorded model.

2. It "show[ed] plainly the effects of habits"; in this regard Gilbreth argued for the habituation of the worker to the right motion.

3. It could be used for comparing the work motions of various workers in connection with the quantity and quality of output achieved.

4. It demonstrated that "fast motions are different from slow motions," in that they occupy different orbital patterns and thus enabled the teaching of a standard speed or the most efficient speed at which work could be conducted.[90]

In Siegfried Giedion's panegyric to the cyclograph, we get a clear articulation of the extent to which, in an analytic geometry of work, the linear path of the cyclograph becomes a source of normative power.

> The very form of the movement, invisible to the naked eye, is now captured. The light patterns reveal all hesitation or habits interfering with the worker's dexterity and automaticity. In a word, they embrace the sources of error as they do the perfect performance.[91]

Photography makes it possible to pierce the apparent opacity of the body bringing to the surface new visibilities: visibilities that help propose a machine analogue for the worker's body, a body redesigned to synchronize with the machine rhythms of industry, that is, automaticity. It makes for a cybernetic disciplining of the body, according to a machine norm of efficiency—the standard by which each body must measure its productivity. Hence, photograph's functioning within discourses of scientific management provides for the illumination and construction of new forms of corporeal permeability. The consequence is that the forces of capital can operate in this discursive terrain of the visible to transform the "interior" of the worker's body according to the rationalities of efficiency and control. The law of efficiency then inscribed into the gestures and acts of the body, becomes the very essence and necessity of the normative working body. Thus, the worker's body in turn is shaped and construed so that its reconstituted boundaries are less corporeal boundaries than they are the exercise and limits of corporate discourse and disciplinary power.

> We have passed . . . to a web that constrains them (gestures). A sort of anatomochronological schema of behavior is defined. The act is broken down into its elements; the position of the body, limbs, articulations is defined; to each movement are assigned a direction, an aptitude; a duration; their order of succession is prescribed. Time penetrates the body and with it all the meticulous controls of power.[92]

As Foucault notes, disciplinary control establishes both "the best relation between a gesture and the overall position of the body," as well as the "relations that the body must have with the object it manipulates."[93] These are the conditions of its efficiency and speed. "Over the whole surface of contact between the body and the object it handles, power is introduced, fastening them to one another."[94]

Hence, discipline seeks out the body in its most intimate details. Every motion of each limb must be on a similar arc, its relative distance and relative time calculated, organized, and incorporated into the broader logistics and heightened temporality of the production space. "Through the study of the motion path . . . and through a comparison of such graphs or models showing the paths of different operators doing the same kind of work, it is possible to deduce the most efficient method and to make this the standard."[95] From the reduction through photography of individual bodies into electrovisual graphs and then from an aggregate of such graphs, the normative working body is constituted to express the efficiency principle (Fig. 35). Moreover, in the case of skilled work, the standard is to be established, according to Gilbreth, by the observation of skilled workers.[96] This would enable the subsequent employing of unskilled workers for the same work because time-motion standards would result in these workers being quickly taught the standardized motions.[97] "Through an intensive study of motion paths followed in doing different kinds of work efficiently, there has come a recognition of the indications of an efficient motion, its smoothness, its lack of hesitation, its regular normal acceleration and retardation and its use of habit."[98] The body is traversed by the fetish of a machine language, and by reducing the body to disembodied motion the disciplinary program takes on the aura of high reason.

In addition, Gilbreth observed that "through a comparison of the motions used in different lines of work, in the industries, in surgery and in other kinds of activity, it can be shown that the same identical motions are used in doing what are usually considered widely different types of work."[99] Thus, in 1916, the Gilbreths identified as a result of their use of the camera, twenty-two elementary units of motion, the building blocks of all work activity. They referred to these elements or units as therbligs (the Gilbreth's name spelled backwards). The elementary units consisted of motions such as pre-position (pp), position (p), grasp (g), select (st), search (sh), assemble (a), transport loaded (tl), transport empty (te), inspect (i), and so forth. According to their schematic taxonomy of motion, "To pick up a pencil, therefore, would involve the proper categories of Transport Empty, Pinch Grasp, and Transport Loaded, each with a standard time value, and the sum of the time categories of these three therbligs, given in ten-thousandths of a minute, constitutes the time for the complete motion."[100] As Braverman points out, "the therblig was only the first of a series of standard data systems, which are now constructed by many large corporations for their internal use."[101]

> Almost compulsively, like the theologian reaching for the perfect metaphysical system with which to encompass all thought, the engineer going beyond the mere breakdown of work into its simplest detail, now reaches out for a simple, comprehensive system to encompass all time and motion. From the correct strokes of the janitor sweeping the floor to the movement of the typist drumming

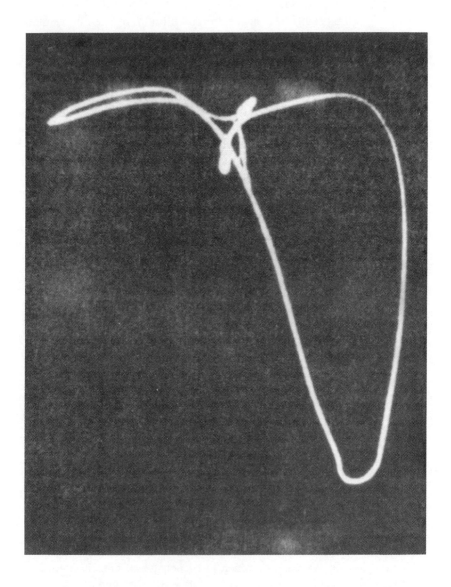

Figure 35. A motion model representing the standard of efficiency and perfection.

rhythmically on the keyboard of her electric typewriter, in each instance the striving is toward the irreducible atom, the nuclear unit which, in alchemic fashion, can be recombined into almost infinite variations, yet be encompassed within the two dimensions of a single card.[102]

Furthermore, through the use of a stereoscope, the Gilbreths also created three-dimensional wire models of a standard motion for the worker's edification (Fig. 36). The pedagogical value inherent in three-dimensional wire models of this nature, is apparent to them, and its rationale should obviously be evident to the worker too: "Through its use he [the worker] can see what he is to do, learn about it through his eye, follow the wire with his fingers, and thus accustom his muscles to the activity that they are expected to perform."[103] Thus we find the worker considering and examining his own labor, face to face with what he has been dispossessed of, which lies before him abstracted, a simulacrum, a signifier whose signified, preconceived, awaits the material receptacle of his body. Their function located outside of them, workers must do their best to simulate it; since their function is standardized, it has become more important than they are.[104]

Gilbreth seemed to be well aware of the particular antagonism with which skilled craftsmen responded to scientific management in general and time-studies specifically, for he notes that there are those

who object to having any observer record what they are doing, believing that the time study man is obtaining knowledge of their skill and giving them no information in return. Other [objections] have come from those who have seen or heard "secret time study" and "watch-book time study" [the technique Taylor advocated], and who regard all observers as spies because of a general lack of understanding and cooperation; and there are some instances where they are right.[105]

And what does Gilbreth advocate for such cases? He advocates the use of a self-activated, automicromotion study whereby the worker makes himself responsible for his own surveillance!

There is also in the Gilbreths' work a clear separation and hierarchy between intellectual and manual labor, between those who conceive and those who execute, between those who visualize and those who emulate. "The average engineer, who becomes, through his train-

Figure 36. Gilbreth holding a three-dimensional wire model.

ing and the necessities of his work, a good visualizer, even though he is not one by nature, often fails to realize the small capacity for visualization, possessed by the average person."[106] Management would operate in the thin air and high altitudes of abstract visualization while workers would occupy the lower reaches, imitating by rote and engaging in good habits. Gilbreth had asserted that time-motion studies "determine(d) the ideal habit for the particular work to be done. This is simply another name for standardizing working conditions and methods."[107] And in response to critics, he claimed that the ideal habit or "the standardized motion paths" or "the one best way of doing work" was not to be confused with monotony.

> The method being used is as "habitual" as is possible, that is to say the body is performing the same activity by as nearly as possible the same method every time, with the least amount of active attention on the work hand. There is a careful allowance for fatigue. There is, therefore, no possibility of the body becoming unduly tired. In the meantime, the active attention and all the higher powers of the mind are free, free for the planning of details, free to plan new work, or free to do what they please.[108]

In this manner the separation between mind and body is presented in the guise of a new freedom, endowed with common sense and valorized. The hidden appeal is that the capitalist now requires from the worker only his body, leaving the mind and hence the worker's individuality intact. But this hardly represents an accurate picture of the benefits of automaticity and standardized motion. In the words of a Chicago factory worker:

> You'd think that it would all become so automatic that you could do a lot of serious thinking on the job. But you've got to be careful in placing the steel under the press. So even "day-dreaming" is dangerous. Six guys on my shift have missing fingers.[109]

What traverses Gilbreth's work so vividly is its utilitarian spirit. Time-motion study was not simply a method of increasing efficiency, it was simultaneously its corollary: reducing waste. "Babbage, Coulomb, Adam Smith—all recognized the importance of the time element in industrial operations, for the purpose of obtaining methods of greatest output, but not methods of least waste."[110] Drawing on an example relevant to the times, the Gilbreths observed:

Stupendous as the financial loss to the entire world is, on account
of the great war [World War I] that is now being waged in many
countries . . . it is as nothing compared to the world's loss of the
human element. . . . It is therefore, a great world problem, demand-
ing the attention of all of us, to conserve and utilize humanity in
every way possible.[111]

Thus, while the mind unencumbered by the body would be granted an
expanded freedom, the body organized according to the higher principle of efficiency would be conserved, such conservation no doubt being
necessary for its continued exploitation and utilization by industry. The
motives, we are however assured, are quite unselfish, for what the efficiency increases provided by time-motion study would ensure, was
"the need for conserving the worker for his own happiness."[112] Finally,
praise is offered up to the discourse that legitimizes the Gilbreths'
activities: "It is a fortunate thing to be born in an age like the present
when the scientific spirit prevails in all fields, and where everything can
be legitimately submitted to measurement."[113] But as Bell has
remarked, "utilitarianism provided us a new definition of rationality:
not the rule of reason, but the rule of measurement. With it, man himself
could now be regulated."[114]

Foucault has argued that it is typical of disciplinary power that it
constitutes "the individual as a describable, analyzable object, not in
order to reduce him to 'specific' features, as did the naturalists in relation to living beings, but in order to maintain him in his individual features, in his particular evolution, in his own aptitudes or abilities, under
the gaze of a permanent corpus of knowledge."[115] Consonant with this,
the Gilbreths boldly declare that "under scientific management the individual is the unit to be measured."[116] And since measurement becomes
the criterion by which individual bodies are understood, known and
judged, these calculations in turn become the measure of individuality.
Hence, a new type of individual is ushered into place, whose willing-
ness to define himself/herself in terms of the dominant logic of efficiency bestows on him/her the valued subjectivity of a machined body.
Thus the Gilbreths claim that scientific management is the desire to
treat each worker as an individual.

Under scientific management the work of each man is arranged so
that his output shows up separately and on the individual records. . . .

The primary purpose of separating the output is to see what the man can do, to record this, and to reward the man according to his work, but this separating of output has also an individual result, which is even more important than the result aimed at, and that is the development of individuality.[117]

These individual records were the basis by which workers were to be hired or promoted, and generally classified and related to a norm. And not unlike the criminal record, they exerted a disciplinary pressure by their very existence. And if the photograph operating in a disciplinary apparatus fragmented the worker's body, it also had its honorific function: "The photographs of the 'high priced men,' copies of which may be given to the workers themselves, allow the worker to carry home a record and thus impress his family with what he has done."[118] Thus the physiology of the worker is provided a new level of individuality; its value and, correlatively, its status, instantiated by a corporate biography or record of utilisability. Not "the chronicle of a man . . . [which] formed part of the rituals of power," but that system of describability which becomes the means for discipline and domination.[119]

To recapitulate the argument, the disciplinary apparatus of capitalism systematically attacked the knowing and constituted body of the worker, whose labor was conceived creatively out of the union of conception and execution. In progressive stages, through detailed division of labor and subsequently through the disciplinary apparatus of scientific management, capitalism alienated labor from its own potential creativity. It analyzed the body of the worker, extracted from the worker that knowledge essential to the worker's ability to conceptualize and incorporated that knowledge in itself; the body of the worker was then left powerless and dependent on the instructions it received from the brain trust of capitalism.

Finally, photography operating inside the disciplinary apparatus of scientific management visually fragmented the body of the worker into a series of quantifiable motions and enabled the machine logic of efficiency to operate from within the body, thereby totalizing capitalism's control over the worker's body. Essentially, photographic practices—by making the skilled worker's body visible, his/her skills apparent and the motion-paths of his/her intrinsic abilities available to management's reductive gaze—made possible a disciplining and standardization of the worker's body. For the skilled worker's knowledge, abstracted and reified in standardized, efficient models of work-motion, is then transferred to hundreds of untrained, unskilled workers, which in turn enables the employment of labor that is made both tractable and cheap. Workers' bodies were thus made "both legible and docile" by the mutually enhancing configuration of knowledge and power. Since photography, as we observed, functioned in an ocularcentric regime identified with Cartesian perspectivalism, it was an eminently suitable instrument for underwriting the geometrization of the worker's body along an axis of conception and execution. Consequently, the subject-object dichotomy of an ocularcentric science was, and is no less today, writ large into the body of the worker.

FIVE

The Visual Order of the Nineteenth Century

INTRODUCTION

The examination of photographic practices and their effects on the body, point to the fact that the nineteenth century involved not only large-scale structural changes in economic and social formations but a tremendous expansion of the field of vision. The addiction to visualism had already been apparent in the classificatory and tabular representations of knowledge and in the sensory bases of conceptualizing intellectual matters which had characterized the emerging scientific languages of the seventeenth century.[1] But the introduction of photography in the nineteenth century and the visual ordering of the public domain which it had engendered, signalled an intensification and heightened functioning of the instumentalities of vision. The hegemony of vision is crucial to an understanding of modernity and points to its "deep structure" because, as Martin Jay asserts, the modern era has been dominated by the sense of sight "in a way that sets it apart from its premodern predecessors and possibly its postmodern successor."[2] It meant that a new kind of subject had to function within regimes of visibility structured not just by the introduction of photography, but by changed urban spaces, new modes of perception and spatial and temporal dislocations initiated by novel forms of mobility.[3] These regimes of visibility involved a transformation in the arrangements of objects, spaces, and bodies, which in turn determined what could be seen and what was made visible.

We have examined the deployment of photographic practices in discourses emanating from different points in the social formation of nineteenth-century bourgeois society, and shown how they made visible to knowledge and power the bodies and spaces they sought to effect and to structure. We must now turn to the general conception of seeing that prevailed in bourgeois societies of the nineteenth century. By doing so we may discover in its general principles, in its arrangements for generating knowledge and power, matrices of sight, spaces and bodies, a clearer understanding of the practices and effects of photography, even as we locate these practices in the larger visual order of the nineteenth century. It then becomes a question of providing what Deleuze identifies in Foucault's approach as "visibilities," that is, linking the way things were made visible by photography to a larger conception of seeing in the nineteenth century.[4] It must be remembered that while the photographic frame provided for a reticulated grid within which bodies could be organized, analyzed, and displayed, there were other grids and frames by means of which the body and what it was disposed to see—as well as how the body was revealed to power and knowledge, that is, those spaces in which bodies and eyes meet—was made possible and available in the nineteenth century. In this regard, to understand modernity may well mean unearthing what Foucault has called its "positive unconscious" of vision, for he has argued that a "period only lets some things be seen and not others."[5]

Even though Foucault enables us to engage in a disclosure of the logic and operations of vision, we must nevertheless avoid reducing modern vision to surveillance. Adhering too closely to Foucault's model, would result in making vision equivalent with supervision. In order properly to situate the expanding practices of photography and their effects on the body within the context of modern vision, we need to take into account the emerging regime of the spectacle. Indeed, there is a significant array and depth of scholarship—including the writings of Walter Benjamin, Richard Sennett, T. J. Clark, and Jonathan Crary— that demonstrates quite unequivocally the increasing presence of the spectacle as a determinant of nineteenth-century vision. Even though surveillance and its correlate, discipline, is a fundamental matrix of modernity, we must be mindful of the fact that by opposing surveillance to the spectacle as Foucault does—"Our society is one not of spectacle, but of surveillance; under the surface of images, one invests bodies in depth"[6]—we devalue the importance of the spectacle and its functioning in modernity.

Understanding the "positive unconscious of vision" of modernity, then, means that instead of opposing one regime of visibility to another, we must take into account the presence of both, so that we may discover their interrelationships. Both these regimes were founded on "the incessant spread of a precise technical rationality"; an outgrowth of that "philosophical project which undertook to comprehend activity in terms of seeing."[7] And a genealogy of modern subjectivity constituted by vision must account for both,[8] especially since, as Deleuze points out, the process of modernization is not a linear, progressive unfolding, but one in which capitalism engages in a continual process of deterritorialization and reterritorialization.[9] That is, in modernization, bodies, spaces, images, and so forth, are provided a high order of exchangeability, but, at the same time, that level of unprecedented exchangeability becomes the basis for reterritorialization into new hierarchies. In the context of vision, this means that subjects engage in greater visibilities and mobility even as they are soon reterritorialized and made visible to both knowledge and power. This is consistent with Foucault's notion that production of modern power rests in constituting individuals as both objects and subjects of knowledge/visibility.

Hence in contrast to the Foucauldian opposition between the regimes of surveillance and spectacle, and even against those who would privilege the spectacle, the construction of a modern subject adequate to the functioning of a nineteenth-century visual order requires that we understand how such a subject is simultaneously constituted within both the fields of spectacle[10] and surveillance. For, in essence, modernity is the constitution of individuals who are both subject-spectators for the spectacular consumption of images and observed-observers within the regime of surveillance: individuals who engage the abundant field of the visible and are in turn made visible, at each instance producing knowledge and power.

Speaking of the spectacle, Debord has observed: "Capital is no longer the invisible center which directs the mode of production: its accumulation spreads it all the way to the periphery in the form of tangible objects. The entire expanse of society is its portrait."[11] In the nineteenth century, the increasing proliferation and democratization of images and spectacles operate as tangible evidence for the joint measure and celebration of capitalist modernity;[12] but, simultaneously and in parallel fashion operating alongside the spectacle, are the barely discernible forms of surveillance, their pervasiveness symptomatic of what we have identified as modernity's dark and melancholic progression. The spectacle and the panopticon are not of opposed orders; inextricably entwined and coadunated, they function on a single plane permeated by the operations of knowledge and power. Both regimes, in fact, signal a radical transformation in the way power will operate non-coercively within modernity. It is to the emergence of these regimes of visibility—the relation between vision and social power—and their increasing coexistence within the nineteenth-century visual order that we must now turn our attention, for they are central to understanding the role of photographic practices and the formation of modern subjectivity.

SPECTACULAR VISION

In the case of photographic practices, operating in juridico-political discourses to provide a bio-political surveillance and categorization of the social, hence apprehending and limiting the circulation of bodies occasioned by capitalism, we are confronted with vision in its realist mode. As John Tagg has observed, the realism of the photograph, its ability to record, reflects the power of the apparatuses of the state which invest and guarantee the images it constructs as evidence.[13] That power to guarantee the identity between signifier and referent is also the product of a coded intertextuality of realism in photography, and "works by the controlled and limited recall of a reservoir of similar 'texts,' by a constant repetition, a constant cross-echoing"[14] of the brute frontality and neutrality of the body that exists in illustrations and photographs in anatomy, psychiatry, phrenology, and so forth.[15] But, most importantly, the transparency of the signifier in the photograph is a product of the fact that the camera became a model in the empirical sciences for how observations made possible truthful inferences about an external world. This model of vision expressed in such technical and discursive predecessors as linear perspective and the camera obscura, regulates the observer's relation to the contents of the world, hence guaranteeing the referential illusion. Consequently, the observer is constituted as a sovereign individual, and what is legislated into place is a transcendental vision unburdened by the observer's body.[16]

But even while photography functioned in the disciplinary and other institutions as a ratification of empiricism, there is no denying that photography simultaneously took its place as an interpretive art form, especially in the portrait practices of such gifted photographers as Nadar and Julia Margaret Cameron.[17] According to Bernard Edelman, that ideological contradiction was negotiated so that the law, by granting recognition to the creative artist, could provide for the ownership of images and their commodification.

> The law recognized only "manual" art—the paintbrush, the chisel—or "abstract" art—writing. The irruption of modern techniques of the (re)production of the real—photographic apparatuses, cameras—surprises the law in the quietude of its categories. . . . Photographer and filmmaker must become creators, or the industry will lose the benefit of legal protection.[18]

Thus photography as art and as the variability and fluidity of its signifiers was guaranteed by its status as a commodity within capitalist market relations. More significantly, photography in its subjective mode is coterminous with the consumption of the photographic sign and the field of serially produced images, which, as in the case of late-nineteenth-century "carte-de-visite" portraiture, circulate and proliferate severed from a referent.

Jonathan Crary has pointed to the development of other nineteenth-century optical devices which, in taking the corporeal subjectivity of the observer as their site, defined a vision that was autonomous, subjective, equivalent, and indifferent. His argument is that there was a general transformation from geometrical optics to physiological optics at the beginning of the nineteenth century, with the consequence that vision underwent a dislocation from "the stable and fixed relations" that characterized the paradigmatic model of the observer in the seventeenth and eighteenth centuries—the camera obscura.[19] However, as I have demonstrated, geometrical optics or Cartesian perspectivalism based on the technical and discursive figures of linear perspective and the camera obscura (the realist model), operated with powerful effects in key institutional apparatuses of nineteenth-century society. The "reality effect" of photography—contrary to Jonathan Crary's claim that "fictions of realism" functioned only at a superficial level[20]—was crucial to the operations and success of disciplinary institutions. Hence, instead of arguing for a wholesale transformation from one model of vision to another, it is more appropriate to speak of the increasing coexistence of two radically distinct models of vision. For the "fictions of realism," wherein vision is grounded to a referent (the regime of surveillance), and the increasing abstraction and mobility of vision (the regime of the spectacle), are both crucial for the construction of a new kind of observer/observed spectator adequate to the emergence and operation of a complex modern visual order.

What were the specific relations that were constructed between visibility, bodies, and spaces in the emerging mode of the spectacle? To begin with, optical experiments conducted into the retinal image and its modulation indicated that the subjective contents of the eye had no external correlate.[21] According to Crary, the developing field of physiological optics provided "an account of a body with an innate capacity, one might even say a transcendental faculty, to 'misperceive'—of an eye that renders differences equivalent."[22] The result of these empirical discoveries and theories is that they produced an observer who was increasingly viewed as susceptible to illusion and open to manipulation; in turn, they provided the grounds on which the introduction of an economy for the spectacular consumption of images could be founded. However, Crary also notes that in light of the referential crisis in meaning and the threat of arbitrariness spawned by the evidence of an autonomous vision, there were concerted attempts to organize the observer as an object of calculated management and regimentation.[23] "The afterimage was to become a crucial means by which observation could be quantified, by which the intensity and duration of retinal stimulation could be measured."[24] In this sense, Crary appears to provide tacit support for the coexistence of two separate but related regimes of representation and visibility.

The optical devices and techniques that were developed for producing an individual amenable to the new productive requirements also doubled as forms of entertainment in popular culture. These included in the nineteenth century, such devices as the thaumatrope, the phenakistiscope,[25] the diorama, and the stereoscope (Fig. 37). Both as spectacle and apparatus they signalled, in rudimentary and microcosmic fashion, the new ubiquity of the observer, who, no longer limited to the localized point of view[26] which characterized the classical models of vision (perspective and the camera obscura), could now partake of a

Figure 37. Holmes-Bates Stereoscope.

visual plentitude. Furthermore, in taking the corporeal subjectivity of the observer as their site and exploiting the disjuncture between perception and its object, they confirmed the hallucinatory nature of the image.[27] In these optical devices, the production of the "real" involved the integration of a passive observer within a mechanical apparatus who is also, as in the case of the phenakistiscope and the stereoscope, separated from the space of the spectacle. Hence, they testify to Debord's observation that the principle of separation "is the alpha and omega of the spectacle"[28] and, furthermore, that the "spectacle's job is to cause a world that is no longer directly perceptible to be seen via different specialized mediations."[29] In general, this model of vision constituted an observer who would be ideally suited to the increasing levels of mobility, exchange, and circulation of the image inherent to modernism's construction of the social.[30]

An examination of the process by which a modern observer amenable to the tasks of specular consumption was created, would also have to take into account the significant presence during the nineteenth century of phantasmagoria spectacles. First presented during the last years of the eighteenth century by the Belgian inventor Etienne-Gaspard Robertson, phantasmagoria referred to the projection of illusions by means of a magic lantern.[31] According to Terry Castle, phantasmagoria operated as a master trope in romantic writings of the nineteenth century and the nature of its use involved a metaphorical displacement, so that which was previously considered to be within the supernatural realm was perceived as the psychological result of delirium, hallucination, and reverie.[32] This blurring of reality and illusion, which was tangibly experienced by spectators of phantasmagoria, was compounded by rationalist discourses in science and philosophy, which in seeking to demystify supernatural phenomena only served to "displace it into the realm of psychology"[33] as the romantics had done. While the argument put forth was that illusions and specters were the products of imagination, by locating illusion in the mind itself, these discourses provided a powerful status to illusion and spectacle in general. But the most important consequence was that thought itself came to be viewed as "a spectral process"[34] and, as such, conducive to the establishment of a spectacular regime.

TRAIN TRAVEL: PANORAMIC PERCEPTION

However, the construction of a spectacular vision was not limited to optical devices only, for the temporal and spatial displacement which accompanied new forms of transportation such as the railroad, both expanded the visible world which erupts in a multiplicity of views and engenders an abstracted vision too. Indeed, what we discover in fact is that the regimes of the spectacle and surveillance are imbricated. Inasmuch as the archival grid of portraiture had imposed a systematic grid of normative representations on the social, the railroad, by assimilating previously inaccessible places into the coordinate geometry of a systematized grid, had transformed landscape space into disciplined and disciplinary geographical space (Fig. 38).[35]

> In a landscape we always get to one place from another place; each location is determined only by its relation to the neighboring place within the circle of visibility. But geographical space is closed, and is therefore in its entire structure transparent. Every place in such a space is determined by its position with respect to the whole and ultimately by its relation to the null point of the coordinate system by which this space obtains its order. Geographical space is systematized.[36]

What is manifest in this systematization of geography is the disciplinary architecture of the panopticon, insofar as it is bound in a nexus of transparency and determined by coordinate points of visibility emanating from the viewpoint of the observer. However, at the same time, from the viewpoint of the traveller, the railroad introduces, enframed by the railway car's window, a "panoramic" perception of the landscape (Fig. 39). The views from the window

> have entirely lost their dimension of depth and have become mere particles of one and the same panoramic world that stretches all around and is, at each and every point, merely a painted surface.[37]

By depthlessness, Schivelbusch is referring to the blurring of the foreground due to the velocity of the train. In preindustrial travel, the foreground had constituted an intimate relationship between traveller and landscape, for travellers had seen themselves as part of the foreground, and that perception had joined them to the landscape. But with

Figure 38. Cutting in the city, 1837.

Figure 39. Panoramic perception of the landscape introduced by train travel.

train travel, the blurring of the foreground, unreconstitutable into a visible whole, forces the traveller/spectator to engage in the distant view or what Benjamin Gastineau has referred to as "la philosophie synthètique du coup d'oeil" (the synthetic philosophy of the glance or panoramic perception).[38] Thus, the velocity of the train radically displaces the spectator from the comprehensive visible space that combines proximity and distance. Hence observers are separated from the space of their seeing—displaced subjectivity—by an almost immaterial barrier in much the same way as "ferrovitreous architecture" employed in the 1867 World Exhibition separated spectators from the space they could nevertheless see (fig. 40).[39] "Panoramic perception, in contrast to traditional perception no longer belongs to the same space as the perceived objects: the traveller sees the objects, landscapes, etc. through the apparatus which moves him through the world."[40]

Significantly, the perception that is organized by railroad travel, which "no longer belongs to the same space as the perceived objects," is the same kind of seeing exhibited by photography. Both photography and the railroad journey mediate discursively and technically between observer/traveller and landscape, providing for a passive spectator who is privy to a world made more visible and whose subjectivity is premised on the collection of views. But the very condition for increased visibility is the isolation of the traveller/viewer from the space of his/her seeing, whether looking out of a railway car window or looking at a photograph. Furthermore, railroad travel, in its temporal appropriation of space, not unlike photography, introduces an elliptical narrative in its trajectory.[41] Also, as Schivelbusch observes, the railroad rushes each of the points on the coordinate system into "each other's immediate vicinity," destroying "the isolation of localities, which was created by spatial distance" and which "was the very essence of their identity, their self-assured and complacent individuality."[42] In this context, invoking Benjamin, he notes, that as photography destroyed the "aura" of individual objects, the railroad annihilated the "aura" of isolated regions.[43]

Panoramic perception, which Schivelbusch identifies with the railroad, became a popular mode of seeing in the nineteenth century (Fig. 41). Panoramic views were not only to be found in the dioramas during the nineteenth century, but, as Benjamin points out, they even characterized the literature of the time.

Figure 40. Interior of the Crystal Palace ("Ferrovitreous architecture").

Figure 41. Fairmount Waterworks, 1848. Courtesy of the George Eastman House.

Contemporary to the panoramas is a panoramic literature. . . . They consist of isolated sketches, the anecdotal form of which corresponds to the plastic foreground of the panorama, and their informational base to its painted background.[44]

In the 1870s, photographers such as Eadweard Muybridge, William Henry Jackson, and Carleton E. Watkins,[45] also engaged in making panoramic or bird's-eye views of such American cities as San Francisco, Boston, and Chicago. The "panoramists,"[46] as they were referred to, utilized the "traffic arteries as internal organizing mechanisms (in their photographs) in much the same way that Baron Haussmann had done with his plan of Paris,"[47] to impose an order and picturesqueness which nonetheless betrayed a particular hierarchy of seeing. The central organizing matrix of these panoramic photographs was the large bourgeois cultural and business monuments which gave "a hierarchical order to the seeming chaos of the urban reality."[48] And if, as in the case of Muybridge's famous panorama of San Francisco, the photographs (multiple photographs pasted together to create the panorama) were taken from the highest point in the city—the house of one of the most powerful members of the city's bourgeoisie—the nature of seeing is no different (Fig. 42).

> The way the streets operate as a pictorial device points up the fundamentally fictive nature of the panorama's "civilizing role" [my quotes]; for the streets seem, falsely, to emanate from Muybridge's vantage point . . . (subsequent photographs revealed that it did not). . . . Yet Muybridge's was a culturally crucial fiction: The streets of his city not only declare his preeminence at the center of his created world but, for his entrepreneurial sponsors, place the heart of the city in the residential neighborhood of the richest and most powerful of San Francisco citizens. For Muybridge, the city might be his; for Hopkins, Stanford, Crocker and the other merchant princes, it was theirs.[49]

Panoramic perception was a crucial component in the organizing of a nineteenth-century visual order, and it is intrinsic to what Richard Sennett has identified as the paradox of isolation and visibility which characterized nineteenth-century bourgeois societies.

Figure 42. Panorama of San Francisco, 1878.

HAUSSMANN'S URBAN PANOPTICON/SPECTACLE

In the reordering of Paris in the mid-nineteenth century by Baron Haussmann, we confront as well, the imposition of a grid which transformed the vital heterogeneity of neighborhoods into homogeneous "social molecules," instituting and legislating into existence what Sennett calls an "ecology of classes."[50] What we find is a geographical grid that classifies in a hierarchical and exclusionary manner in order to consolidate the bourgeoisie, in much the same way as the archival grid of portraiture situated the social in discourse categories of physiognomy and phrenology. Grid space is the prototypical space of a disciplinary economy, the analyzed space of formalization and systematization, whether it inhabits Bertillon's criminal archive designed to arrest the criminal body or Haussmann's geographic grid instituted to regulate and classify urban populations. The source and stimulus for the two grids is identical: the need to discipline and govern the social, characterized as it was by urban pressure, dislocation, crime, and sudden influxes of population, and to impose demographically and socially by the means of the logic of the grid, a fixed and arbitrary personality of bourgeois order that would provide for unobstructed spaces open to vision and surveillance. These, then, are spaces and bodies made increasingly visible to sustain the mutually enhancing logic of knowledge and power.

"Haussmannization" meant that the urban experience of free movement from one part of the city to another was restricted largely to the bourgeoisie, while localism fused with the working classes.[51] If the "right to the city" was something that accrued only to the bourgeoisie,[52] then it only served to emphasize the fact, as Kristin Ross has noted, that the social space of everyday life "is always political and strategic."[53] That space must be understood politically, is clearly elucidated by the fact that a significant percentage of the Communards who entered into the center of Paris and seized the government and declared Paris an autonomous Commune on 18 March 1871, were "the semiskilled day laborers who had migrated from the provinces to work on Haussmann's massive and fantastic urban renewal projects."[51] Their revolt is literally a transgressive inscription in space.

> The [Communards'] redescent into the center of Paris followed in part from the political significance of the city center within a tradition of political insurgency, and in part from their desire to reclaim

the public space from which they had been expelled, to reoccupy streets that once were theirs.[55]

There is no disputing the fact that one of the primary reasons motivating the Haussmannization of Paris was the overarching desire to put an end to insurrection:

> It meant the disembowelling of the old Paris, the quartier of uprisings and barricades, by a wide central street piercing through this almost impossible maze. . . . The subsequent completion of the Rue de Turbigo made the Rue Transnonian [symbolic capital of the barricades] disappear from the map of Paris.[56]

That, in fact, Haussmann had intended the tactical and political use of space is testified to in Benjamin's own comments:

> Haussmann seeks to prevent barricades in two ways. The breadth of the streets is intended to make their erection impossible, and new thoroughfares are to open the shortest route between the barracks and the working-class districts.[57]

But the Communards did erect barricades, for as Benjamin jubilantly observed: "The barricade is resurrected in the Commune. It is stronger and better secured than ever."[58] Even as the Communards tore down the imperial column at the Place Vendome in the center of Paris—"whose aura (derived) from its isolation and stability"[59] and from its "unique, proper place"—they substituted an architectural space punctuated by barricades (Fig. 43). Barricades in contrast are antithetical to any notion of a unique "proper place," and not made of materials of "duration or immortality"[60] but instead constitute a "bricolage"— objects torn out of their everyday context and haphazardly erected. And if Haussmann's streets were "unveiled like monuments,"[61] the Communards appear in photographs posing in front of the barricades they erected.[62] Three months later, twenty-five thousand Communards (most of them working-class) were massacred, their identification and elimination by the authorities, ironically enough, made efficient and thorough by the fact that many of them had been photographed (Fig. 44). These, then, are the tales of bodies and spaces, of visibilities that can be fatal.

But to speak of Haussmannization solely in the language of surveillance, is to foreclose the possibility of understanding its function in

Figure 43. Statue of Napoleon I on the Vendome column after being pulled down by the Communards, May 1871.

Figure 44. Communards in their coffins, May 1871.

producing spectacular spaces for consumption. No doubt Haussmann's remaking of the city organized the segregation of the city along class lines and provided for a neutral space of pure surveillance—"Boulevards without turnings, without chance perspectives, implacable in their straight lines"[63]—but these same boulevards were also a space given over to generalized display, colorful illusions, uncertainty, and spectacle.

> It is here that Paris makes one of its grandest impressions . . . rue de la Plaix, all gleaming with gold and jewels . . . the Avenue de l'Opéra inundated with electric light; rue Quartre Septembre shining with its thousand gas jets, and seven continuous carriages issuing from two Boulevards and five streets, crossing each other rapidly on the square, and a crowd coming and going under a shower of rosy and whitest lights diffused from the great ground-glass globes, which produce the effect of wreaths and garlands of full moons, coloring the trees, high buildings and the multitude with the weird and mysterious reflections of the final scene of a fancy ballet. Here one experiences for the moment the sensations produced by Hasheesh.[64]

Thus, we are faced with a city in which the ambiguity which attended the free play of signs and display coexisted with the rigid disciplining of space. Because Haussmann sought to discipline Paris, it was no longer plural and brimming with real differences, as when the bourgeois and worker worked and lived in close proximity to one another; eviscerated of a certain "density of life," the streets had lost their presence,[65] and everyday life made and remade in social practice had been transformed into a single unified spectacle to be passively consumed. But even as Haussmann had encouraged the city to "be consumed in the abstract, as one convenient fiction,"[66] he was only exacerbating a trend already in place. Indeed, according to T. J. Clark, Haussmann's project colluded in the collective desire to visualize and make manifest a social process that was already underway. "Part of Haussmann's purpose was to give modernity a shape . . . he built a set of forms in which the city appeared to be visible, even intelligible."[67] It was in this sense that Paris was becoming both a modern spectacle and a site for surveillance.

An ineluctable aspect of that social process was that the city was being shaped and made visible according to the logic and transformations of mid-nineteenth-century capitalism. To the critics of the period who had little notion of the relationship between these newly emergent forms of capitalism and Haussmannization, this fact remained inenarrable and instead they directed their ire and hostility at that which was vividly available—the city itself.[68] But they were not incorrect in ascribing blame to Haussmann's city, upon which nevertheless the form of capital had been deeply inscribed. The *grands magasins* that had been erected on profits derived from property speculation and the construction of the new boulevards,[69] introduced new forms of capitalist exchange and production into Paris that resulted in destroying the workshop economy and the pattern of relationships on which the working-class quartier had depended. Capital had destroyed a form and pattern of social life which had helped construct notions of social place and personal identity, and in its place a new Paris emerged: a "Paris in which it appears there *are* no relations, only images arranged in their place."[70]

> [The city] belonged to them now simply as an image, something occasionally and casually consumed in spaces expressly designed for that purpose—promenades, panoramas, outings on Sundays, great exhibitions, and official parades.[71]

If Haussmannization meant that under the aegis of capitalist modernism the city had been given over to spectacle, the regime of surveillance and discipline was a necessary corollary of that same order. For Haussmann's introduction of wide boulevards linked to the railway stations meant not only that goods could be rapidly shipped to the provinces but that troops could be swiftly transported into the city.[72] Along with the general circulation of images and people put into play with the expansion of the logic of the commodity and its encroachment upon everyday life—that mode that we have identified as the deterritorialization of the social—there is an accompanying recuperation of the social system under the sign of surveillance, which delineates, territorializes, and regulates individual bodies.

THE OBSERVED/SPECTATOR: THE PARADOX OF ISOLATION AND VISIBILITY

Richard Sennett, in his study of the social psychology of capitalism, identifies the genealogical transmutation of the social into an all-encompassing notation for an economy of the gaze with the emergence of the secular belief in a self immanent in appearances. On the other hand, Judith Wechsler has identified this shift in terms of Tönnies' description of the onset of "Gesselschaft."[73] However, they both emphasize the similar consequences that engender this arrival of the positivist dream of a visual order. According to Sennett's account, with the emergence of the doctrine of secular immanence, immediacy of sensation and perception became increasingly important. As a consequence, people began to attach greater significance to the impressions they made on each other, and personality immanent in appearances became a social category in the public domain. Unlike the Enlightenment belief in natural character, the nineteenth-century construct of personality, solely predicated on outward appearances, was taken as an index of inner feeling and character. Since one knew in public only through what was manifested in appearances, people began to examine each other with a new closeness for every clue and sign that would indicate the nature of inner character. Consequently, the body outfitted in a careful repertory of gestures and clothed with a circumspect sense for detail, became an elaborate signification system—a text to be both coded and decoded with infinite care if one was to avoid being ostracized.[74]

> All visible things are emblems; what thou seest is not there on its own account; strictly taken, is not there at all: matter exists only spiritually, and to represent some Idea and "body" it forth. Hence "clothes," as despicable as we think them, are so unspeakably significant.[75]

The decoding of the body as emblematic of the social itself, was undertaken through the dual process of miniaturization and inflation: "Details of workmanship now show how 'gentle' a man or woman is. . . . The tying of cravats becomes an intricate business."[76] Thus, what emerged was not dissimilar from the mystification that accompanied the transformation of goods into commodities, for the secular belief in personality had now posited the body as a new locus for fetishistic practices and correspondingly elevated the bourgeois body from sign to mysterious symbol.

The divining of class in a subtly orchestrated signification system which could reveal even as it concealed, was a special source of anxiety for the bourgeoisie. The worker's body was construed as both a significant resource and a source of potential transgression against a system which had systematically nourished itself at the expense of the lower classes. Within the fluid milieu of signifiers that characterized the social, it therefore became increasingly important that the bourgeoisie be able to identify and apprehend the particular significations that attended that body and its circulations. "The problem of how to identify a worker absorbed the attention and energy of a considerable number of people and was addressed in a variety of ways."[77] As an example of this bourgeois anxiety, Ross points to Dénis Poulot's work *Le Sublime, ou le travailleur comme il est en 1870, et ce qu'il peut être*, written just before the Paris Commune revolt. In this book, Poulot sought to establish a "pathologic diagnostic" which would make it possible to identify the "bad" worker on sight. The determining characteristic for a judgment of "bad" was, of course, based on a set of categories comprised of what was considered unproductive behavior.[78]

In time, it became a requirement, in a public which operated on a vernacular of the eye, that "one must impose no coloration of one's own, of one's own commitments; this meant silence in public in order to understand it, objectivity in scientific investigation, a gastronomy of the eye. Voyeurism was the logical complement of 19th century secularity."[79] To paraphrase Balzac's eulogy to the Observer, it meant that: "The observer's genius in public is incontestably his silence in public."[80] The specular nature of the new social order is also captured remarkably well in Benjamin's description of Paris as "the city of mirrors," where men and women bring to bear upon one another a hyper-reflexivity of display, reflecting off each other their elaborately constructed images—"even the eyes of passers-by are hanging mirrors"—hence emphasizing in Susan Buck-Morss' words "the contradictory extremes of visibility and anonymity of the city-dweller."[81] This emergence of the paradox of isolation and visibility is evocatively illustrated by E.T.A. Hoffman's story, "The Cousin's Corner Window." The cousin, paralyzed, looks out of his corner window which frames the passing urban crowd, fully absorbed and yet distanced from what he sees, for he has no wish to join the people parading below. As Benjamin, in commenting on this modern figure, notes:

To a visitor he says he would like to induct the man who can use his legs "to the principles of the art of seeing." The visitor is made to realize that he will never understand the crowd until he too is paralyzed, until he watches but does not move himself.[82]

Benjamin's figure of the "flâneur" is emblematic as well of this transformation in the perception of modern subjectivity. For the "flâneur" (loiterer/spectator) "who goes botanizing" on the new boulevards built by Haussmann, the city presents itself in sharply delineated ways: "it opens itself to him as a landscape; it encloses him as a room."[83] Here the paradox of isolation and visibility manifests itself in the reverie of the "flâneur" whose projection onto or textualizing of the visible world always involved incorporating it as fantasy images within his interior world.[84] Likewise, the literature of "flâneurie"—"physiologies"—pocket-size paperbacks devoted to identifying the "types that may be encountered,"[85] encourages the privatization of social space and gives "assurance that the individual's passive observation was adequate for knowledge of social reality."[86]

In the commodity-filled dream world of the *grands magasins*,[87] the "flâneur"/consumer ascends to his/her rightful place. The utilization of transparent display windows and the introduction of systems of artificial lighting, including electricity by the 1880s, "created a spectacular effect, a sense of theatrical excess"[88] in department stores. Within this sublime economy of the gaze, democratic in its access,[89] the commodity took center stage. The inception of *spectacle de la marchandise* meant that the process to reify the commodity as image was fully underway; its content rendered polymorphous, the commodity began to inhabit voluptuous and "dreamlike surroundings."[90] In turn, the "flâneur"/consumer's primarily reactive/consumerist (Erlebnis) mode, expressed in the textual reverie of surfaces, encouraged an erotic cathexis onto commodities—hence Benjamin's cryptic observation that "Erlebnis is the phantasmagoria of the idler."[91] In this prehistory of the spectacle, the nineteenth-century observer is initiated into a cultural economy of mobile, equivalent, and abstracted signs. In time, with the ubiquity of the photographic image, the spectacle circulating within a perpetual present, annihilates history and apotheosizes itself as "the general abstract equivalent of all commodities."[92]

If the body had achieved a heightened level of significance and public visibility, it had also simultaneously acquired a new potential for betrayal. Since the barrier between inner character and outer appearances had been erased and since it was believed that control over personality could only be retrospective, the fear of involuntary disclosure became a permanent feature of interaction in the public domain.[93] A paranoiac order of the visual had ensued. In speaking of the emergence of the spectator into the public realm as a representative figure of the nineteenth-century paradox of isolation and visibility, Sennett notes:

> In the 1850s a Parisian or London theatergoer had no compunction about talking to a neighbor in the midst of the play, if he or she had just remembered something to say. By 1870, the audience was policing itself. Talking now seemed in bad taste and rude.[94]

Thus, the gaze internalized becomes the disciplinary complement of the practices engaged in by the state apparatuses at other sites in the social formation. "It was perfectly reasonable for men and women who were having trouble 'reading' each other in the street to worry about feeling the right emotions in the theater or concert hall."[95] In this sense, appearances as a social indicator of personality brought into play a cybernetics of the social predicated on the other's gaze. Control over oneself could only be established by a constant policing of feelings which involved a cogitative distanciation from self. This is corroborated by Susan Buck-Morss' study of Benjamin's Arcades project, in which she observes that in a specular order in which the self is perpetually on display, "viewing oneself as constantly being viewed" is a form of self-surveillance."[96] In this manner, surveillance and display correlatively established a more silent public domain. Simultaneously, silence and passive observation became symptomatic of public order and synonymous with an orderly set of representations.

No doubt even in our own modern century, we correlate silence with order, which may well be the product of the fact that we have based our notions of order on vision. From the classificatory tables of the seventeenth century to the humble file of the nineteenth century, from Galton's photographs to Bentham's panopticon, from the railroad grid to the modern twentieth-century highway, the positivist dream repeats itself monotonously. The grand boulevards that were the epitome of Haussmann's disciplinary grid, enabled the spread of outdoor cafés from which the bourgeoisie silently gazed at one another. Privacy had become a right not easily infringed upon and fundamental to the new secularism; it represented a permeation of the social by a powerful visual order. Simultaneously the space of visibility so revealed, divulges a wonderful and visible spectacle, a profusion of views juxtaposing people and objects offered unsparingly for consumption by the specular consciousness of the observer.

CONCLUSION

Sennett's paradox of isolation and visibility characterizes our modern public domain; for, as we watch the world made visible and transformed into a spectacle on television, our capacity for political action diminishes. However, isolation and visibility is only paradoxical when viewed superficially, for the fact of the matter is that the paradox is less a paradox than it is a principle essential to the very functioning of the knowledge/power dynamic which Foucault has identified. What, after all, is Bentham's panopticon if not an architectural embodiment of isolation and visibility? And as for the observer, constituted at the center of this design, what does s/he behold if not the spectacle of power?

Whether it is case of the observer/observed located within the geometry of disciplinary architecture or the spectator disposed within the arrangements of the spectacle, s/he is bound by the principle of isolation and visibility. In the case of the subject isolated and made visible by surveillance or the spectacle that isolates, power is produced by a knowledge which takes as its basis the hegemony of vision. Originating from the same desire, but operating in adjacent geographies of power, surveillance and spectacle function as mutually reciprocal orders. It is often within the clearing of surveillance, within those areas it has opened to unobstructed vision, that the spectacle is provided its autonomous existence (for example, train travel). And the spectators in their reverie, lured by the delights of the spectacle, its seeming innocence, its flattery, remain unaware of the blueprint of surveillance.

In surveillance, the realist/objective model of vision dominates, while the regime of the spectacle derives its power from the autonomy and abstraction of subjective vision. In its abstraction—the referent's apparent groundlessness—spectacular vision is provided a mobility, equivalence, and circulation. In contrast, the regime of surveillance possesses a fixity; it is an anti-nomadic technique. In the spectacle, disparate zones of experience, dynamic flux, and the structured yet unexpected juxtaposition of elements all provide for a seductive power. Hence, the spectacle radiates deliriously and associated with it is spectral excess, the nonrecuperable expenditure. Moreover, the spectacle produces the subject of visuality, whose pleasure as subject is in the multiple surfaces, views, and vistas to which s/he is privileged; s/he is the subject of consumption—traveller, tourist, spectator—site of desires and collector of sights, whose seeming autonomy functions as an alibi for the exercise of knowledge and power.

The regime of surveillance, however, posits a transparency that is identified with a homogenous space, a declared referent. Associated with the masterly overview, the regime of surveillance deploys bodies in space, its design constituted by a disembodied vision. The spectacle, in contrast, exploits the observer's capacity for misperception, disclosing fragmentary views and encouraging a dispersed subjectivity. In surveillance, vision invests bodies in depth; in spectacle, vision is invested in the play of surfaces. Surveillance functions to territorialize, colonize, and regulate the social, while the regime of the spectacle deterritorializes the social, producing new distributions and multiplying the exchanges between bodies, spaces, and representations.

In examining a host of material and discursive practices besides photography—including optical devices, train travel, urban reconstruction, and so on, operating at different sites within the social formation of nineteenth-century society—we discover that they are all embedded in a larger visual discourse—"a positive unconscious vision"—of modernism. This "positive unconscious vision," its visible horizon imbricated by the isogonal regimes of spectacle and surveillance (whose logic and deployment serve the generative and regulative powers of capitalism), simultaneously functions to guarantee access to a semiotic and material plentitude, even as it seeks to make visible the social order, its operations permeated throughout by the isolation and individuation of bodies.

As we have seen in the case of photography, the disciplinary apparatuses situated in juridico-political discourses of crime and punishment, sought through the utilization of photography to isolate and make visible the criminal's body, thereby eliciting knowledge through identification, which, in turn, enabled the increasing regulation and permeation of power in and across the social body. The case of the skilled worker was no different, for the disciplinary apparatus of scientific management utilized photography to isolate, make visible, appropriate, and divest skilled workers of the knowledge they embodied, so that the same knowledge could be transferred in standardized, efficient models of work-motion to hundreds of untrained, unskilled, poorly-paid workers. These, then, are bodies surveilled, isolated, enframed, and made visible in photographic space. And whether it is the case of the worker, the prisoner, or the insane, each arrives in an apparatus of writing, examined, and individuated in a record or file. Furthermore, photography simultaneously assisted in making visible and constituting the bourgeois body as subject of moral and social meaning. In all these cases, the body isolated, made visible, and individuated, is, in turn, transformed into an object or subject of knowledge and power.

Foucault has argued that with the emergence of the modern human sciences—criminology, demographics, statistics, and we may add, scientific management—"Man appears in his ambiguous position as an object of knowledge and as a subject that knows; enslaved sovereign, observed spectator."[97] In the arrival of this "strange empirico-transcendental doublet,"[98] human beings are both isolated objects made visible by the ocularcentric discourses of the sciences, and neutral metasubjects of knowledge engaging the visible field of the social. Thus, "the veritable technological take-off in the productivity of power,"[99] represented a constituting of human beings as both subjects and objects of knowledge/visibility. Photography in the nineteenth century was consequently embedded in the larger visual discourse—"a positive unconscious of vision"—of the period, characterized by practices which sought, in their specificity, not only to make visible the social order through the isolation and individuation of bodies but also to produce subjects who had access to new levels of visibility.

How then are we to understand the ubiquitous role of vision in the construction of modern power and, concomitantly, the creation of a modern observer/observed spectator necessary for the successful circulation and exchange of that power? Power operating in the grids of photographic space, urban space, transport space, produced iconic bodies, analyzed bodies, mobile bodies, spectator bodies, and regulated bodies, eliciting and disseminating knowledge with each frame of space. In each case, individuals were constituted either as isolated subjects or isolated objects, enjoying greater visibilities or being made more visible to the dynamic of power and knowledge as it initiates the social order within a returning matrix of deterritorialization and reterritorialization.

It is in this sense that the model of the modern observer is constituted in terms of a split subjectivity which makes the observer suitable for functioning within both the regimes of spectacle and surveillance. In this process of isolation and individuation, of visibilities and being made visible, discourses proliferate, knowledge is informed, and power is produced correlatively. Thus what Sennett calls the paradox of isolation and visibility, is the real basis on which the modern arrangement of power and knowledge comes into play. Simultaneously, it is the same site that is haunted by the lamentations of a mind-body dualism. Enslaved sovereign, observed spectator, this empirico-transcendental doublet produced by ocularcentric knowing, creates lines of great visibility across social spaces increasingly mediated and reticulated by conjoining grids of knowledge and power, which, capillary-like, drain deep into the social body.

NOTES

CHAPTER ONE. A THEORETICAL FRAMEWORK

1. Hannah Arendt, *The Life of the Mind* (New York: Harcourt Brace Jovanovich, 1978), 110–11.
2. Martin Heidegger, *The Question Concerning Technology and Other Essays*, trans. William Lovitt (New York: Harper & Row), 1977.
3. Jacques Derrida, "Sending on Representation," *Social Research* 49 (1982).
4. Friedrich Nietzsche, *The Genealogy of Morals* (New York: Doubleday Anchor Books, 1956); also Friedrich Nietzsche, *The Birth of a Tragedy*, trans. Walter Kaufmann (New York: Penguin, 1967).
5. Friedrich Nietzsche, *The Genealogy of Morals*; Friedrich Nietzsche, *Thus Spoke Zarathustra*, trans. Walter Kaufmann, (New York: Penguin Books, 1978).
6. Jonathan Crary, *Techniques of the Observer: On Vision and Modernity in the Nineteenth Century* (Cambridge, Mass.: MIT Press, 1991), 6–8.
7. Michel Foucault, *Discipline and Punish: The Birth of the Prison*, trans. Alan Sheridan (New York: Vintage Books, 1979).
8. Even though for the sake of convenience in periodization I speak of photographic practices in the nineteenth century, the period I am addressing extends from the time of photography's invention in the 1830s, when a number of the technical innovations necessary for its development were made, to the early part of the twentieth century, which witnessed its important use as a disciplinary technology.
9. Martin Jay, "In the Empire of the Gaze: Foucault and the Denigration of Vision in Twentieth-century French Thought," in *Foucault: A Critical Reader*, ed. David Couzens Hoy (Oxford: Basil Blackwell, 1986), 179.
10. In chapter 5, I will, however, take up the emergence and existence of another model of vision that came into existence only in the nineteenth century. As the century wore on, photography began to function within this particular regime as well, producing such effects as would correspond with the prehistory of the spectacle.

11. According to Samuel Edgerton: "it seems from the evidence of perspective constructions in pictures from this period that no such applications of rules derived from Brunelleschi's demonstrations occurs in any known example before 1425; after that date painters increasingly depended on perspective constructions." Samuel Y. Edgerton, *The Renaissance Rediscovery of Linear Perspective* (New York: Basic Books, 1975), 126.

12. In the Florentine metrology of the time, a "half-braccio" was a little less than one foot in length. Edgerton, *Renaissance Rediscovery*, 127.

13. Ibid., 145.

14. A "half-braccio" separated the mirror from the painted panel and the ratio of this viewing distance to the size of painted panel was the same as that between the distance of the Baptistery from the viewing standpoint and the height of the Baptistery. Ibid., 151.

15. Pirenne speculates that the use of the mirror assisted in providing a convincing illusion because the mirror dispels awareness of the surface, thus creating a three-dimensional effect on a two-dimensional surface. In this regard, the subsidiary awareness of picture surface is more likely to occur in the case of a painting than a mirror. M.H. Pirenne, *Optics, Painting and Photography* (London: Cambridge University Press, 1970), 44.

16. Ibid., 40.

17. See David C. Lindberg, "Alkindi's Critique of Euclid's Theory of Vision," *Isis* 62 (1971): 469–89; and David C. Lindberg, "Alhazen's Theory of Vision and its Reception in the West," *Isis* 58 (1967): 321–41.

18. Charles Homer Haskins, *The Renaissance of the Twelfth Century* (Cambridge, Mass.: Harvard University Press, 1927), 35–47.

19. Leon Battista Alberti, *On Painting and On Sculpture: The Latin Texts of DePictura and De Statua*, ed. and trans. Cecil Grayson (London: Phaidon, 1972), 40–41.

20. Ibid., 48–49.

21. Ibid., 50–51.

22. Norman Bryson, *Vision and Painting: The Logic of the Gaze* (New Haven: Yale University Press, 1983), 94.

23. Ibid., 21.

24. Ibid., 8.

25. E.H. Gombrich, *Art and Illusion: A Study in the Psychology of Pictorial Representation* (New York: Bollingen Foundation, 1961), 241–57.

26. Martin Jay, "Scopic Regimes of Modernity," in *Vision and Visuality: Discussions in Contemporary Culture* Ser. 2, ed. Hal Foster (Seattle: Bay Press, 1988), 8.

27. Marshall McLuhan and Harley Parker, *Through the Vanishing Point: Space in Poetry and Painting* (New York: Harper & Row, 1968), 16.

28. Jan B. Deregowski, "Pictorial Perception and Culture," *Scientific American* 227.5 (1972): 82–90; Marshall H. Segall, Donald T. Campbell, and Melville J. Herskovits, *The Influence of Culture on Visual Perception* (New York: Bobbs-Merrill Co., 1966); and Rudolf Arnheim, "Inverted Perspective in Art: Display and Expression," *Leonardo* 5 (1972): 123–35.

29. McLuhan, *The Vanishing Point*, 4.

30. Ibid.

31. Ibid., 261.

32. Robert Belle Burke, *The Opus Majus of Roger Bacon* (Philadelphia, 1928), I: 232; quoted in Edgerton, *Renaissance Rediscovery*, 17.

33. Ibid., 18.

34. Ibid., 86.

35. Edgerton, *Renaissance Rediscovery*, 56.

36. Ibid., 86.

37. Edward Peragallo, *Origin and Evolution of Double-Entry Bookkeeping: A Study of Italian Practice from the Fourteenth Century* (Concord, N.H.: Rumford Press, 1938), 55–56; Raymond de Roover, "The Development of Accounting prior to Luca Pacioli according to Account Books of Medieval Merchants" in *Studies in the History of Accounting*, ed. A.C. Littleton and B.S. Yamey (Homewood, Ill.: R.D. Irwin, 1956).

38. Edgerton, *Renaissance Rediscovery*, 39.

39. John Berger, *Ways of Seeing* (London: British Broadcasting Corp. and Penguin Books, 1987), 109.

40. W.J. Thomas Mitchell, *Iconology: Image, Text, Ideology* (Chicago: University of Chicago Press, 1986), 37.

41. Ibid.

42. William M. Ivins, *Art and Geometry: A Study in Space Intuitions* (Cambridge, Mass.: Harvard University Press, 1946), 84–87.

43. Beaumont Newhall, *The History of Photography, from 1839 to the Present Day* (New York: Museum of Modern Art, 1964), 1; Naomi Rosenblum, *A World History of Photography* (New York: Abbeville Press, 1984), 192.

44. Ibid. The first published account of the utilization of the "camera obscura" as an aid to draftsmen appeared in Giovanni Baltista della Porta's *Natural Magic*, a popular compendium of sixteenth-century science. Newhall, *History of Photography*, 1.

45. Arthur Goldsmith, *The Camera and Its Images* New York: Newsweek Books, 1979), 13. On occasion, in order to demonstrate the veridicality of their representations, painters incorporated an image of the camera obscura in the painting itself. Rosenblum, *A World History*, 193.

46. Jonathan Crary, "Modernizing Vision," in *Vision and Visuality. Discussions in Contemporary Culture* Ser. 2, ed. Hal Foster (Seattle: Bay Press, 1988), 31.

47. Mitchell, *Iconology*, 168.

48. John Locke, *An Essay Concerning Human Understanding*, ed. Peter H. Nidditch (Oxford: Clarendon Press, 1975), ch. 17, 162–63.

49. Richard Rorty, *Philosophy and the Mirror of Nature*, Princeton (Princeton University Press, 1979), 50.

50. Ibid., 45.

51. Crary, "Modernizing Vision," 32.

52. Ibid.

53. Ibid., 33.

54. Jay, "Scopic Regimes of Modernity," 11.

55. Ibid.

56. Crary, "Modernizing Vision," 33.

57. Rosenblum, *A World History*, 194.

58. The "Diorama" consisted of three proscenia, on which were placed 45½-by-71½-foot paintings. The intent was to surround the audience with circular painted views, and, through the effect of lights and other atmospheric effects, to provide a three-dimensional, illusionary view of storms and sunsets. Rosenblum, *A World History*, 17, 36, 96; Newhall, *History of Photography*, 14.

59. Rosenblum, *A World History*, 194.

60. Goldsmith, *Camera and Its Images*, 26.

61. Michel Braive, for instance, argues for greater recognition to be granted to Niépce's role in the invention of photography. He also cites Hippolyte Bayard, another French experimenter—whom he notes made photographs on paper and who according to Braive had the world's first photography exhibition in 1839—as co-inventor along with Daguerre. Michel F. Braive, *The Era of the Photograph: A Social History* (New York: Random House, 1966), 22.

62. Bill presented to the Chamber of Deputies, France, 15 June 1839, in *Photography in Print: Writings from 1816 to the Present*, ed. Vicki Goldberg (New York: Simon and Schuster, 1981), 33.

63. In effect, the French government renounced its monopoly rights to the invention, but as Gisele Freund points out, this was typical of the times. In fact, "the gesture actually meant little: since the process was so simple, it would have been difficult to protect by any patent." Gisele Freund, *Photography and Society* (Boston: David R. Godine, 1980), 26.

64. Ibid., 25.

65. *Les comptes rendus des séances de l'Academie des sciences* 19 (August 1839), vol. IX, 257–66; quoted in Freund, *Photography and Society*, 26.
66. Ibid.
67. Ibid., 26–27.
68. Beaumont Newhall, ed, "The First News Accounts of the Daguerreotype, January 6, 1839," *Photography Essays and Images: Illustrated Readings in the History of Photography* (New York: Museum of Modern Art, 1980), 19.
69. Ibid., 18.
70. Martin Heidegger, *The Question Concerning Technology and Other Essays*, trans. William Lovitt (New York: Harper & Row, 1977).
71. Edgerton, *Renaissance and Rediscovery*, 104.
72. Newhall, *Photography Essays and Images*, 18.
73. Walter Benjamin, *Illuminations*, ed. Hannah Arendt, trans. Harry Zohn (New York: Schocken, 1969), 223.
74. John Fowles, *The Collector* (St. Albans: Brown and Company, 1976), 24.
75. Goldberg, *Photography in Print*, 64.
76. Walter Benjamin, "On the Mimetic Faculty," *Reflections: Essays, Aphorisms, Autobiographical Writings*, ed. and intro. Peter Demetz, trans. Edmund Jephcott (New York: Harcourt Brace Jovanovich, 1978), 336. Even though Benjamin refers to the mimetic faculty of language as "the most complete archive of non-sensuous similarity," I have taken the liberty of applying the concept to the photographic image, which insofar as it represents a disembodied vision, engenders an aesthetic distanciation of the object and not a multisensuous experience of it.
77. Walter Benjamin, *Charles Baudelaire: A Lyric Poet in the Era of High Capitalism*, trans. Harry Zohn (London: Suhrkamp Verlag, 1973), 166.
78. Ibid., 167.
79. Ibid.
80. Ibid.
81. In this context, it is interesting to note that Marx viewed the camera obscura as a metaphor for the functioning of ideology: "If in all, ideology men and their relations appear upside-down as in a 'camera obscura,' the phenomenon arises just as much from their historical life process as the inversion of objects on the retina does from their physical life process" (23). Mitchell, in examining Marx's use of the camera obscura as a metaphor for ideology, has argued that the same metaphor of the camera obscura may be used to explain Marx's notion of fetishism of the commodity—that which disguises the social character of men's labor and "assumes in their eyes the fantastic form of a relation between things" (189)—providing for a central optical and metaphorical link between the

mind-body, ideology-commodity axis on which Marx's dialectic revolves. Thus, "the idols of the mind" (185) that Marx saw projected in the camera obscura take their material, incarnate form in the legal and aesthetic status of the photograph as a capitalist fetish. Karl Marx, *Capital: The Communist Manifesto and Other Writings*, ed. and intro. Max Eastman (New York: The Modern Library, 1932); quoted in Mitchell, *Iconology*, 168.

82. For instance, the Krokers point to the ubiquitous presence of a post-modern body, which as a consequence of "the cultural politics of advanced capitalism" is processed into a "semiurgy of floating body parts" or technologically "subordinated to the two-fold hypothesis of hyperfunctionality and ultra refuse" (21). At one moment it is technologically ablated and simultaneously made obsolete (32). However in arguing that the body has been deprived of a worthy concept of corporeality, they succumb to a nostalgia for some "natural" or pre-cultural body, whose disappearance is then mourned. Arthur Kroker and Marilouise Kroker, "Theses on the Disappearing Body in the Hyper-Modern Condition," in *Body Invaders: Panic Sex in America*, eds. Arthur Kroker and Marilouise Kroker (New York: St. Martin's Press, 1987).

83. Jay, "Empire of the Gaze," 179.

84. David Michael Levin, *The Opening of Vision: Nihilism and the Post-modern Situation* (New York: Routledge, 1988), 267; also Jean-Paul Sartre, *The Transcendence of the Ego*, trans. F. Williams and R. Kirkpatrick (New York: Noonday Press, 1957), 37–38, 41–42.

85. Edmund Husserl *Cartesian Meditations*, trans. D. Carns (The Hague: Martinus Nijhoff, 1970).

86. Jean-Paul Sartre, *Being and Nothingness: An Essay on Phenomenological Ontology*, trans. Hazel E. Barnes (New York: Philosophical Library 1956), 318, 225.

87. James Schmidt, *Maurice Merleau-Ponty: Between Phenomenology and Structuralism* (New York: St. Martin's Press, 1985), 91.

88. Mark C. Taylor, *Altarity* (Chicago: University of Chicago Press, 1987), 69.

89. Marc Richir, "La defenestration," *L'Arc* 46, (1971): 31–42, cit. James Schmidt, *Between Phenomenology and Structuralism*, 99–100.

90. Jay, "Empire of the Gaze," 179.

91. Michel de Certeau, *Heterologies: Discourse on the Other*, trans. Brian Massumi (Minneapolis: University of Minnesota Press, 1986), 192.

92. Ibid., 191.

93. In all of this as well, there is a degree of ambivalence towards vision. With regard to *Discipline and Punish*, Certeau observes, that there is "an internal tension between his [Foucault's] historical thesis (the triumph of a panoptical system) and his [Foucault's] own way of writing (the subversion of a panoptical discourse)" (192). Thomas R. Flynn also addresses this ambivalence in Foucault's work: "Foucault and the Eclipse of Vision," in *Modernity and the Hegemony of Vision*, ed. David Michael Levin (Berkeley: University of California Press, 1993), 273.

94. Jay "Empire of the Gaze, 177–79.

95. Michel Foucault, *Madness and Civilization: A History of Insanity in the Age of Reason* (New York: Vintage Books, 1988), 70.

96. Ibid., 35.

97. Ibid.

98. Ibid., 70.

99. Ibid., 108.

100. Ibid., 108–9.

101. Michel Foucault, *The Birth of the Clinic*, trans. A. M. Sheridan Smith (New York: Vintage Books, 1975), 107.

102. Ibid., 120.

103. Ibid., xiii.

104. Ibid., 39.

105. Ibid., 142.

106. Ibid., 143.

107. Ibid., 166.

108. Ibid., 171.

109. Ibid., 197.

110. John Rajchman, "Foucault: Art of Seeing," *October* 44 (Spring 1988): 91.

111. Rajchman, "Art of Seeing," 91.

112. Ibid.

113. Gilles Deleuze, *Foucault,* trans. Sean Hand (Minneapolis: University of Minnesota Press, 1986), 63.

114. Rajchman, "Art of Seeing," 92.

115. Ibid., 98.

116. Deleuze, *Foucault,* 58.

117. Jay, "Scopic Regimes of Modernity," 13.

118. For Foucault, Jeremy Bentham's 1787 proposal for the panopticon or Inspection House—an architectural system of social discipline, applicable to prison, factory, workhouse, asylum and school—was a central figure of modern disciplinary power based on isolation, individuation, and

supervision through visibility. Within the architectural scheme of the panopticon, inmates held in a ring of individual cells would be unable to view the central observation tower and would have to assume that they were being observed, inasmuch as they were open to a chain of observation by other prisoners. The panopticon is the concrete embodiment of a temporal-spatial disciplinary technology with its cellular organization, its detailed hierarchical architecture, its temporal cataloguing of the body, and its componential systematized gridlike view of reality to surveil, train, and discipline bodies in one and the same movement.

119. *Michel Foucault, Power/Knowledge: Selected Interviews and Other Writings, 1972–1977*, ed. Colin Gordon and trans. Colin Gordon et al. (New York: Pantheon Books, 1980), 152.

120. Foucault, *Discipline and Punish*, 200.

121. Jay, "Empire of the Gaze," 191.

122. Foucault, *Power/Knowledge*, 151.

123. Deleuze, *Foucault*, 34. For the normative implications of architecture, see Francois Ewald, "A Power without an Exterior," in *Michel Foucault, Philosopher: Essays*, trans. Timothy J. Armstrong New York: Routledge, 1992), 171.

124. Foucault, *Power/Knowledge*, 150.

125. Ibid., 149.

126. Foucault, *Discipline and Punish*, 228.

127. Deleuze, *Foucault*, 94.

128. Ibid., 98.

129. Ibid., 57. Given Foucault's affinity for visibilities and spatialities, Deleuze has also referred to him as a modern cartographer. Ibid., 44.

130. Ibid., 59.

131. Foucault, *Discipline and Punish*, 25.

132. Michel Foucault, *History of Sexuality I: An Introduction*, trans. Robert Hurley (New York: Pantheon, 1978), 143.

133. Ibid., 86.

134. Michel Foucault Lectures delivered at Stanford University, October 1979, quoted in Hubert Dreyfus and Paul Rabinow, *Michel Foucault: Beyond Structuralism and Hermeneutics*, second edition (Chicago: University of Chicago Press, 1992), 138.

135. Foucault, *Power/Knowledge*, 172.

136. Foucault, *History of Sexuality*, 139.

137. Ibid. "Bio-politics of the population" and the accompanying field of intervention and regulatory controls becomes the basis of Foucault's attempt to study the "governmentalization of the state." It also receives

prominent attention in *The History of Sexuality*, in which Foucault describes the coming together of these two disciplinary technologies in the nineteenth-century discourse of sex. Anatomo-politics, on the other hand, is analyzed in detail in *Discipline and Punish*.

138. Foucault, *Discipline and Punish*, 26

139. Ibid., 210.

140. Ibid., 211.

141. Ibid., 216.

142. Ibid., 222.

143. Ibid., 26.

144. Ewald, "A Power without an Exterior," 170.

145. Ibid.

146. Foucault, *Power/Knowledge*, 194.

147. Gilles Deleuze, "What is a dispositif?" *Michel Foucault Philosopher: Essays*, trans. Timothy J. Armstrong (New York: Routledge, 1992), 160.

148. Ibid., 160.

149. Ibid., 160–61.

150. Foucault, *Discipline and Punish*, 176.

151. Ibid., 170.

152. Ibid., 192.

153. Ibid., 305.

154. Ibid., 226.

155. Judith Butler, *Gender Trouble: Feminism and the Subversion of Identity* (New York: Routledge, 1990), 129.

156. Michel Foucault "Nietzsche, Genealogy, History," in *Language, Counter-Memory, Practice: Selected Essays and Interviews* by Michel Foucault, trans. Donald F. Bouchard and Sherry Simon, ed. Donald F. Bouchard (Ithaca: Cornell University Press, 1977), 148.

157. Ibid.

158. Foucault, *The History of Sexuality*, 31.

159. Ibid., 34.

160. Butler, *Gender Trouble*, 130.

161. Mary Douglas, *Purity and Danger: An Analysis of Concepts of Pollution and Taboo* (London: Routledge and Kegan Paul, 1969). According to Douglas, since bodies constitute a region of unruliness, cultural discourses seek to establish the boundaries of the body by means of social taboos regarding appropriate posture and modes of exchange (4). While Douglas, operating within a structuralist orientation, presumes the body's unruliness to be of a "natural" sort, Butler rightly points out that

the body's untidiness must be viewed as a region of cultural unruliness (*Gender Trouble*, 131).

162. Ibid., 134.

163. Foucault, *Discipline and Punish*, 29.

164. Butler, *Gender Trouble*, 135.

165. David Couzens Hoy, "Power, Repression, Progress: Foucault, Lukes, and the Frankfurt School," in David Couzens Hoy, ed., *Foucault: A Critical Reader* (Oxford: Basil Blackwell, 1986), 129.

166. Foucault, *Power/Knowledge*, 122.

167. Mark Poster, *Foucault, Marxism and History* (Cambridge, UK: Polity Press; New York: Basil Blackwell, 1984, 79); also see Hoy, "Power, Repression," in Hoy, ed., *Foucault: A Critical Reader*, 141.

168. Hoy, "Power, Repression," in Hoy, ed., *Foucault: A Critical Reader*, 129.

169. Poster, *Foucault, Marxism and History*, 79.

170. Foucault, *Power/Knowledge*, 117.

171. Ibid., 58.

172. Poster, *Foucault, Marxism and History*, 86–87. Deleuze similarly notes that Foucault's "functional microanalysis" of power transforms "whatever is still pyramidal in the Marxist image and replaces it with a strict immanence." Deleuze, *Foucault*, 27.

173. Foucault, *The History of Sexuality*, 49.

174. Ibid., 102.

175. Ibid., 92.

176. Foucault, *Power/Knowledge*, 221.

177. Ibid., 59.

178. Foucault, *The History of Sexuality*, 136.

179. Foucault, *Discipline and Punish*, 27.

180. Foucault, *Knowledge/Power*, 118.

181. Foucault, *The History of Sexuality*, 84.

182. Jana Sawicki, "Feminism and the Power of Foucaldian Discourse," in *After Foucault*, ed. Jonathan Arac (New Brunswick: Rutgers University Press, 1988), 167.

183. Foucault, *The History of Sexuality*, 84.

184. Poster, *Foucault, Marxism and History*, 90–91.

185. Deleuze, *Foucault*, 25.

186. Foucault, *Power/Knowledge*, 53.

187. Barry Smart, "The Politics of Truth and the Problem of Hegemony," in Hoy, ed., *Foucault: A Critical Reader*, 162, 158.

188. Foucault, *The History of Sexuality*, 125.

189. Ibid., 141.

190. Smart, "The Politics of Truth," in Hoy, ed., *Foucault: A Critical Reader*, 160.
191. Ibid., 163–65.
192. Foucault, *Power/Knowledge*, 81.
193. Ibid., 190.
194. Hoy, "Power, Repression," in Hoy, ed., *Foucault: A Critical Reader*, 138.
195. Foucault, *Power/Knowledge*, 49.
196. Deleuze, *Foucault*, 29.
197. Foucault, "The Subject and Power," in Dreyfus and Rabinow, *Foucault: Beyond Structuralism*, 222–23.
198. Foucault, *Discipline and Punish*, 152.

CHAPTER 2. PHOTOGRAPHY AND THE BOURGEOIS BODY

1. Freund, *Photography and Society*, 9.
2. Jean Baudrillard, *Simulations*, trans. Paul Foss (New York: Semiotexte, 1983), 84–85.
3. Rosenblum, *A World History*, 39.
4. Freund, *Photography and Society*, 10.
5. Ibid.
6. Ibid., 11.
7. The silhouette, the poor person's miniature, consisted of a tracing from a cast shadow which was then either inked in or cut from shiny black paper and mounted on a lighter background. The silhouette, like the miniature, was a unique object, and duplicates could not be made from it. However, unlike the miniature, the making of a silhouette required little training or interpretive skill. With Gilles Louis Chrétien's invention of the physiontrace, the process of representation was mechanized, albeit in a crude and rudimentary fashion. Aesthetically speaking, the portraits obtained with the physiontrace are flat, expressionless, stylized, and mathematically precise. Furthermore, a single session with the sitter was all that was necessary and so the portraits moderately priced were easily accessible to many. Newhall, *History of Photography,* 11–12.
8. Freund, *Photography and Society*, 29; Tagg, *Burden of Representation*, 49.
9. Freund, *Photography and Society*, 29.
10. Ibid., 30.
11. Newhall, *History of Photography*, 22.

12. Charles Baudelaire, "The Salon of 1859," trans. Jonathan Maynre, in Goldberg, *Photography in Print*, 124.

13. Freund, *Photography and Society*, 35.

14. Rosenblum, *A World History*, 42.

15. Ibid., 47.

16. Richard Rudisill, *Mirror Image: The Influence of the Daguerreotype on American Society* (Albuquerque: University of Mexico Press, 1971), 62.

17. Rosenblum, *A World History*, 47–48.

18. Ibid., 50.

19. The albumen coating came into use at the same time as the colodion negative and improved the quality of the print produced by the collodion wet-plate process, providing it with stronger contrasts, better tonal values, and a generally glossy surface. Edward Lucie-Smith, *The Invented Eye: Masterpieces of Photography, 1839-1914* (New York: Paddington Press, 1975), 66.

20. Walter Benjamin, *Illuminations*, ed. Hannah Arendt, trans. Harry Zohn (New York: Schocken, 1969), 226.

21. Rosenblum, *A World History*, 39.

22. J. C. Lavater, *Essays on Physiognomy*, 3 vols. (London, 1789), commentary to plate 36, vol. 3; cited in Richard Hunter and Ida Macalpine, *Three Hundred Years of Psychiatry, 1535–1860,* (London: Oxford University Press, 1963), 521.

23. Marie-Christine Leps, *Apprehending the Criminal* (Durham: Duke University Press, 1992), 27.

24. Louis Chevalier, *Laboring Classes and Dangerous Classes* (New York: Howard Fertig, 1973), 411.

25. Ibid., 412.

26. Judith Wechsler, *A Human Comedy: Physiognomy and Caricature in 19th-Century Paris* (Chicago: University of Chicago Press, 1982); John Davies, *Phrenology: Fad and Science: A Nineteenth-Century American Crusade* (New Haven: Yale University Press, 1955); Walter Benjamin, *Charles Baudelaire: A Lyric Poet in the Era of High Capitalism,* trans. Harry Zohn (Frankfurt am Main: Suhrkamp Verlag, 1973; originally published in 1969).

27. Wechsler, *A Human Comedy*, 23–24, 30.

28. Ibid.

29. Rudisill, *Mirror Image*, 233.

30. Nathaniel Hawthorne, *The House of the Seven Gables* (New York: Modern Library, 1961), 85.

31. Rudisill, *Mirror Image*, 237.

32. James F. Ryder, *Voigtlander and I* (Cleveland: Cleveland Printing & Publishing Co., 1901), 16.
33. Ibid., xi.
34. Rudisill, *Mirror Image*, 229.
35. Ibid.
36. Ibid.
37. Rosenblum, *A World History*, 49.
38. Ibid.
39. Allan Sekula, "The Body and the Archive," *October* 36–39 (1986): 9.
40. Alan Trachtenberg, "Brady's Portraits," *Yale Review* 73. 2 (1983–1984), 251.
41. John Tagg, *The Burden of Representation* (Amherst: University of Massachusetts Press, 1988), 35.
42. Rudisill, *Mirror Image*, 232.
43. U.S. Congress, *U.S. House of Representatives Report*, 41st Congress, 3rd sess., no. 46, p. 1, cit. Rudisill, *Mirror Image*, 229.
44. Ibid.
45. U.S. Congress, *U.S. House of Representatives Report*, 41st Cong., 3rd sess., no. 46, p. 2, cit. Rudisill, *Mirror Image*, 229.
46. Marcus Aurelius Root, *The Camera and the Pencil* (Philadelphia: J. B. Lippincott & Co., 1864; reprint, Pawlett, Vermont: Pawlett Helios, 1971), cit. in Goldberg, *Photography in Print*, 149.
47. Ibid.
48. Rudisill, *Mirror Image*, 231.
49. Mary Poovey, *Uneven Developments* (Chicago: University of Chicago Press, 1988); Anita Levy, *Other Women: The Writing of Class, Race, and Gender, 1832–1898* (Princeton: Princeton University Press, 1991).
50. Sheila Rowbotham, *Women, Resistance and Revolution* (London: Allen Lane, 1972); Katharine Rogers, *Feminism in Eighteenth-Century England* (Urbana: University of Illinois Press, 1982); Maurice Bloch and Jean Bloch, "Women and the Dialectics of Nature in Eighteenth-Century French Thought," in *Nature, Culture and Gender*, ed. Carol P. MacCormack and Marilyn Strathern, (Cambridge: Cambridge University Press, 1980), 25–41; Joan Kelly, "Early Feminist Theory and Querelle des Femmes, 1400-1789," *Signs* 8.1 (1982).
51. Jean-Jacques Roussaeu, *Emile*, trans. Allan Bloom (New York: Basic Books, 1981), book 5, 362–63.
52. Thomas Laqueur, *Making Sex: Body and Gender from the Greeks to Freud* (Cambridge, Mass.: Harvard University Press, 1990), 194.
53. *Encyclopédie ou Dictionnaire Raisonné des Sciences, des Arts, et des Métriers* (Neuchatel, 1765), cit. in Londa Schiebinger, "Skeletons in the

Closet: The First Illustrations of the Female Skeleton in Eighteenth-Century Anatomy," *The Making of the Modern Body,* ed. Catherine Gallagher and Thomas Laqueur (Berkeley: University of California Press, 1987), 68.

54. Schiebinger, "Skeletons in the Closet," 64–65. As Londa Schiebinger has observed, the anatomists' search for sex differences coincided with the professionalization of medicine and its usurpation of medical care from the traditional networks of knowledge represented by female midwifes. Declaring their concern for specifically female health problems, these physicians produced, under the guise of a "value neutral" discourse, a distinctive anatomy for women that served the interests of a male-dominated public sphere (70-72). As a consequence, over the course of the period between 1780 and 1830, in both France and Germany, medical manuals for women began to base their advice on the new findings of sexual difference (69). According to Thomas Laqueur, professional politics and the imperatives of science had a significant role to play in the propagation of sex differences. They reflected the physicians' desire to wrest control from the clergy and to exercise the power to determine women's bodies, "to substitute" as it were "the physician for the priest as the moral preceptor of society." Laqueur, *Making Sex,* 215–16.

55. Auguste Comte *Cours de philosophie positive,* vol. 4 (Paris, 1839), 569–70, cit. in Schiebinger, "Skeletons in the Closet," 69.

56. Joan Landes, *Women and the Public Sphere* (Ithaca: Cornell University Press, 1988), 11.

57. Laqueur, *Making Sex,* 211.

58. Ibid., 200.

59. Ibid., 195–96.

60. Poovey, *Uneven Developments,* 6–7; Cynthia Eagle Russett, *Sexual Science* (Cambridge, Mass.: Harvard University Press, 1989), 30.

61. Peter Gaskell, *The Manufacturing Population of England, Its Moral, Social, and Physical Conditions, and the Changes Which Have Arisen from the Use of Steam Machinery; with an examination of Infant Labour* (1833; reprint, New York: Arno Press, 1972), 144.

62. Mary Poovey, *Uneven Developments* (Chicago: University of Chicago Press, 1988), 8. A discussion of the domestic ideal and its evolution can be found in Catherine Gallagher's *The Industrial Reformation of English Fiction: Social Discourse and Narrative Form, 1832–1867* (Chicago: University of Chicago Press, 1985); see also Leonore Davidoff and Catherine Hall, *Family Fortunes: Men and Women of the English Middle Class, 1780–1850* (Chicago: University of Chicago Press, 1987). Ironically, even when feminists contested the dominant discourse of the period and

argued for the social equality of women, they did so by basing their case on the physical and moral differences between the sexes. For example, utopian socialists such as Anna Wheeler embraced the devaluation of female passion, because in their view the Enlightenment's progress rested on the elimination of passion and the triumph of reason, hence predicting for women a vanguard position. The conservative domestic ideologists, while advancing the notion of a separate, unhierarchical, but nevertheless radically different sphere for women, also resorted to the idea of women's superior moral power. Insofar as women exerted their moral influence in the domestic sphere, the primary arena for the shaping of proper conduct, domestic ideologists argued that women exercised tremendous public influence. Laqueur, *Making Sex*, 202–4.

63. Poovey, *Uneven Developments*, 76.
64. Gaskell, *The Manufacturing Population,* 165.
65. Poovey, *Uneven Developments,* 10. Not unlike their mothers, daughters too were represented as embodying a feminine purity that was implicitly asexual. And like their mothers, they functioned to provide solace, comfort, and spiritual guidance to a male, who would first be the father and later the husband. The theme of the good and dutiful daughter who aids her father both physically and spiritually is a recurring one in Anglo-American fiction of the nineteenth century. Deborah Gorham, *The Victorian Girl and the Feminine Ideal* (London: Croom Helm, 1982), 38–44.
66. Poovey, *Uneven Developments*, 8–9.
67. Gorham, *The Victorian Girl*, 77.
68. Gregg's suggestion in his article titled, "Why are Women Redundant?" was that such sexually aggressive women be sent to the colonies lest they become prostitutes. Poovey, *Uneven Developments,* 15.
69. Clifford Geertz, "Art as a Cultural System," *MLN* 91 (1978): 1478.
70. Judith Butler, *Bodies that Matter* (New York: Routledge, 1993), 13.
71. Michel Borch-Jacobsen, *The Freudian Subject*, trans. Catherine Porter (Stanford: Stanford University Press, 1988), cit. Butler, *Bodies that Matter*, 13.
72. In order to understand photographic portraiture's functioning in the expanding ideological and disciplinary complex that began to surround the middle-class family, it is important to confront the increasing isolation faced by that family. Isolated from both the world of work and from larger kinship structures, the middle-class family was slowly and surely being "conceived as an inward-turning and self-contained unit." Steven Mintz, *A Prison of Expectations* (New York: New York University Press, 1983), 14. The period between the mid-eighteenth century and the 1850s wit-

nessed a dramatic decline in household industries and in the economic self-sufficiency of households, all of this accompanied by increasing economic specialization and the expansion of a market-oriented economy. Perkin, *Modern English Society,* 149–60. The increasing withdrawal of the conjugal unit is also described in James A. Henretta, *The Evolution of American Society, 1700–1815* (Lexington, 1973), 213–14. On the increasing length of residence of children in their parents' home, see Anne Foner, "Age Stratification and the Changing Family," *American Journal of Sociology* (1978), Supplement 349. For an explanation of the disappearance of apprentices from the middle-class home, see Paul E. Johnson, *A Shopkeeper's Millenium: Society and Revivals in Rochester, New York, 1815–1837* (New York: Hill and Wang, 1978), 43–48, 59.

73. Richard Brodhead has pointed out that a number of middle-class reformers and writers concerned that the unrestrained pursuit of individual self-interest would result in social disruption and, believing that the family could serve as a bulwark against such chaos, began to articulate in innumerable tracts, home management manuals, and novels a theory of family government. This theory of family government, which Brodhead has called "disciplinary intimacy," took as its subject the normative formation and socialization of the child. In its rejection of corporal punishment and in its wish to secure the voluntary obedience of children through disciplinary technologies less visible but more effective, disciplinary intimacy represented a stigmatization of the older mode of punishment that Foucault has detailed in *Discipline and Punish.* But unlike Foucault's description of a depersonalized power, this disciplinary model required the personalization of authority (69–71). What the program advocated was an emotional intensification of the relationship between parent and child: "enmeshing the child in strong bonds of love is the way authority introduces its charge to its imperatives and norms." It was believed that through the process of introjection, the discipline of love would extend its regulatory hold on the child (72). As one reformer expressed it candidly: "there is no constraint like that of love" (72). In keeping with the middle-class paradigm, the domestic tutelary complex defined the mother as the repository of maternal affection and hence the agent of authority and discipline (74). Richard H. Brodhead, "Sparing the Rod: Discipline and Fiction in Antebellum America," *Representations* 21 (Winter 1988): 67–96.

74. Alan Thomas, *The Expanding Eye: Photography and the Nineteenth-Century Mind* (London: Croom Helm, 1978), 68.

75. Judith Williamson, *Consuming Passions: The Dynamics of Popular Culture* (London: Marion Boyars, 1985), 116.

76. Ibid., 116, 118.

77. Marcus Auelius Root, *The Camera and the Pencil* (Philadelphia: J.B. Lippincott & Co., 1864; reprint, Pawlett, Vermont: Helios, 1971); cit. Goldberg, *Photography in Print*, 149.

78. Tagg, *The Burden of Representation*, 36.

79. Richard Sennett, *The Fall of the Public Man: On the Social Psychology of Capitalism* (New York: Vintage Books, 1978).

80. Trachtenberg, "Brady's Portraits," 245.

81. Root, *The Camera and the Pencil* (1864), cit. Trachtenberg, "Brady's Portraits," 245.

82. Trachtenberg, "Brady's Portraits," 251.

83. David Bate, "The Occidental Tourist: Photography and Colonizing Vision," *Afterimage* 20. 1, (Summer 1992): 11.

84. This was not necessarily surprising considering that Lane himself was read and heavily cited by Flaubert as well as Burton, while Nerval's own writings were influenced by Lamartine, who had in turn been influenced by Chateaubriand. "From these complex rewritings the actualities of the modern Orient were systematically excluded, especially when gifted pilgrims like Nerval and Flaubert preferred Lane's description to what their eyes and minds showed them immediately." Edward W. Said, *Orientalism* (New York: Vintage Books, 1979), 177.

85. Ibid., 8.

86. Linda Nochlin, "The Imaginary Orient," *Art in America* 71 (May 1983): 119–91.

87. Nissan N. Perez, *Focus East: Early Photography in the Near East 1839–1885* (New York: Harry N. Abrams, Inc. in association with the Domino Press, Jerusalem, and the Israel Museum, Jerusalem, 1988), 102–3.

88. Ibid., 97.

89. Ibid., 102.

90. Ibid., 50.

91. Ibid., 105.

92. Bate, "The Occidental Tourist," 13.

93. Peter Wollen, *Reflections on Twentieth-Century Culture* (Bloomington: Indiana University Press, 1993), 6.

94. Perez, *Focus East*, 107.

95. Said, *Orientalism*, 190.

96. Homi K. Bhabha, *Out There: Marginalization and Contemporary Culture,* ed. Russell Ferguson, Martha Gever, Trinh T. Minh-ha, and Cornel West (Cambridge, Mass.: MIT Press, 1992), 81.

97. Said, *Orientalism* 150.

98. Bate, "The Occidental Tourist," 13.

99. Alan Grosrichard, *Structure du Serail* (Paris: Seuil, 1979), cit. Peter Wollen, *Raiding the Icebox* (Bloomington: Indiana University Press, 1993), 7.

100. Ibid.

101. Oliver Wendell Holmes, "The Stereoscope and the Stereograph," in Goldberg, *Photography in Print*, 113.

102. Rosenblum, *A World History*, 62; Max Kozloff, "Nadar and the Republic of Mind," in Goldberg, *Photography in Print*, 130.

103. Freund, *Photography and Society*, 56.

104. Ibid., 37; Tagg, *Burden of Representation*, 49.

105. Freund, *Photography and Society*, 61.

106. Rosenblum, *A World History,* 63; Goldsmith, *Camera and Its Images*, 73.

107. Thomas, *The Expanding Eye*, 82; Tagg, *Burden of Representation*, 50.

108. Goldsmith, *Camera and Its Images*, 74.

109. Freund, *Photography and Society*, 55.

110. At this point, I only wish to point out the emergence of a new regime of visibility. Later I take up more fully the discussion of the regime of the spectacle and its relationship to the regime of discipline and surveillance.

111. Jean Baudrillard, *L'échange symbolique et la mort* (Paris: Gallimard, 1976), 86.

112. Freund, *Photography and Society*, 64.

113. Ibid., 71. Out of the tension of photographic verisimilitude and art was born a hybrid portraiture. Photographers seeking to give their images the status and prestige of hand-painted portraits, painted over their photographic images while retaining the underlying trace of the photograph; and the painter seeking the apparent verisimilitude of the camera image and knowing well the bourgeois desire for the same, projected from glass positives the camera image onto the canvas and then painted over it.

114. Nigel Gosling, *Tournachon Felix Nadar 1820–1910* (London: Seecker and Warburg, 1976), 39.

115. Tagg, *Burden of Representation*, 54.

116. Ibid., 56.

CHAPTER THREE. PHOTOGRAPHY AND THE DEVIANT BODY

1. Foucault, *Power/Knowledge*, 39.

2. Cesare di Beccaria, *An Essay on Crimes and Punishments*. Translated from the Italian with a Commentary Attributed to Mons. de Voltaire, Translated from the French, 4th edition (London: Newberry, 1785), 9.
3. Leon Radzinowicz, *Ideology and Crime* (New York: Columbia University Press, 1966), 8.
4. Foucault, *Discipline and Punish*, 48–49.
5. For example, under the Black Act it had become a capital offense for a small farmer or cottager to avail himself of some firewood from the master's land. What had previously been a customary right recognized by the gentry was criminalized because of the overwhelming desire of the landlords to make a profit from their lands. Michael Ignatieff, *A Just Measure of Pain* (New York: Pantheon Books, 1978), 16.
6. Leon Radzinowicz, *A History of English Criminal Law and Its Administration from 1750* (London: Stevens, 1948), vol. I, 3, 35.
7. Jerome Hall, *Theft, Law and Society* (Indianapolis: Bobbs-Merrill, 1952), 118.
8. Ibid., 132.
9. Ignatieff, *A Just Measure of Pain*, 28.
10. Radzinowicz, *Ideology and Crime*, 25.
11. Foucault, *Discipline and Punish*, 73.
12. Ibid., 61.
13. Jeremy Bentham, *An Introduction to the Principles of Morals and Legislation*, 1823 (New York: Hafner Publishing Co., 1948), 171.
14. Ibid., 170.
15. Carl L. Becker, *The Heavenly City of the Eighteenth-Century Philosophers* (New Haven, Conn.: Yale University Press, 1961), 45.
16. Leps, *Apprehending the Criminal*, 20.
17. Ysabel Rennie, *The Search for Criminal Man* (Lexington, Mass: D.C. Heath and Company, 1978), 23; Leps, *Apprehending the Criminal*, 19; Ignatieff, *A Just Measure of Pain*, 28.
18. Leps, *Apprehending the Criminal*, 18.
19. Clive Emsley, *Crime and Society in England, 1750–1900* (London: Longmann, 1987), 115–16.
20. Foucault, *Discipline and Punish*, 114.
21. Ignatieff, *A Just Measure of Pain*, 15. However the existence of Elizabeth Bridewells or "houses of correction" foreshadowed the modern penitentiary. Their purpose was to inculcate in the poor the values of industry and hard work. Masters in such outwork trades as textiles and ropemaking would contract with the various counties to exploit this labor power, and the experiences they gained in managing an extended division of labor were crucial in the subsequent emergence of factories (11). Hence the

bridewell became a model for the future development of the factory. Sidney Pollard, *The Genesis of Modern Management* (Cambridge, Mass.: Harvard University Press, 1965), 46.

22. Sidney and Beatrice Webb, *English Prisons under Local Government* (1927), 11.

23. Ignatieff, *A Just Measure of Pain*, 46.

24. Radzinowicz, *A History of English Criminal*, 330.

25. Foucault, *Discipline and Punish*, 23.

26. Ibid., 29.

27. Ibid., 28.

28. Ignatieff, *A Just Measure of Pain*, 53.

29. Ibid., 62; see also Dario Melossi and Massimo Pavarini, *The Prison and the Factory: Origins of the Penitentiary System*, trans. Glynis Cousin (London: Macmillan Press, 1981), 26.

30. Ignatieff, *A Just Measure of Pain*, 54–59.

31. Ibid., 60.

32. Ibid., 67. Other reformers of the time such as Bentham denied the existence of original sin, embracing instead both Hartley and Locke's notion that ideas were derived externally. Hence they tended to view socialization in mechanistic terms involving a tinkering and adjustment of the self through a graduated disciplining of the body. Bentham, for instance, was given to describing his panopticon as a "machine for grinding rogues honest." Bentham had no trouble asserting, on the one hand, that criminals were free agents while at the same time referring to them as defective mechanisms. Bentham, *Rationale of Punishment*, 28, cit. Ignatieff, *A Just Measure of Pain*, 71.

33. Ibid., 72.

34. Ibid. Benthan even went as far as to suggest the construction of a whipping machine that would bring not only a degree of precision to punishment but mete it out in a wholly impersonal manner. Bentham, *Rationale of Punishment*, 82, cit. Ignatieff, *A Just Measure of Pain*, 76.

35. Ibid., 75–77.

36. Leps, *Apprehending the Criminal*, 21.

37. Ignatieff, *A Just Measure of Pain*, 146, 168, 113.

38. Patricia O'Brien, *The Promise of Punishment: Prisons in Nineteenth-Century France* (Princeton,: Princeton University Press, 1982), 54.

39. Ibid., 66. In France, the organization La Société Générales des Prisons was formed in 1877. Consisting of officials from prison, judicial, and government agencies, it published a journal entitled the *Revue Pénitentiaire et de Droit Pénal*.

40. Ignatieff, *A Just Measure of Pain*, 185–87.

41. O'Brien, *The Promise of Punishment*, 54, 58. O'Brien points out that in nineteenth-century France, while women were in prison for generally the same types of crimes as men—e.g., petty theft (prostitution being the exception)—studies of women's criminality, limited though they were, largely linked the source of women's crimes to biological and moral factors rather than social or class factors. This was not surprising since women were viewed as biologically determined and not open to the influences of socialization. In general, then, women make their appearance in these studies not as social subjects, but as moral and sexual creatures. The moral and sexual causes of women's crime were neatly entwined. Women who neglected their "natural" duties as mothers and wives were capable of "corrupting the social order." Furthermore, their moral failure was traced to their sexuality. Consequently, there were studies which sought to establish correlations between a woman's menstrual cycle and shoplifting. Since the prevailing view was that women's physical inferiority, including the possession of smaller brains, made them emotionally susceptible, women's prisons, in addition to emphasizing work and discipline, included religious instruction and religious ceremonies. "Women, after all, were 'affective beings' who would be reached more successfully by these means" (64–71).

42. Leps, *Apprehending the Criminal*, 21.

43. Ibid., 26.

44. John V. Grauman, "Population Growth," in *International Encyclopedia of the Social Sciences*, 1968, vol. 9, 379.

45. Rennie, *The Search for Criminal Man*, 40.

46. H. A. Frégier. *Des classes dangereuses de la population dans les grandes villes et des moyens de les rendre meilleures*, 2 vols. (Paris, 1840), vol. 1, 6–7, cit. Rennie, *The Search for Criminal Man*, 3.

47. Eugène Buret, *De la misère des classes laborieuses en Angleterre et en France* (Paris, 1840), cit. Louis Chevalier, *Laboring Classes and Dangerous Classes*, 360.

48. Chevalier, *Laboring Classes and Dangerous Classes*, 262.

49. Leps, *Apprehending the Criminal*, 23.

50. Ibid., 132.

51. Ibid., 130.

52. Gareth Stedman Jones, *Outcast London* (Oxford: Clarendon Press, 1971), 13.

53. Chevalier, *Laboring Classes and Dangerous Classes*, 359.

54. Ibid., 383.

55. Ibid., 409.

56. Ibid., 414–15.

57. Ibid., 413.
58. Henry Mayhew, *London Labor and the London Poor: A Cyclopedia of the Conditions and Earnings of Those that Will Work, Those that Cannot Work and Those that Will Not Work*, 4 vols. (1851); (London, 1967), 4:3.
59. Leps, *Apprehending the Criminal*, 25.
60. Jones, *Outcast London*, 100.
61. Ibid., 244–46.
62. Ibid., 256–60.
63. Ibid., 257.
64. Ibid., 255.
65. Ibid., 262.
66. Michel Foucault, "Lectures delivered at Stanford University October 1979," cit. Dreyfus and Rabinow, *Foucault: Beyond Structuralism*, 138.
67. Foucault, *Power/Knowledge*, 172.
68. Foucault, *The History of Sexuality*, vol. I, 138.
69. Ian Hacking, "Biopower and the Avalanche of Printed Numbers," *Humanities in Society* 5 (1982): 281.
70. Ibid., 279.
71. Ibid., 280.
72. Rennie, *The Search for Criminal Man*, 34.
73. Ibid., 44.
74. Hacking, "Biopower," 287.
75. Chevalier, *Laboring Classes and Dangerous Classes*, 1.
76. Frank H. Haskins, "Adolphe Quetelet as Statistician," Ph.D. dissertation, Columbia University, 1908, 36.
77. Ibid., 37.
78. Ibid., 38–39.
79. Ibid., 40.
80. Ibid., 41.
81. Ibid.
82. Ibid., 49.
83. Rennie, *The Search for Criminal Man*, 35.
84. Nouv. Mem. vol. V, 35–36, quoted in Haskins, "Adolphe Quetelet," 55.
85. Ibid., 56.
86. L.A. Quetelet, *A Treatise on Man and the Development of His Faculties*, trans. R. Knox (1835; Edinburgh, 1842; reprint, Westmeed, 1973), 6.
87. Leps, *Apprehending the Criminal*, 25.
88. Nouv. Mem. vol. V, 35–36, quoted in Haskins, "Adolphe Quetelet," 57.
89. Ibid., 53.
90. Ibid., 62.
91. Ibid.

92. Ibid., 68–69.
93. Tagg, *Burden of Representation*, 62.
94. Ibid., 63.
95. Ibid.
96. Tony Bunyan, *The Political Police in Britain* (London: Julien Friedmann, 1976), 58–59.
97. Tagg, *Burden of Representation*, 72.
98. Sidney L. Harring, *Policing a Class Society* (New Brunswick: Rutgers University Press, 1983), 8.
99. Ibid.
100. Cloward and Piven, *Regulating the Poor* (London: Travistock, 1972), ch. 1; see also Leon Radzinowicz, *A History of English Criminal Law*, vol. II (London: Stevens, 1956), 83–127.
101. Ian MacDonald, *Race Today* (December 1973), quoted in Bunyan, *Political Police*, 62.
102. Julian Symons, *A Pictorial History of Crime* (New York: Crown Publishers, 1966), 12.
103. Tagg, *Burden of Representation*, 73.
104. Steven Spitzer, "The Rationalization of Crime Control in Capitalist Society," *Contemporary Crises* 3 (April 1979): 187–206.
105. Harring, *Policing a Class Society*, 8.
106. Ibid., 9–10.
107. Marx, *Capital*, 742, quoted in Harring, *Policing a Class Society*, 13.
108. Bunyan, *Political Police*, 63.
109. Symons, *A Pictorial History of Crime*, 12.
110. Bunyan, *Political Police*, 65.
111. Harring, *Policing a Class Society*, 10–11.
112. Bunyan, *Political Police*, 63.
113. T. A. Critchley, *A History of the Police in England and Wales 1900–1966* (London: Constable, 1967), 163.
114. Harring, *Policing a Class Society*, 18.
115. Bunyan, *Political Police*, 65.
116. Harring, *Policing a Class Society*, 15.
117. Bunyan, *Political Police*, 66.
118. Ibid., 67.
119. Ibid., 68.
120. Philip John Stead, *The Police of France* (New York: Macmillan, 1983), 11.
121. Ibid., 16, 26, 27.
122. Ibid., 67.
123. Ibid., 68.

124. Foucault, "Lectures," in Dreyfus and Rabinow, *Foucault: Beyond Structuralism*, 139.
125. Sekula, "Body and the Archive," 18.
126. Henry T. F. Rhodes, *Alphonse Bertillon* (New York: Abelard-Schuman, 1956), 73.
127. Ibid., 74.
128. Alphonse Bertillon, "The Bertillon System of Identification," *Forum* 2.3 (May 1891): 335, quoted in Sekula, "Body and the Archive," 26.
129. Rhodes, *Alphonse Bertillon*, 74.
130. Ibid., 82.
131. Ibid., 75.
132. Ibid., 89.
133. Ibid., 83.
134. Ibid., 103.
135. Sekula, "Body and the Archive," 30.
136. Thomas Byrnes, *1886 Professional Criminals of America* (New York: Chelsea House Publishers, 1969), 53.
137. Sekula, "Body and the Archive," 30.
138. Rhodes, *Alphonse Bertillon*, 90–93; Sekula, "Body and the Archive," 28.
139. Rhodes, *Alphonse Bertillon*, 90.
140. Ibid., 90–91.
141. Ibid., 91.
142. Sekula, "The Body and the Archive," 18.
143. Rhodes, *Alphonse Bertillon*, 105; Sekula, "Body and the Archive," 30.
144. Rhodes, *Alphonse Bertillon*, 105; Sekula, "Body and the Archive," 28.
145. Sekula, "The Body and the Archive," 33.
146. Tagg, *Burden of Representation*, 89–92.
147. Foucault, *Discipline and Punish*, 185.
148. Ibid.
149. Ibid., 189.
150. Ibid., 191.
151. Ibid.
152. Ibid., 192.
153. Sekula, "Body and the Archive," 34.
154. Rhodes, *Alphonse Bertillon*, 107.
155. Ibid.
156. O'Brien, *The Promise of Punishment*, 88.
157. Ibid., 80; Cesare Lombroso *Criminal Man* (New York: G.P. Putnam & Sons, 1911); see also Gina Lombroso-Ferrero *Criminal Man: According to the Classification of Cesare Lombroso* (New York: G.P. Putnam & Sons, 1911).

158. Alexandre Lacassagne, *Précis de médecine légale* (Paris, 1906), 185–189, cit. O'Brien, *The Promise of Punishment*, 86.

159. Ibid.

160. Ibid., 87.

161. Ibid., 79.

162. According to O'Brien, among male prisoners the practices of homosexuality and the selling of favors was a fundamental component of the barter system, but among female prisoner such relationships took on a more maternal form, finding expression in "marriage" and parent-child relationships. O'Brien, ibid., 107.

163. Ibid., 88.

164. Ignatieff, *A Just Measure of Pain*, 204.

165. O'Brien, *The Promise of Punishment*, 226.

166. Ibid., 233–34.

167. Ignatieff, *A Just Measure of Pain*, 204.

168. According to Patricia O'Brien, even though theories of criminality did not focus on women to any great extent, the view that women's crime was the result of such factors as instinct and nature "spread to analyses of crime in general." O'Brien, *The Promise of Punishment*, 69–70.

169. See Sekula, "Body and the Archive," 19.

170. Jones, *Outcast London*, 128–51. Jones identifies the significance and popularity of theories of degeneration in London during the 1880s; see also Sekula, "Body and the Archive," 40.

171. Chevalier, *Laboring Classes and Dangerous Classes*, 410–17; see also Wechsler, *A Human Comedy*, 16.

172. Greta Jones, *Social Darwinism and English Thought: The Interaction between Biological and Social Theory* (Atlantic Highlands, N.J.: Humanities Press, 1980), 146.

173. Ibid., 137.

174. David Green, "Veins of Resemblance: Photography and Eugenics," *The Oxford Art Journal* 7.2 (1984): 8.

175. Karl Pearson, *The Life, Letters and Honours of Francis Galton* (Cambridge: Cambridge University Press, 1924), 225.

176. Francis Galton, *Hereditary Genius*, (London: Julian Fiedmann, 1978), 339.

177. Pearson, *Life, Letters and Honours*, 352–53.

178. Donald A. Mackenzie, *Statistics in Britain 1865–1930: The Social Construction of Scientific Knowledge* (Edinburgh: Edinburgh University Press, 1981), 15.

179. Galton, *Hereditary Genius*, 32.

180. Mackenzie, *Statistics in Britain*, 58.

181. Ibid., 17.
182. Galton, *Hereditary Genius*, 17.
183. Francis Galton, "Eugenics: Its Definition, Scope and Aims," *Sociological Papers* (1905), 50.
184. Leonard Darwin, *The Need for Eugenic Reform* (London: John Murray, 1926), 164, cit. Mackenzie, *Statistics in Britain*, 20.
185. Ibid.
186. Ibid.
187. Ibid.
188. Ibid., 21.
189. Jones, *Outcast London*, 283.
190. Ibid., 287.
191. Ibid., 284.
192. Ibid., 303.
193. Ibid., 289.
194. Jones, *Social Darwinism*, 103.
195. Francis Galton, "Hereditary Improvement," *Frazers Magazine* 7 (1873): 116–30, quoted in Green, "Veins of Resemblance," 9.
196. Francois Galton, *Inquiries into Human Faculty and its Development* (London: Macmillan, 1883), 16, quoted in Green, "Veins of Resemblance," 9.
197. Green, "Veins of Resemblance," 9.
198. T.S. Clauston, "The Developmental Aspects of Criminal Anthropology," *Journal of the Anthropological Institute* 23 (1893): 194, 215–24, quoted in Green, "Veins of Resemblance," 11.
199. Francis Galton, *Essays in Eugenics* (London: Eugenics Education Society, 1909), 8–9.
200. Francis Galton, "Generic Images," *The Nineteenth Century: A Monthly Review* 6 (July–December, 1879): 161; see also Sekula, "Body and the Archive," 47.
201. Galton, "Generic Images," 162.
202. Sekula, "Body and the Archive," 48.
203. Galton, *Inquiries into Human Faculty*, 15, quoted in Sekula, "Body and the Archive," 50.
204. Sekula, "Body and the Archive," 42.
205. Mackenzie, *Statistics in Britain*, 22; G. R. Searle, *Eugenics and Politics in Britain, 1900–1914* (Leyden: Hoordhoff, 1976), 121.
206. Mackenzie, *Statistics in Britain*, 22-23.
207. Searle, *Eugenics and Politics*, 129.
208. Mackenzie, *Statistics in Britain*, 25.

209. Harold Perkin, *The Origins of Modern English Society, 1780–1880* (London: Routledge and Kegan Paul, 1972), 258.
210. Mackenzie, *Statistics in Britain*, 41.
211. Ibid., 33.
212. Ibid., 31.
213. L. Levidow, "A Marxist Critique of the IQ Debate," *Radical Science Journal* 6/7 (1978): 64–65, quoted in Mackenzie, *Statistics in Britain*, 34.
214. Foucault, *Madness and Civilization*, 253.
215. Sander L. Gilman, ed., *The Face of Madness: Hugh W. Diamond and the Origin of Psychiatric Photography* (Secaucas, N.J.: Brunner-Mazel, 1976), 20.
216. Ibid., 21.
217. *The Photographic Journal* 3 (1857): 289, quoted in Sander L. Gilman, *Seeing the Insane* (New York: John Wiley & Sons, 1982), 166.
218. Ibid., 167.
219. Dietrich Georg Kieser, *Elemente der Psychiatrik* (Breslau and Bonn: Kaiserliche L.-C. Akademie, 1855), op. cit. 173.
220. Ibid., 167–68.
221. Ruth Levy, "Types of One: Adolph Meyer's Life Chart and the Representation of Individuality," *Representations* 34 (Spring 1991): 12.
222. Gilman, *Seeing the Insane*, 166, 174.
223. Ibid., 171.
224. Gilman, ed., *The Face of Madness*, 21.
225. John C. Bucknill and Daniel Hack Tuke, *A Manual of Psychological Medicine* (New York, 1968), 282, cit. in Gilman, *Seeing the Insane*, 176.
226. William Noyes, "Composite Portraiture of the Insane," *Science* 9 (1888): 252–53; "Composite Portraits of General Paresis and of Melancholia," *Journal of Nervous and Mental Diseases*, 13 (1888): 1-2 , op. cit. 188.
227. Ibid., 188–89.

CHAPTER FOUR. PHOTOGRAPHY AND THE
BODY OF THE WORKER

1. Marx, *Capital*, vol I, 173.
2. Foucault, *Discipline and Punish*, 224.
3. Ibid., 138.
4. Ibid.
5. Ibid., 137.

6. Ibid., 224.

7. Ibid., 194.

8. Roland Barthes, "The Plates of the Encyclopedia," in *New Critical Essays*, trans. Richard Howard (New York: Hill & Wang, 1980), 29.

9. Pollard, *The Genesis*, 31, 39, 46.

10. Harry Braverman, *Labor and Monopoly Capital: The Degradation of Work in the Twentieth Century* (New York: Monthly Review Press, 1974), 60.

11. Pollard, *The Genesis*, 38.

12. Daniel Nelson, *Managers and Workers: Origins of the New Factory System in the United States, 1880–1920* (Madison, Wis.: University of Wisconsin Press, 1975), 38.

13. U.S. Department of Commerce, Bureau of the Census, *Historical Statistics of the United States, Colonial Times to 1954* (Washington, D.C., 1960), Series P 138, 413; cit. in Nelson, *Managers and Workers*, 4.

14. *Twelfth Census of the United States*, vol. 7: *Manufactures*, part I (Washington, D.C., 1902), lxxii; ibid.

15. Nelson, *Managers and Workers*, 6.

16. Braverman, *Labor and Monopoly Capital*, 65.

17. Nelson, *Managers and Workers*, 41, 43.

18. Craft unions opposed piece work since it often went hand in hand with the "driving method." Thomas S. Adams and Helen L. Sumner, *Labor Problems: A Text Book* (New York: Macmillan, 1905), 259.

19. In formulating a coherent theory of value, classical political economy often took the value of labor to be both the wage paid and the value produced by labor. Marx in *Capital*, vol. I (chs. 6 and 19) dissipates the confusion by dividing the concept of labor into the subcategories of labor and labor power in order to explain the source of surplus value, that is, labor power is what workers sell to capitalists for a monetary wage but labor is the process by which the use value is altered and value added to commodity.

20. Jesse S. Robinson, *The Amalgamated Association of Iron, Steel, and Tin Workers* (Baltimore: Johns Hopkins University Press, 1920), 114.

21. H.M. Gitelman, "Perspectives on American Industrial Violence," *Business History Review* 47 (1973): 8–16.

22. Philip Taft and Philip Ross, "American Labor Violence: Its Causes, Character, and Outcome," in Hugh Davis Graham and Ted Robert Gurr, eds., *The History of Violence in America: Historical and Comparative Perspectives* (New York: Bantam Books, 1969), 281–344; see also David Montgomery, *Workers' Control in America: Studies in the History of*

Work, Technology and Labor Struggles (Cambridge: Cambridge University Press, 1979).

23. Foucault, *Discipline and Punish*, 164.

24. Ibid., 189.

25. David F. Noble, *America by Design: Science, Technology, and the Rise of Corporate Capitalism* (New York: Knopf, 1977), 33. As Noble points out and as Frederick Taylor's own background supports, most early mechanical engineers were formerly "skilled mechanics who had worked their way up, to become shop managers" (36).

26. Ibid., 34.

27. According to Noble, "two-thirds of all engineering graduates were becoming managers in industry within fifteen years after graduation." Ibid., 32, 41.

28. A perusal through the technical literature of the last quarter of the nineteenth century indicates a growing interest by engineers in managerial methods. Joseph A. Litterer in his survey observes that while there was little evidence of writings on management in the United States prior to 1870, there was a marked increase after that (64). While before 1880 only fifteen articles on the subject were written, from 1880 to 1885 sixty articles appeared, between 1885 and 1890, ninety-three articles and in the last ten years of the nineteenth century 253 articles were published (66). Two journals figured prominently as vehicles for these publications, the *American Machinist*, and *The Engineering Magazine* (68), indicating the extent to which engineers dominated the emerging study of management. Joseph A. Litterer, "The Emergence of Systematic Management as Indicated by the Literature of Management from 1870 to 1900," Ph.D dissertation, University of Illinois, 1959.

29. Otto S. Beyer, "Engineering," in *Civilization in the United States,* ed. Harold E. Stearns (New York: Harper & Row, 1959), 419.

30. Noble, *America by Design*, 31.

31. Judith A. Merkle, *Management and Ideology* (Berkeley: University of California Press, 1980), 98; Cecelia Tichi, *Shifting Gears* (Chapel Hill: University of North Carolina Press, 1987), 133.

32. Merkle, *Management and Ideology*, 18.

33. Merkle's argument is that scientific management, in seeking such a reconciliation in terms of a rationality interpreted by middle-class technicians (like Taylor himself), paved the way for middle-class mobility and the growth of a new professionalism. Ibid., 21.

34. Braverman, *Labor and Monopoly Capital*, 86.

35. Lyndall Urwick and E.F.L. Brech, *The Making of Scientific Management,* vol. 1 (New York: Harper & Row, 1954), 17.

36. Merkle, *Management and Ideology*, 11.
37. Daniel Bell, "Work and its Discontents," in *The End of Ideology* (New York: The Free Press of Glencoe, 1961), 224–27; and Merkle, *Management and Ideology*, 93.
38. Frederick W. Taylor, *Scientific Management* (Westport: Conn.: Greenwood Press, 1972), 34–35.
39. Frederick W. Taylor, *The Principles of Scientific Management* (New York: Norton, 1967), 32.
40. Taylor, *Scientific Management*, 33.
41. Taylor, *The Principles of Scientific Management*, 32.
42. Ibid., 36.
43. Ibid.
44. Peter F. Drucker, *The Practice of Management* (New York: Harper, 1954), 280; see Lyndall Urwick and E.F.L. Buch, *The Making of Scientific Management*, 27.
45. Braverman, *Labor and Monopoly Capital*, 90.
46. Noble, *America by Design*, 6.
47. Frederick W. Taylor, *On the Art of Cutting Metals* (New York: The American Society of Mechanical Engineers, 1906), 4–5.
48. Braverman, *Labor and Monopoly Capital*, 97, 113.
49. Taylor, *Scientific Management*, 169.
50. Ibid.
51. Focault, *Discipline and Punish*, 151.
52. Taylor, *Scientific Management*, 24.
53. As Braverman so rightly points out: "Why a 'fair day's work' should be defined as a physiological maximum is never made clear . . . it would make just as much if not more sense to express a fair day's work as the amount of labor necessary to add to the product a value equal to the worker's pay. But that would be to deny the capitalist his surplus value." Braverman, *Labor and Monopoly Capital*, 97.
54. Merkle, *Management and Ideology*, 13.
55. Taylor, *Scientific Management*, 32.
56. Foucault, *Discipline and Punish*, 170.
57. Taylor, *Scientific Management*, 152
58. Foucault, *Discipline and Punish*, 207.
59. Taylor, *Scientific Management*, 110.
60. Ibid., 110, 117.
61. Ibid., 98–99.
62. Foucault, *Discipline and Punish*, 192.
63. Ibid., 190.
64. Ibid., 187.

65. Ibid., 173.
66. As Marx noted in *Capital*: "The work of superintending and adjusting becomes one of the functions of capital, from the moment that the labor under the control of capital, becomes cooperative. Once a function of capital, it requires special characteristics." Marx, *Capital,* vol. I, 175.
67. Foucault, *Discipline and Punish*, 174.
68. Ibid., 177.
69. Taylor, *Scientific Management*, 109.
70. Ibid.
71. Foucault, *Discipline and Punish*, 171.
72. Taylor, *Scientific Management*, 105.
73. Foucault, *Discipline and Punish*, 219.
74. Ibid., 220.
75. Ibid.
76. Marey, for instance, had photographed the movements of his model, clad in black and with luminous tape attached to their bodies against a black backdrop. Etienne Jules Marey, *Movement,* trans. Prichard (New York: Heinemann, 1895).
77. Bruce Kaiper, "The Cyclograph and Work-Motion Model," *Still Photography: the Problematic Model*, eds. Lew Thomas and Peter D'Agostino (San Francisco: NFS Press, 1981), 58.
78. Frank B. Gilbreth, *Motion Study: A Method for Increasing the Efficiency of the Workman* (New York: Van Nostrand, 1911), 19–21.
79. Frank B. Gilbreth and L. M. Gilbreth, *Applied Motion Study: The Efficient Method to Industrial Preparedness* (New York: Sturgis & Walton, 1917), 64.
80. Gilbreths, *Applied Motion Study*, 19–20.
81. Ibid., 63–64.
82. Ibid., 64.
83. Ibid., 79.
84. Kaiper, "The Cyclograph and Work-Motion Model," 59.
85. Ibid.
86. Gilbreths, *Applied Motion Study*, 80.
87. Ibid., 67.
88. Ibid.
89. Ibid., 87.
90. Ibid., 117–21.
91. Siegfried Giedion, *Mechanization Takes Command* (New York: Oxford University Press, 1968), 103.
92. Foucault, *Discipline and Punish*, 152.
93. Ibid., 152–53.

94. Ibid., 153.
95. Gilbreths, *Applied Motion Study*, 91.
96. Ibid., 184.
97. Ibid., 82.
98. Ibid., 91.
99. Ibid., 92.
100. Braverman, *Labor and Monopoly Capital*, 174.
101. Ibid., 175; see also Benjamin W. Niebel, *Motion and Time Study* (Homewood, Ill.: Richard D. Irwin, Inc., 1976).
102. Bell, "Work and Its Discontents," 231–32.
103. Gilbreths, *Applied Motion Study*, 128.
104. Kaiper, "The Cyclograph and Work-Motion Model," 62.
105. Gilbreths, *Applied Motion Study*, 70.
106. Ibid., 83.
107. Ibid., 181.
108. Ibid.
109. Bell, "Work and Its Discontents," 232.
110. Gilbreths, *Applied Motion Study*, 60.
111. Ibid., 74.
112. Ibid., 75.
113. Ibid., 78.
114. Bell, "Work and Its Discontents," 224.
115. Foucault, *Discipline and Punish*, 190.
116. L.M. Gilbreth, *The Psychology of Management: The Function of the Mind in Determining, Teaching and Installing Methods of Least Waste* (New York: Sturgis & Walton, 1918), 27.
117. Ibid., 33.
118. Ibid., 42.
119. Foucault, *Discipline and Punish*, 191.

CHAPTER FIVE. THE VISUAL ORDER OF THE NINETEENTH CENTURY

1. Walter Ong has provided a list of visually based terms commonly applied in matters of intellection, for example: observe, demonstrate, discern, evidence, analyze, illuminate, explicate, clarity, and so on. Walter Ong, *Rhetoric, Romance, and Technology* (Ithaca and London: Cornell University Press, 1971), 78.
2. Jay, "Scopic Regimes of Modernity," 3.

3. Crary, *Techniques of the Observer*, 10–11.

4. Deleuze, *Foucault*, 58; Rajchman, "Art of Seeing," 9.

5. Rajchman, "Art of Seeing," 92.

6. Foucault, *Discipline and Punish*, 217.

7. Guy Debord, Society of the Spectacle (Detroit: Black & Red, 1983), 19.

8. Jonathan Crary has undertaken a genealogical study of the nineteenth-century observer as well. Even though my thinking has been influenced by his work, and in some sense is a response to it, our approaches are quite distinct. See Crary, *Techniques of the Observer*.

9. Gilles Deleuze and Felix Guattari, *Anti-Oedipus: Capitalism and Schizophrenia*, preface Michel Foucault, trans. R. Hurley, M. Seem, and H. Lane (Minneapolis: University of Minnesota Press, 1983), 257.

10. Even though for stylistic purposes I may preface the term "spectacle" with the definite article, I am in no way suggesting that there is a single, monovalent notion that can be applied across time. Jonathan Crary makes the same very point in his "Spectacle, Attention, Counter-Memory," *October* 50 (Fall 1989): 97–107. Clearly, nineteenth-century spectacles are quite different from present-day spectacles. See Baudrillard, *Simulations*.

11. Debord, *Society of the Spectacle*, 50; see Susan Buck-Morss, *The Dialectics of Seeing: Walter Benjamin and the Arcades Project* (Cambridge, Mass.: MIT Press, 1989), 87–88.

12. Baudrillard, *La Societé de Consommation*, 60.

13. Tagg, *The Burden of Representation*, 64.

14. Ibid., 99.

15. It also recalls the larger domain of "realism" prevalent in the literature and arts of the time, and in the journalism of the nineteenth century, where writers or interpreters were called upon to disappear behind their lenses. Tagg, *The Burden of Representation*, 100.

16. Crary, *Techniques of the Observer*, 39-41.

17. Charles Gibbs-Smith, "Mrs. Julia Margaret Cameron, Victorian Photographer," in Coke, *One Hundred Years*, 70–76.

18. Bernard Edelman, *The Ownership of the Image: Elements for a Marxist Theory of the Law*, trans. Elizabeth Kingdom (London: Routledge & Kegan Paul, 1979), 44.

19. Crary, *Techniques of the Observer*, 71.

20. Ibid., 14.

21. Ibid., 75.

22. Ibid., 90.

23. Ibid., 101.

24. Ibid., 102.

25. The phenakistiscope constructed by Plateau in the 1830s comprised at its simplest of a disc divided into eight or sixteen equal segments, each segment containing a slit on which a figure was drawn. When the phenakistiscope was held in front of a mirror with the side of the wheel with the figures drawn on it facing the mirror and the disc was turned, the observer caught a glimpse of a figure in the mirror as he or she peered through the slits. Because of retinal persistence the figures appeared to be in continuous motion.

26. Crary, *Techniques of the Observer*, 113.

27. Ibid., 106.

28. Debord, *Society of the Spectacle*, 25.

29. Ibid., 18.

30. Crary, *Techniques of the Observer*, 14, 96.

31. A tube with a convex lens at each end and a groove at its center on which an image was painted, was attached to a lantern containing a candle and a concave mirror. The first convex lens functioned to focus the light on the image, while the second lens magnified the illuminated image and projected it onto a wall or screen. In the darkness, the mediating screen was not discernible and the images appeared as luminous forms suspended above the spectators. In the last decades of the nineteenth century, when staged phantasmagoria had become quite elaborate, the commercialization of small models and do-it-yourself manuals made magic lanterns accessible even to middle-class Victorians. Terry Castle, "Phantasmagoria: Spectral Technology and the Metaphorics of Modern Reverie," *Critical Inquiry* 15 (Autumn, 1988): 42.

32. Ibid. 43–47.

33. Ibid., 52.

34. Ibid., 56.

35. See Carl Condit, *The Railroad and the City* (Columbus, Ohio: Ohio State University Press, 1977).

36. Wolfgang Schivelbusch, *The Railway Journey: Trains and Travel in the 19th Century* (New York: Basil Blackwell, 1979), 58.

37. Ibid., 64.

38. Ibid., 63; see Dolf Sternberger, "Panorama of the 19th Century," *October* 40 (Fall 1977): 3–20.

39. Schivelbusch, *The Railway Journey*, 51–53.

40. Ibid., 66.

41. In preindustrial travel—with its mimetic relation to the space traversed, organically embedding the traveller in the space travelled—the spaces between arrivals and departures is experienced as a living entity. This is no longer possible in the new time-space continuum established by the

railroad. "They [the railways] only serve the points of departure, the way stations, and the terminals, which are mostly at great distance from each other [but] they are of no use whatsoever for the intervening spaces, which they traverse with disdain and provide only with useless spectacle." Ibid., 44–45.

42. Ibid., 45.
43. Ibid., 47.
44. Benjamin, *Charles Baudelaire*, 161.
45. Peter B. Hales, *Silver Cities: The Photography of American Urbanization, 1839–1915* (Philadelphia: Temple University Press, 1984), 82.
46. According to Peter Hales, the work of the panoramists was a reflection of "urban boosterism." Ibid., 90.
47. Ibid., 70.
48. Ibid., 90.
49. Ibid., 82.
50. Richard Sennett, *The Fall of Public Man: On the Social Psychology of Capitalism* (New York: Vintage Books, 1978), 135.
51. Ibid., 136.
52. Ibid., 137.
53. Kristin Ross, *The Emergence of Social Space: Rimbaud and the Paris Commune* (Minneapolis: University of Minnesota Press, 1988), 9.
54. Ibid., 30.
55. Ibid., 41.
56. Baron Haussmann, *Memoires* (Paris, 1890–1893), 3:54 in T.J. Clark, *The Painting of Modern Life: Paris in the Art of Manet and His Followers* (New York: Knopf, 1985), 39.
57. Walter Benjamin, *Reflections: Essays, Aphorisms, Autobiographical Writings*, ed. and intro. Peter Demetz, trans. Edmund Jephcott (New York: Harcourt Brace Jovanovich, 1978), 160; see Eugene Lunn, *Marxism and Modernism: An Historical Study of Lukacs, Brecht, Benjamin and Adorno* (Berkeley: University of California Press, 1982).
58. Ibid., 160.
59. Ross, *Emergence of Social Space*, 37.
60. Ibid., 36.
61. Benjamin, *Reflections*, 139.
62. Ibid.
63. Edmond and Jules de Goncourt, *Journal des Goncourts,* vol. I, 345–46, in Clark, *The Painting of Modern Life*, 35.
64. N. Evenson, *Paris, A Century of Change: 1878–1978* (New Haven: Yale University Press, 1979), 75–76.
65. Clark, *The Painting of Modern Life*, 43–46.

66. Ibid., 36.
67. Ibid., 66.
68. Ibid., 58.
69. Ibid., 55.
70. Ibid., 66.
71. Ibid., 36.
72. Ibid., 39.
73. Wechsler, *A Human Comedy*, 15–16.
74. Sennett, *The Fall of Public Man*, 150–53.
75. Ibid., 153.
76. Ibid, 165–66.
77. Ross, *Emergence of Social Space*, 15.
78. Ibid.
79. Sennett, *Fall of Public Man*, 153.
80. In one of his studies attached to *La Comedie Humaine*, Balzac notes that "The observer is incontestably the man of genius." Ibid., 160.
81. Susan Buck-Morss, "The Flâneur, the Sandwichman, and the Whore: The Politics of Loitering," in *New German Critique* 39 (Fall 1986): 128.
82. Benjamin, *Illuminations*, 173.
83. Walter Benjamin, *Gesmmelte Schriften (Passagen-Werk*, vol. v), ed. Rolf Tiedemann and Hermann Schweppenhauser (Frankfurt am Main, 1972), cited Buck-Morss, "The Flâneur," 129.
84. Buck-Morss, "The Flâneur," 122. Whereas the male who loiters is a flâneur, women who loitered ran the risk of being labelled whores or as they were termed in Haussmann's planar era—"Les grandes horizon-tales"; and while the flâneur signals a transformation in perception, the figure of the whore represents the transformation of the world of things, for she simultaneously embodies both the seller and the spectacle/commodity. Buck-Morss, "The Flâneur," 119–20.
85. Benjamin, *Charles Baudelaire*, 35.
86. Buck-Morss, "The Flâneur," 103.
87. Following Aristide Boucicaut's Bon Marche in 1852, department stores were soon established elsewhere in Paris (La Belle Jardiniere) and also spread abroad to England (Harrod's), as well as the United States (Wannamakers, Macy's), where they became central institutions of the emerging consumer culture. Rachel Bowlby, *Just Looking* (New York: Methuen, 1985), 2; see Michael B. Miller *The Bon Marche: Bourgeois Culture and the Department Store, 1869–1920* (Princeton: Princeton University Press, 1981).
88. Bowlby, *Just Looking*, 2.

89. The department stores were characterized both by open entry which severed the connection between the moral requirement of entering a shop and making a purchase, as well as by the presence of assistants who, paid by commission, sought to politely flatter rather than urge a transaction. In this manner, the stores installed a democratic access by the eye. Ibid., 3–6.

90. William Leach, "Strategists of Display and the Production of Desire," in *Consuming Visions: Accumulation and Display of Goods in America, 1880–1920*, ed. Simon J. Bronner (New York & London: Norton, 1989), 117; see Jackson Lears, "Beyond Veblen: Rethinking Consumer Culture" in ibid.

91. Buck-Morss, "The Flâneur," 106.

92. Debord, *Society of the Spectacle*, 49. For Debord, the primary effect of the spectacle is its destruction of historical knowledge. The same "crisis in perception" motivates Benjamin's search for "afterimages"—images of collective historical memory which he believed had the dialectical power to reawaken society.

93. Sennett, *Fall of Public Man*, 150–52.

94. Ibid., 206.

95. Ibid., 210.

96. Buck-Morss, "The Flâneur," 125; see also Susan Buck-Morss, *The Dialectics of Seeing: Walter Benjamin and the Arcades Project* (Cambridge, Mass.: MIT Press, 1989), 267.

97. Foucault, *The Order of Things*, 312.

98. Ibid., 318.

99. Foucault, *Power/Knowledge*, 119.

SELECTED BIBLIOGRAPHY

Adams, Thomas S., and Helen L. Sumner. *Labor Problems: A Text Book.* New York: Macmillan, 1905.

Alberti, Leon Battista. *On Painting and On Sculpture: The Latin Texts of De Pictura and De Statua.* Ed. and trans. Cecil Grayson. London: Phaidon, 1972.

Arendt, Hannah. *The Life of the Mind.* New York: Harcourt Brace Jovanovich, 1978.

Arnheim, Rudolf. "Inverted Perspective in Art: Display and Expression. *Leonardo* 5 (1972): 123–35.

Bakhtin, Mikhail. *Rabelais and His World.* Trans. Helene Iswolsky. Cambridge, Mass.: MIT Press, 1968.

Barker, Francis. *The Tremulous Private Body: Essays on Subjection.* London and New York: Methuen, 1984.

Barthes, Roland. *Camera Lucida: Reflections on Photography.* Trans. Richard Howard. New York: Noonday Press, 1981.

———. "The Plates of the Encyclopedia." In *New Critical Essays.* Trans. Richard Howard. New York: Hill & Wang, 1980.

Bataille, Georges. *Visions of Excess: Selected Writings, 1927–1939.* Ed. and intro. Allan Stoekl. Trans. Allan Stoekl, Carl R. Lovitt, and Donald M. Leslie, Jr. Minneapolis: University of Minnesota Press, 1985.

Bate, David. "The Occidental Tourist: Photography and Colonizing Vision." *Afterimage* 20.1 (Summer 1992).

Baudelaire, Charles. "The Salon of 1859." Trans. Jonathan Maynre. In *Photography in Print: Writings from 1816 to the Present*. Ed. Vicki Goldberg. New York: Simon and Schuster, 1981.

Baudrillard, Jean. *For a Critique of the Political Economy of the Sign*. Trans. and ed. Charles Levin. St. Louis: Telos Press, 1981.

————. *L'échange symbolique et la mort*. Paris: Gallimard, 1976.

————. *La Société de Consommation*. Paris: Gallimard, 1970.

————. *Simulations*. Trans. Paul Foss. New York: Semiotexte, 1983.

Beccaria, Cesare Bonsana, marchese di. *An Essay on Crimes and Punishments*. Translated from the Italian with a Commentary Attributed to Mons. de Voltaire. Translated from the French. 4th Edition. London: F. Newberry, 1775.

Becker, Carl L. *The Heavenly City of the Eighteenth-Century Philosophers*. New Haven: Yale University Press, 1961.

Bell, Daniel. "Work and its Discontents." In *The End of Ideology*. New York: The Free Press of Glencoe, 1961.

Benjamin, Walter. *Charles Baudelaire: A Lyric Poet in the Era of High Capitalism*. Trans. Harry Zohn. London: Suhrkamp Verlag, 1973.

————. *Illuminations*. Ed. Hannah Arendt. Trans. Harry Zohn. New York: Schocken, 1969.

————. *Reflections: Essays, Aphorisms, Autobiographical Writings*. Ed. and intro. Peter Demetz. Trans. Edmund Jephcott. New York: Harcourt Brace Jovanovich, 1978.

Bentham, Jeremy. *An Introduction to the Principles of Morals and Legislation*. A reprint of the 1823 edition. New York: Hafner Publishing Co., 1948.

Berger, John. *Ways of Seeing*. British Broadcasting Corp. and Penguin Books, 1972.

Beyer, Otto S. "Engineering." In *Civilization in the United States*. Ed. Harold E. Stearns. New York: Harper & Row, 1959.

Bhabha, Homi K. *Out There: Marginalization and Contemporary Culture*. Ed. Russell Ferguson, Martha Gever, Trinh T. Minh-ha, Cornel West. Cambridge, Mass.: MIT Press, 1992.

Bloch, Herbert A., and Gilbert Geis. *Man, Crime, and Society: The Forms of Criminal Behavior.* New York: Random House, 1962.

Bloch, Maurice, and Jean Bloch. "Women and the Dialectics of Nature in Eighteenth-Century French Thought." In *Nature, Culture, and Gender*. Ed. Carol P. MacCormack and Marilyn Strathern. New York: Cambridge University Press, 1980.

Bottomore, Tom, ed. *A Dictionary of Marxist Thought*. Cambridge, Mass.: Harvard University Press, 1983.

Bowlby, Rachel. *Just Looking: Consumer Culture in Dreiser, Gissing, and Zola*. New York: Methuen, 1985.

Braive, Michel F. *The Era of the Photograph: A Social History*. New York: Random House, 1966.

Braverman, Harry. *Labor and Monopoly Capital: The Degradation of Work in the Twentieth Century*. New York: Monthly Review Press, 1974.

Brodhead, Richard. "Sparing the Rod: Discipline and Fiction in Antebellum America." *Representations* 21 (Winter 1988): 67–96.

Bryson, Norman. *Vision and Painting: The Logic of the Gaze*. New Haven: Yale University Press, 1983.

Buck-Morss, Susan. *The Dialectics of Seeing: Walter Benjamin and the Arcades Project*. Cambridge, Mass.: MIT Press, 1989.

———. "The Flâneur, the Sandwichman, and the Whore: The Politics of Loitering." *New German Critique* 39 (Fall 1986): 128.

Bunyan, Tony. *The Political Police in Britain*. London: Julien Friedmann, 1976.

Butler, Judith P. *Bodies that Matter: On the Discursive Limits of "Sex."* New York: Routledge, 1993.

———. *Gender Trouble: Feminism and the Subversion of Identity*. New York: Routledge, 1990.

Byrnes, Thomas. *1886 Professional Criminals of America*. New York: Chelsea House Publishers, 1969.

Castle, Terry. "Phantasmagoria: Spectral Technology and the Metaphorics of Modern Reverie." *Critical Inquiry* 15 (Autumn 1988): 42.

Certeau, Michel de. *Heterologies: Discourse on the Other*. Trans. Brian Massumi. Minneapolis: University of Minnesota Press, 1986.

Chevalier, Louis. *Laboring Classes and Dangerous Classes*. New York: Howard Fertig, 1973.

Clark, T.J. *The Painting of Modern Life: Paris in the Art of Manet and His Followers*. New York: Knopf, 1985.

Cloward, Richard A., and Frances Fox Piven. *Regulating the Poor*. London: Travistock, 1972

Coke, Van Deren, ed. *One Hundred Years of Photographic History: Essays in Honor of Beaumont Newhall*. Albuquerque: University of New Mexico Press, 1975.

Condit, Carl. *The Railroad and the City: A Technological and Urbanistic History of Cincinnati*. Columbus, Ohio: Ohio State University Press, 1977.

Cousins, Mark, and Akthar Hussain. *Michel Foucault*. London: Macmillan, 1984.

Crary, Jonathan. "Modernizing Vision." In *Vision and Visuality*. Discussions in Contemporary Culture Ser. 2. Ed. Hal Foster. Seattle: Bay Press, 1988.

————. "Spectacle, Attention, Counter-Memory." *October* 50 (Fall 1989).

————. *Techniques of the Observer: On Vision and Modernity in the Nineteenth Century*. Cambridge, Mass.: MIT Press, 1991.

Critchley, T.A. *A History of the Police in England and Wales, 1900–1966*. London: Constable, 1967.

Davidoff, Leonore, and Catherine Hall. *Family Fortunes: Men and Women of the English Middle Class, 1780–1850*. Chicago: University of Chicago Press, 1987.

Davies, John. *Phrenology: Fad and Science, a Ninteenth-Century American Crusade*. New Haven: Yale University Press, 1955.

De Roover, Raymond. "The Development of Accounting Prior to Luca Pacioli according to Account Books of Medieval Merchants." In *Studies in the History of Accounting*. Ed. A.C. Littleton and B.S. Yamey. Homewood, Ill.: R.D. Irwin, 1956.

Debord, Guy. *Society of the Spectacle*. Detroit: Black & Red, 1983.

Deleuze, Gilles. *Foucault*. Trans. Sean Hand. Minneapolis: University of Minnesota Press, 1986.

————. "What is a dispositif?" *Michel Foucault, Philosopher: Essays*. Trans. Timothy J. Armstrong. New York: Routledge, 1992.

Deleuze, Gilles, and Felix Guattari. *Anti-Oedipus: Capitalism and Schizophrenia*. Preface Michel Foucault. Trans. R. Hurley, M. Seem, and H. Lane. Minneapolis: University of Minnesota Press, 1983.

Deregowski, Jan B. "Pictorial Perception and Culture." *Scientific American* 227.5 (1972): 82–90.

Derrida, Jacques. "Sending on Representation." *Social Research* 49 (1982).

Douglas, Mary. *Purity and Danger: An Analysis of Concepts of Pollution and Taboo*. London: Routledge & Kegan Paul, 1969.

Dreyfus, Hubert, and Paul Rabinow. *Michel Foucault: Beyond Structuralism and Hermeneutics*. Second edition. Chicago: University of Chicago Press, 1992.

Edelman, Bernard. *The Ownership of the Image: Elements for a Marxist Theory of the Law*. Trans. Elizabeth Kingdom. London: Routledge & Kegan Paul, 1979.

Edgerton, Samuel Y. *The Renaissance Rediscovery of Linear Perspective*. New York: Basic Books, 1975.

Elias, Norbert. *The Civilizing Process: The History of Manners*. Trans. Edmund Jephcott. New York: Urizen Books, 1978.

Ellul, Jacques. *The Technological Society*. Intro. Robert Merton. Trans. John Wilkinson. New York: Vintage Books, 1964.

Emsley, Clive. *Crime and Society in England 1750–1900*. London: Longman, 1987.

Evans, Hilary, and Mary Evans. *The Victorians at Home and at Work*. New York: Arco Publishing, 1973.

Evenson, Norma. *Paris, A Century of Change: 1878–1978*. New Haven: Yale University Press, 1979.

Ewald, Francois. "A Power without an Exterior." In *Michel Foucault, Philosopher: Essays*. Trans. Timothy J. Armstrong. New York: Routledge, 1992.

Flynn, Thomas R. "Foucault and the Eclipse of Vision." In *Modernity and the Hegemony of Vision*. Ed. David Michael Levin. Berkeley: University of California Press, 1993.

Foner, Anne. "Age Stratification and the Changing Family." *American Journal of Sociology* 1978 (Supplement 349).

Foucault, Michel. *Discipline and Punish*. Trans. Alan Sheridan. New York: Vintage Books, 1979.

———. *History of Sexuality I: An Introduction*. Trans. Robert Hurley. New York: Pantheon, 1978.

———. *Madness and Civilization: A History of Insanity in the Age of Reason*. New York: Vintage Books, 1988.

———. Nietzsche, Genealogy, History." In *Language, Counter-Memory Practice: Selected Essays and Interviews*. Trans. Donald F. Bouchard and Sherry Simon. Ed. Donald F. Bouchard. Ithaca: Cornell University Press, 1977.

———. *Power/Knowledge: Selected Interviews and Other Writings, 1972–1977*. Ed. Colin Gordon. Trans. Colin Gordon et al. New York: Pantheon Books, 1980.

———. *The Birth of the Clinic: An Archeology of Medical Perception*. Trans. A.M. Sheridan Smith. New York: Vintage Books, 1975.

———. *The Order of Things: An Archeology of the Human Sciences*. Trans. Alan Sheridan. New York: Vintage Books, 1973.

Foster, Hal, ed. *Vision and Visuality*. Discussions in Contemporary Culture Ser. 2. Seattle: Bay Press, 1988.

Fowles, John. *The Collector*. St. Albans: Brown and Company, 1976.

Freund, Gisele. *Photography and Society*. Boston: David R. Godine, 1980.

Gallagher, Catherine. "The Body versus the Social Body in the Works of Thomas Malthus and Henry Mayhew." In *The Making of the Modern Body: Sexuality and Society in the Nineteenth Century*. Ed. Catherine Gallagher and Thomas Laqueur. Berkeley: University of California Press, 1987.

————. *The Industrial Reformation of English Fiction: Social Discourse and Narrative Form, 1832–1867*. Chicago: University of Chicago Press, 1985.

Galton, Francis. *Essays in Eugenics*. London: Eugenics Education Society, 1909.

————. "Eugenics: Its Definition, Scope, and Aims." *Sociological Papers*, 1905.

————. "Generic Images." *The Nineteenth Century: A Monthly Review* 6 (July-December 1879): 161.

————. *Hereditary Genius*. London: Julian Fiedmann, 1978.

————. "Hereditary Improvement." *Frazers Magazine* 7 (1873): 116–30. Quoted in David Green, "Veins of Resemblance: Photography and Eugenics." *The Oxford Art Journal* 7.2 (1984): 8.

Gaskell, Peter. *The Manufacturing Population of England, Its Moral, Social, and Physical Conditions, and the Changes Which Have Arisen from the Use of Steam Machinery; with an Examination of Infant Labour*. 1833 Reprint, New York: Arno Press, 1972.

Geertz, Clifford. "Art as a Cultural System." *MLN* 91 (1978): 1478.

Gernsheim, Helmut, and Alison Gernsheim. *L.J.M. Daguerre*. New York: Dover, 1968.

Gibbs-Smith, Charles. "Mrs. Julia Margaret Cameron, Victorian Photographer." In *One Hundred Years of Photographic History*. Ed. Van Deren Coke. Albuquerque: University of New Mexico Press, 1975.

Giedion, Siegfried. *Mechanization Takes Command.* New York: Oxford University Press, 1968.

Gilbreth, Frank B. *Motion Study: A Method for Increasing the Efficiency of the Workman.* New York: Van Nostrand Company, 1911.

Gilbreth, Frank B., and Lillian M. Gilbreth. *Applied Motion Study: The Efficient Method to Industrial Preparedness.* New York: Sturgis & Walton, 1917.

Gilbreth, Lillian M. *The Psychology of Management: The Function of the Mind in Determining, Teaching, and Installing Methods of Least Waste.* New York: Sturgis & Walton, 1918.

Gilman, Sander L. *Seeing the Insane.* New York: John Wiley & Sons, 1982.

Gilman, Sander L., ed. *The Face of Madness: Hugh W. Diamond and the Origin of Psychiatric Photography.* Secaucas, N.J.: Brunner-Mazel, 1976.

Gitelman, H.M. "Perspectives on American Industrial Violence." *Business History Review* 47 (1973): 8–16.

Goldberg, Vicki, ed. *Photography in Print: Writings from 1816 to the Present.* New York: Simon and Schuster, 1981.

Goldsmith, Arthur. *The Camera and Its Images.* New York: Newsweek Books, 1979.

Gombrich, Ernst Hans. *Art and Illusion.* New York: Bollingen Foundation, 1961.

Gorham, Deborah. *The Victorian Girl and the Feminine Ideal.* London: Croom Helm, 1982.

Gosling, Nigel. *Tournachon Felix Nadar, 1820–1910.* London: Seecker and Warburg, 1976.

Graham, Hugh Davis, and Ted Robert Gurr, eds. *The History of Violence in America: Historical and Comparative Perspectives.* New York: Bantam Books, 1969.

Gras, Norman Scott Brien. *Industrial Evolution.* New York: Augustus M. Kelley, 1969.

Grauman, John V. "Population Growth." In *International Encyclopedia of the Social Sciences.* Ed. David L. Sills. New York: Macmillan, 1968. Vol. 9, 379.

Green, David. "Veins of Resemblance: Photography and Eugenics." *The Oxford Art Journal* 7.2 (1984): 8.

Hacking, Ian. "Biopower and the Avalanche of Printed Numbers." *Humanities in Society* 5 (1982): 281.

Hales, Peter B. *Silver Cities: The Photography of American Urbanization, 1839–1915.* Philadelphia: Temple University Press, 1984.

Hall, Jerome. *Theft, Law, and Society.* Indianapolis: Bobbs-Merrill, 1952.

Harland, Richard. *Superstructuralism: The Philosophy of Structuralism and Post-Structuralism.* New York: Methuen, 1987.

Harring, Sidney L. *Policing a Class Society: The Experience of American Cities, 1865–1915.* New Brunswick: Rutgers University Press, 1983.

Haskins, Charles Homer. *The Renaissance of the Twelfth Century.* Cambridge, Mass.: Harvard University Press, 1927.

Haskins, Frank H. "Adolphe Quetelet as Statistician." Ph.D. dissertation, Columbia University, 1908.

Hawthorne, Nathaniel. *The House of the Seven Gables.* New York: Modern Library, 1961.

Heidegger, Martin. *The Question Concerning Technology and Other Essays.* Trans. William Lovitt. New York: Harper & Row, 1977.

Henretta, James A. *The Evolution of American Society, 1700–1815.* Lexington, Mass.: Heath, 1973.

Holmes, Oliver Wendell. "The Stereoscope and the Stereograph." In *Photography in Print: Writings from 1816 to the Present.* Ed. Vicki Goldberg. New York: Simon and Schuster, 1981.

Houghton, Walter E. *The Victorian Frame of Mind, 1830–1870.* New Haven: Yale University Press, 1957.

Hoy, David Couzens. "Power, Repression, Progress: Foucault, Lukes, and the Frankfurt School." In *Foucault: A Critical Reader.* Ed. David Couzens Hoy. Oxford: Basil Blackwell, 1986.

Hunter, Richard, and Ida Macalpine. *Three Hundred Years of Psychiatry, 1535–1860.* London: Oxford University Press, 1963.

Husserl, Edmund. *Cartesian Meditations: An Introduction to Phenomenology.* Trans. Dorion Cairns. The Hague: Martinus Nijhoff, 1970.

Ignatieff, Michael. *A Just Measure of Pain: The Penitentiary in the Industrial Revolution, 1750–1850.* New York: Pantheon Books, 1978.

Ivins, William M. *Art and Geometry: A Study in Space Intuitions.* Cambridge, Mass.: Harvard University Press, 1946.

Jay, Martin. "In the Empire of the Gaze: Foucault and the Denigration of Vision in Twentieth-Century French Thought." In *Foucault: A Critical Reader.* Ed. David Couzens Hoy. Oxford: Basil Blackwell, 1986.

———. *Marxism and Totality: The Adventures of a Concept from Lukacs to Habermas.* Berkeley: University of California Press, 1984.

———. "Scopic Regimes of Modernity." In *Vision and Visuality.* Discussions in Contemporary Culture Ser. 2. Ed. Hal Foster. Seattle: Bay Press, 1988.

Johnson, Paul E. *A Shopkeeper's Millenium: Society and Revivals in Rochester, New York, 1815–1837.* New York: Hill and Wang, 1978.

Jones, Gareth Stedman. *Outcast London: A Study in the Relationship between Classes in Victorian Society.* Oxford: Clarendon Press, 1971.

Jones, Greta. *Social Darwinism and English Thought: The Interaction between Biological and Social Theory.* Atlantic Highlands, N.J.: Humanities Press, 1980.

Kaiper, Bruce. "The Cyclopgraph and Work-Motion Model." In *Still Photography: The Problematic Model.* Ed. Lew Thomas and Peter D'Agostino. San Francisco: NFS Press, 1981.

Kelly, Joan. "Early Feminist Theory and Querelle des Femmes, 1400–1789." *Signs* 8.1 (1982).

Kozloff, Max. "Nadar and the Republic of Mind." In *Photography In Print: Writings from 1816 to the Present.* Ed. Vicki Goldberg. New York: Simon and Schuster, 1981.

Kroker, Arthur, and Marilouise Kroker. "Theses on the Disappearing Body in the Hyper-Modern Condition." In *Body Invaders: Panic Sex in America.* Ed. Arthur Kroker and Marilouise Kroker. New York: St. Martin's Press, 1987.

Landes, Joan B. *Women and the Public Sphere.* Ithaca: Cornell University Press, 1988.

Laqueur, Thomas. *Making Sex: Body and Gender from the Greeks to Freud.* Cambridge, Mass.: Harvard University Press, 1990.

———. "Orgasm, Generation, and the Politics of Reproductive Biology." In *The Making of the Modern Body: Sexuality and Society in the Nineteenth Century.* Ed. Catherine Gallagher and Thomas Laqueur. Berkeley: University of California Press, 1987.

Lavater, J.C. *Essays on Physiognomy.* 3 vols. London: 1789.

Leach, William. "Strategists of Display and the Production of Desire." In *Consuming Visions: Accumulation and Display of Goods in America, 1880–1920.* Ed. Simon J. Bronner. New York: Norton, 1989.

Lears, Jackson. "Beyond Veblen: Rethinking Consumer Culture." In *Consuming Visions: Accumulation and Display of Goods in America, 1880–1920.* Ed. Simon J. Bronner. New York: Norton 1989.

Lemert, Charles, and Garth Gillan. *Michel Foucault: Social Theory and Transgression.* New York: Columbia University Press, 1982.

Leps, Marie-Christine. *Apprehending the Criminal: The Production of Deviance in Nineteenth-Century Discourse.* Durham: Duke University Press, 1992.

Levin, David Michael. *The Opening of Vision: Nihilism and the Post-Modern Situation.* New York: Routledge, 1988.

Levy, Anita. *Other Women: The Writing of Class, Race, and Gender, 1832–1898.* Princeton: Princeton University Press, 1991.

Levy, Ruth. "Types of One: Adolph Meyer's Life Chart and the Representation of Individuality." *Representations* 34 (Spring 1991).

Lindberg, David C. "Alhazen's Theory of Vision and Its Reception in the West." *Isis* 58 (1967): 321–41.

———. "Alkindi's Critique of Euclid's Theory of Vision." *Isis* 62 (1971): 469–89.

Litterer, Joseph A. "The Emergence of Systematic Management as Indicated by the Literature of Management from 1870 to 1900." Ph.D. dissertation, University of Illinois, 1959.

Littleton, A.C., and B.S. Yamey, eds. *Studies in the History of Accounting.* Homewood, Ill.: R.D. Irwin, 1956.

Locke, John. *An Essay Concerning Human Understanding*. Ed. Peter H. Nidditch. Oxford: Clarendon Press, 1975.

Lombroso, Cesare. *Criminal Man*. New York: G.P. Putnam's Sons, 1911.

Lombroso-Ferrero, Gina. *Criminal Man: According to the Classification of Cesare Lombroso*. New York and London: G.P. Putnam's Sons, 1911.

Lucie-Smith, Edward. *The Invented Eye: Masterpieces of Photography, 1839–1914*. New York: Paddington Press, 1975.

Lunn, Eugene. *Marxism and Modernism: An Historical Study of Lukacs, Brecht, Benjamin, and Adorno*. Berkeley: University of California Press, 1982.

MacCormack, Carol P., and Marilyn Strathern, eds. *Nature, Culture, and Gender*. Cambridge: Cambridge University Press, 1980.

Mackenzie, Donald A. *Statistics in Britain, 1865–1930: The Social Construction of Scientific Knowledge*. Edinburgh: Edinburgh University Press, 1981.

Marx, Karl. *Capital: The Communist Manifesto and Other Writings*. Ed. and intro. Max Eastman. New York: The Modern Library, 1932.

Mayhew, Henry. *London Labour and the London Poor: A Cyclopedia of the Conditions and Earnings of Those that Will Work, Those that Cannot Work, and Those that Will Not Work*. 4 vols. (1851); London, 1967.

McLuhan, Marshall, and Harley Parker. *Through the Vanishing Point: Space in Poetry and Painting*. New York: Harper Row, 1968.

Merkle, Judith A. *Management and Ideology*. Berkeley: University of California Press, 1980.

Melossi, Dario, and Massimo Pavarini. *The Prison and the Factory: Origins of the Penitentiary System.* Trans. Glynis Cousin. London: Macmillan Press, 1981.

Miller, D.A. *"Cage aux folles*: Sensation and Gender in Wilkie Collins's *The Woman in White.*" In *The Making of the Modern Body: Sexuality and Society in the Nineteenth Century.* Ed. Catherine Gallagher and Thomas Laqueur. Berkeley: University of California Press, 1987.

Miller, Michael B. *The Bon Marche: Bourgeois Culture and the Department Store, 1869–1920.* Princeton: Princeton University Press, 1981.

Mintz, Steven. *A Prison of Expectations: The Family in Victorian Culture.* New York: New York University Press, 1983.

Mitchell, W.J. Thomas. *Iconology: Image, Text, Ideology.* Chicago: University of Chicago Press, 1986.

Montgomery, David. *Workers' Control in America: Studies in the History of Work, Technology and Labor Struggles.* Cambridge: Cambridge University Press, 1979.

Nelson, Daniel. *Managers and Workers: Origins of the New Factory System in the United States, 1880–1920.* Madison, Wis.: University of Wisconsin Press, 1975.

Newhall, Beaumont. *The History of Photography, from 1839 to the Present Day.* New York: Museum of Modern Art, 1964.

———. Ed. "The First News Accounts of the Daguerreotype, January 6, 1839." *Photography Essays and Images: Illustrated Readings in the History of Photography.* New York: Museum of Modern Art, 1980.

Niebel, Benjamin W. *Motion and Time Study.* Homewood, Ill.: Richard D. Irwin, 1976.

Nietzsche, Friedrich. *The Birth of Tragedy*. Trans. Walter Kaufmann. New York: Penguin Books, 1967.

———. *The Genealogy of Morals*. New York: Doubleday Anchor Books, 1956.

———. *Thus Spoke Zarathustra*. Trans. Walter Kaufmann. New York: Penguin Books, 1978.

Noble, David F. *America by Design: Science, Technology and the Rise of Corporate Capitalism*. New York: Alfred A. Knopf, 1977.

Nochlin, Linda. "The Imaginary Orient." *Art in America* 71 (May 1983): 119–91.

O'Brien, Patricia. *The Promise of Punishment: Prisons in Nineteenth-Century France*. Princeton: Princeton University Press, 1982.

Ong, Walter. *Rhetoric, Romance, and Technology: Studies in the Interaction of Expression and Culture*. Ithaca: Cornell University Press, 1971.

Pearson, Karl. *The Life, Letters and Honours of Francis Galton*. Cambridge: Cambridge University Press, 1924.

Peragallo, Edward. *Origin and Evolution of Double Entry Bookkeeping: A Study of Italian Practice from the Fourteenth Century*. Concord, N.H.: Rumford Press, 1938.

Perez, Nissan N. *Focus East: Early Photography in the Near East, 1839–1885*. New York: Harry N. Abrams in association with the Domino Press, Jerusalem, and the Israel Museum, Jerusalem, 1988.

Perkin, Harold. *The Origins of Modern English Society, 1780–1880*. London: Routledge and Kegan Paul, 1972.

Pirenne, Maurice Henri. *Optics, Painting, and Photography*. London: Cambridge University Press, 1970.

Pollard, Sidney. *The Genesis of Modern Management: A Study of the Industrial Revolution in Great Britain.* Cambridge, Mass.: Harvard University Press, 1965.

Poovey, Mary. *Uneven Developments.* Chicago: University of Chicago Press, 1988.

Poster, Mark. *Foucault, Marxism, and History.* Cambridge, UK: Polity Press; New York: Basil Blackwell, 1984.

Quetelet, L.A. *A Treatise on Man and the Development of His Faculties.* Trans. R. Enox. 1835. Edinburgh, 1842; reprint, Westmeed, 1973.

Rabinow, Paul, ed. *The Foucault Reader.* New York: Pantheon Books, 1984.

Radzinowicz, Leon. *A History of English Criminal Law and Its Administration from 1750.* 4 vols. London: Stevens, 1948–1968.

———. *Ideology and Crime.* New York: Columbia University Press, 1966.

Rajchman, John. "Foucault: Art of Seeing." *October* 44 (Spring 1988).

Rennie, Ysabel. *The Search for Criminal Man: A Conceptual History of the Dangerous Criminal.* Lexington, Mass.: D.C. Heath and Company, 1978.

Rhodes, Henry T.F. *Alphonse Bertillon.* New York: Abelard-Schuman, 1956.

Robinson, Jesse S. *The Amalgamated Association of Iron, Steel, and Tin Workers.* Baltimore: Johns Hopkins University Press, 1920.

Rogers, Katharine M. *Feminism in Eighteenth-Century England.* Urbana: University of Illinois Press, 1982.

Root, Marcus Aurelius. *The Camera and the Pencil, or, The Heliographic Art.* Philadelphia: J.B. Lippincott & Co., 1864; reprint, Pawlett, Vt.:

Helios, 1971. Cited in *Photography in Print: Writings from 1816 to the Present*. Ed. Vicki Goldberg. New York: Simon and Schuster, 1981.

Rorty, Richard. *Philosophy and the Mirror of Nature*. Princeton: Princeton University Press, 1979.

Rosenblum, Naomi. *A World History of Photography*. New York: Abbeville Press, 1984.

Ross, Kristin. *The Emergence of Social Space: Rimbaud and the Paris Commune*. Minneapolis: University of Minnesota Press, 1988.

Rousseau, Jean-Jacques. *Emile*. Trans. Allan Bloom. New York: Basic Books, 1981.

Rowbotham, Sheila. *Women, Resistance, and Revolution*. London: Allen Lane, 1972.

Rudisill, Richard. *Mirror Image: The Influence of the Dauguerreotype on American Society*. Albuquerque: University of New Mexico Press, 1971.

Russett, Cynthia Eagle. *Sexual Science: The Victorian Construction of Womanhood*. Cambridge, Mass.: Harvard University Press, 1989.

Ryder, James F. *Voigtlander and I*. Cleveland: Cleveland Printing & Publishing Co., 1901.

Said, Edward W. *Orientalism*. New York: Vintage Books, 1979.

Sartre, Jean-Paul. *Being and Nothingness: An Essay on Phenomenological Ontology*. Trans. Hazel E. Barnes. New York: Philosophical Library, 1956.

———. *The Transcendence of the Ego: An Existenialist Theory of Consciousness*. Trans. F. Williams and R. Kirkpatrick. New York: Noonday Press, 1957.

Sawicki, Jana. "Feminism and the Power of Foucaldian Discourse." In *After Foucault: Humanistic Knowledge, Postmodern Challenges.* Ed. Jonathan Arac. New Brunswick: Rutgers University Press, 1988.

Schiebinger, Londa. "Skeletons in the Closet: The First Illustrations of the Female Skeleton in Eighteenth-Century Anatomy." In *The Making of the Modern Body.* Ed. Catherine Gallagher and Thomas Laqueur. Berkeley: University of California Press, 1987.

Schivelbusch, Wolfgang. *The Railway Journey: Trains and Travel in the 19th Century.* New York: B. Blackwell, 1979.

Schmidt, James. *Maurice Merleau-Ponty: Between Phenomenology and Structuralism.* New York: St. Martin's Press, 1985.

Searle, G.R. *Eugenics and Politics in Britain, 1900–1914.* Leyden: Hoordhoff, 1976.

Segall, Marshall H., Donald T. Campbell, and Melville J. Herskovits. *The Influence of Culture on Visual Perception.* New York: Bobbs-Merrill, 1966.

Sekula, Allan. "The Body and the Archive." *October* 36–39 (1986): 9.

Sennett, Richard. *The Fall of the Public Man: On the Social Psychology of Capitalism.* New York: Vintage Books, 1978.

Smart, Barry. "The Politics of Truth and the Problem of Hegemony." In *Foucault: A Critical Reader.* Ed. David Couzens Hoy. Oxford: Basil Blackwell, 1986.

Sontag, Susan. *On Photography.* New York: Farrar, Straus and Giroux, 1977.

Spiegel, Alan. *Fiction and the Camera Eye: Visual Consciousness in Film and the Modern Novel.* Charlottesville: University Press of Virginia, 1976.

Spitzer, Stephen P. "The Rationalization of Crime Control in Capitalist Society." *Contemporary Crises* 3 (April 1979): 187–206.

Stead, Philip John. *The Police of France.* New York: Macmillan, 1983.

Stein, Sally. "The Composite Photographic Image and the Composition of Consumer Ideology." *Art Journal* 61 (Spring 1981): 39–45.

Sternberger, Dolf. "Panorama of the 19th Century." *October* 40 (Fall 1977): 3–20.

Symons, Julian. *A Pictorial History of Crime.* New York: Crown Publishers, 1966.

Tagg, John. *The Burden of Representation: Essays on Photographies and Histories.* Amherst: University of Massachusetts Press, 1988.

Taylor, Frederick Winslow. *On the Art of Cutting Metals.* New York: The American Society of Mechanical Engineers, 1906.

———. *Scientific Management.* Westport, Conn.: Greenwood Press, 1972.

———. *The Principles of Scientific Measurement.* New York: Norton, 1967.

Taylor, Mark C. *Altarity.* Chicago: University of Chicago Press, 1987.

Thomas, Alan. *The Expanding Eye: Photography and the Nineteenth-Century Mind.* London: Croom Helm, 1978.

Thompson, E.P. *The Making of the English Working Class.* Hammondsworth: Penguin, 1968.

———. "Time, Work-Discipline and Industrial Capitalism." *Past and Present* 38 (December 1967): 56–97.

Tichi, Cecelia. *Shifting Gears: Technology, Literature, Culture in Modernist America.* Chapel Hill: University of North Carolina Press, 1987.

Trachtenberg, Alan. "Brady's Portraits." *Yale Review* 73.2 (1983–1984).

———. *The Incorporation of America: Culture and Society in the Gilded Age*. New York: Hill and Wang, 1982.

Urwick, Lyndall, and E.F.L. Brech. *The Making of Scientific Management*. Vol. 1. New York: Harper & Row, 1954.

Wechsler, Judith. *A Human Comedy: Physiognomy and Caricature in 19th Century Paris*. Chicago: University of Chicago Press, 1982.

Williamson, Judith. *Consuming Passions: The Dynamics of Popular Culture*. London: Marion Boyars, 1985.

Wollen, Peter. *Raiding the Icebox: Reflections on Twentieth-Century Culture*. Bloomington: Indiana University Press, 1993.

INDEX